ECONOMICS
and the good life

Bertrand de Jouvenel

ECONOMICS
and the good life

Essays on Political Economy

edited & with an introduction by
Dennis Hale & Marc Landy

Transaction Publishers
New Brunswick (U.S.A.) and London (U.K.)

Library of Congress Catalog Number: 98-30889
ISBN: 0-7658-0428-X
Printed in the United States of America

Library of Congress Cataloging-in-Publication Data

Jouvenel, Bertrand de, 1903–
    [Essays. English. Selections]
    Economics and the good life : essays on political economy / Bertrand de Jouvenel ; edited and with an introduction by Dennis Hale and Marc Landy.
        p. cm.
    Includes bibliographical references and index.
    ISBN 0-7658-0428-X (alk. paper)
    1. Economics—Political aspects.   2. Reconstruction (1939–1951).
3. Natural resources. 4. Welfare economics. I. Hale, Dennis. II. Landy, Marc, 1950–   . III. Title.
HB74.P65J68213   1998
338.9—dc21   98-30889
                                                                    CIP

Contents

Preface

Edouard Bertrand de Jouvenel des Ursins was born in 1903, and raised in a household that was deeply involved in the political and intellectual currents sweeping through France and Europe. His father, Henri, was the son of a baron, Raoul de Jouvenel, from Corrèze. Bertrand's mother, Sarah Claire Boas, was the daughter of a wealthy industrialist. Henri and Sarah met while both were working to defend Alfred Dreyfus. And although de Jouvenel's parents divorced when he was young, he remained close to both his parents, and participated in their active political, social, and literary circles. Henri was France's representative to the League of Nations, was elected to the French Senate, and was married to the novelist Colette—giving Bertrand access, simultaneously, to the worlds of diplomacy, party politics, and letters. Sarah presided over a salon of great prestige and importance, and was instrumental in getting the French government to support the cause of an independent Czechoslovakia—as a result of which the young Bertrand was able to work as a private secretary to Eduard Benes, Czechoslovakia's first prime minister.

After his service to Benes, de Jouvenel took up a journalistic career which he was to follow until the Second World War. He was a widely read correspondent for a variety of newspapers and magazines identified, generally, with the French Left. He called himself a progressive and ran (unsuccessfully) as a Radical Socialist candidate for the National Assembly. His interests in those days included international reconciliation, especially between Germany and France, and economic reform aimed at curing the "evil of unemployment." His was one of the few voices on the French Left urging international support for schemes to improve the German economy, on the prophetic grounds that economic dislocation would lead to the collapse of Germany's democratic government.

Breaking first with the Radical Socialists and then with the Parti Populaire Francaise over their refusal to oppose German militarism, de Jouvenel withdrew from political activism into reflection on the esca-

lating disasters of totalitarianism and war. Late in 1943, fearing immi-
nent arrest, de Jouvenel fled, with his wife, to Switzerland, where he
remained for the duration of the war. It was there that he composed the
book that first brought him to the attention of an American audience:
On Power: Its Nature and the History of its Growth, published in French
in 1945 and in English in 1948.

De Jouvenel is therefore known in the United States—to the extent
that he is known at all—primarily as a political scientist. His best-known
works—*On Power*; *Sovereignty*; and *The Pure Theory of Politics*—all
make distinctive contributions to our understanding of the modern state,
and to the crafting of a political science whose aim is to civilize that
state. De Jouvenel was also invited, during the 1950s and 1960s, to
lecture at American universities (Yale, the University of Chicago, and
the University of California at Berkeley) where he developed close
friendships with several American intellectuals and left a lasting impression on some of their students.[1]

But in France, de Jouvenel was known primarily as an economist—
especially in the last three decades of his life. He founded and directed
the Society for Economic, Industrial, and Social Research, and the
Futuribles Institute, devoted to forecasting. He edited and contributed to
the journals published by the institutes—*Bulletin SEDEIS*, *Analyse et
Prévision,* and *Futuribles*—which earned him a wide reputation as a public
intellectual with broad interests in social, political, and economic problems and developments. This reputation earned him appointments to several commissions organized to give advice to the French government,
and one of his last public appointments was to a commission organized
to study France's national forests. Up to the final years of his life (he died
in 1987), de Jouvenel was still travelling to international conferences to
deliver papers on a wide range of topics, including forecasting, environmental regulation, marine economics, and democratic reform.

While de Jouvenel's work in economics is relatively unknown in the
United States, it is an important companion to his work as a political
scientist. But unlike so many writers in the contemporary field of
political economy, de Jouvenel was not interested in expanding the
claims of the economy at the expense of the polity. On the contrary; his
economic writing was governed in the first instance by the oldest and
most fundamental of political concerns, namely, the definition of the
good life.

This was among the earliest concerns of thinkers, such as Aristotle,
who sought to distinguish between the private and the public house-

holds, and to understand how the economy of the public household shaped, or interfered with, the creation of the good life—the chief and noblest aim of the City. The study of politics, and the study of the public household, are properly one study and not two.

The good life, however, is not a product of the marketplace, but of deliberate and collective decision. It is a task for thoughtful citizens and statesmen, and not simply the sum of millions of separate and amoral "consumer preferences." De Jouvenel was well-known for his opposition to the distended State; but he was no anarchist. His eloquent warnings to keep the State in its proper sphere were accompanied by a richly sophisticated discussion of what that proper sphere is—an aspect of his work that comes through very clearly in the pages of these essays.

That discussion is informed by de Jouvenel's own generous and humane understanding of the good life, and in the pages of this book the reader will encounter an intelligence that is gracious, wise, and hopeful—remarkably catholic in its concerns, and a happy contrast to the austere minimalism of more widely read political economists. The essays—which appeared between 1952 and 1980, in journals both obscure and well-known—range from a discussion of technology to reflections on such fundamental economic concepts as "amenity" and "welfare." They include the deeply theoretical as well as the practical and the concrete, all informed by de Jouvenel's insistence that a science which seeks to understand the production and distribution of "goods" must be concerned in the first place with the Good itself.

* * *

We would like to take this opportunity to thank Irving Louis Horowitz, Mary Curtis, and Transaction Books for their willingness to republish de Jouvenel's essays. The preservation of the best intellectual labors is sometimes a financially thankless task, but a publisher can do no more important service.

Dennis Hale
Marc Landy

Note

1. See, for example, Wilson Carey McWilliams' discussion of de Jouvenel as a teacher in his preface to *The Nature of Politics: Selected Essays of Bertrand de Jouvenel*, edited by Dennis Hale and Marc Landy (Transaction Publishers, 1992).

Introduction

*"Intellectuals resemble Rabelais's Panurge
more than one would like to admit, and while
many intellects combine to make a well-known
problem with rapidly decreasing yields their
quarry, another problem which is important for
society remains unexplored. Thus the attention
given to problems of productivity certainly
exceeds the golden mean, while the problem of
'the good life' suffers from neglect."*
—*"A Better Life in an Affluent Society,"* 1961.

I

The writings collected in this volume represent a small selection—the principle of selection being their availability in English–of the essays on political economy of Bertrand de Jouvenel (1903–1987), a man who practiced many professions in his richly productive life: reporter, soldier, diplomatic correspondent, novelist, historian, political scientist, economist, and public servant.

Unfortunately, few American scholars are familiar with de Jouvenel's work, and these few are largely political scientists; he is virtually unknown to American economists.[1] But de Jouvenel was an avid "reader" (to use his term) of economic literature, and in addition to teaching law and politics at the Faculty of Law and the Fondation Nationale des Sciences Politiques in Paris, he gave lectures on both economics and political science at Manchester, Oxford, Cambridge, Berkeley, Yale, and the Sorbonne. The research institute that he founded and directed—SEDEIS[2]—took the study of economic problems as one of its chief missions, and de Jouvenel was a member of several national commissions organized to give economic advice to the French government, including the French Commission of National Accounts and the Commission for Planning. One of his last public services was to direct a government study of his country's forestry resources.[3] And much of de Jouvenel's writing, from the beginning to the end of his professional career, was concerned with "political economy," in the old sense of the term—the coordination of political and economic arrangements toward a common end.[4]

The subjects and titles of de Jouvenel's books and essays in the field of political economy give an immediate indication of the direction of his thinking, or at least of the particular part of the field in which he preferred to roam. Nominally, he was concerned with natural resources, national accounting, planning, and employment: all matters with obvious, and sometimes not so obvious, political implications; he also did much work on the history of the "controlled economy" and its role in the evolution of modern states.

Yet it must be acknowledged that most economists, even if they were acquainted with his work, would be loathe to accept de Jouvenel as a brother in the craft—and not only because he was an autodidact, in economics as in political science. What truly makes de Jouvenel a stranger to the economics profession is his insistence on the natural alliance between economics and political science—even, in some sense, the natural *subordination* of economics to political science.

"The term 'political' all but disappeared from many economic treatises a long time ago," he writes, "even though governments around the world have been steadily assuming an increasingly important role in the economic realm."[5] But there is a more important reason for insisting upon the affinity of economics and political science, and it reveals de Jouvenel's debt to classical political science, and especially to Aristotle: the private economy has a profound effect on the public order—and vice versa; economic arrangements can either supplement and support political arrangements, or they can undermine them and bring down the regime, in the process destroying the private household along with the public. Another way of putting this is to say that there are *goods*—the collection of services and products supplied by the private economy— and there is the Good—that arrangement of laws and institutions that is most productive of human happiness in a particular place at a particular time. De Jouvenel believed that it was important for economists to broaden their horizons so that their science could include in a single glance not just the "goods" of conventional analysis but the Good itself.

De Jouvenel adopted a similar strategy with political scientists, who were only slightly more willing than economists to accept him into their guild. While embracing the methods and the spirit of "empirical" political science, de Jouvenel tried to turn especially American political scientists to a more classical understanding of the ends of political life: as Wilson Carey McWilliams has put it, de Jouvenel, "like Theseus who slew the Minotaur,... would bring the old gods to a new city."[6]

To attempt in one lifetime the turning of two professions—especially one as rightly prideful as modern economics—is surely a hurculean effort, and it would be folly to pretend that de Jouvenel made significant progress with either group of pupils. Still, as long as we have libraries, no wisdom is permanently out of reach; and it is in that spirit that we collect these essays in book form, to be planted where they will someday, we hope, bear fruit.

II

It was catastrophe that led de Jouvenel to the study of *both* economics and political science. No public event was more important to his political education than the economic dislocations of the 1920s and 1930s and their fatal consequences in Europe: the collapse of liberal democracy, the rise of totalitarianism, the apocalypse of World War II. From that experience came the reflections that grew into de Jouvenel's first major work of political science, *Du pouvoir* (1945), published in English as *On Power: Its Nature and the History of its Growth* (1948).[7]

In the rise of fascism, it was impossible to ignore the impact of two tragic and puzzling economic developments: hyperinflation and mass unemployment. In addition to the phenomenal waste of resources such problems caused, they undermined confidence in democratic institutions and drove citizens into the arms of tyrants. They would do so again, if given the chance. The postwar project was therefore as obvious as it was daunting: to civilize the nation-state and to rationalize the economy, simultaneously, so that limited government and steady economic growth could together prevent a recurrence of the nightmares of the Depression and the Second World War.

Such thinking naturally led de Jouvenel to a consideration of the United States.[8] In America, fascism had failed to take root; American institutions had proved durable enough to weather the storms that had overwhelmed European democracies, without losing completely their liberal and constitutional spirit. And America was, above all, the great exemplar of economic growth. What America had managed, what Great Britain had managed earlier—this is what the whole world would now attempt to achieve.

While universal economic growth on the American pattern was unlikely, because of the unequal distribution of natural resources among the nations of the world, no nation would be completely immune to the growing prosperity of the world economy. Growth would bring challenges, but it had already brought about, in Europe, North America, and a few other parts of the world, a profound and unprecedented social transformation.

> The great new idea is that it is possible to enrich all the members of society, collectively and individually, by gradual progress in the organization of labor, its methods and its implements; that this enrichment provides the means for a greater development of the individual; and that this development can be rapid and unlimited. This idea is an enormous innovation.[9]

The transformation is both political and economic. The possibility of abundance transforms the regime by making what was once impossible (widespread wealth) seem not just a *good* but a *right*. That expectation, in turn, inspires greater individual effort and increased economic growth. On the political side, the growth of an economy of abundance creates tasks that can only be performed by governments that are relatively centralized and integrated compared to previous regimes (in part because society must sustain much larger populations). The market might be free, but its freedom is supported by an elaborate structure of rules, regulations, and public institutions. And governments must also be strong enough to prevent the kind of turmoil that destroyed liberal regimes in the 1930s. The modern state, for all its dangers, cannot be abolished, therefore, but only *tamed*.

Given these facts of life, it is essential that citizens, and especially intellectuals, learn to appreciate—to value properly—the moral and constitutional restraints on the power of government, a lesson they had not fully learned even after the experience of fascism and totalitarianism in Europe.[10] Similarly, those intellectuals devoted to the science of economics must learn to appreciate the full nature of their task as advisors and counsellors to statesmen: how to make economic institutions serve the end of promoting the Good Life under the supremely difficult conditions imposed by modernity.

III

As de Jouvenel was well aware, mention of the Good Life provokes in most of our contemporaries an immediate retreat into relativism. Do not social and moral "goods" merely reveal *preferences* that are every bit as subjective as our preferences for material goods?

How can we claim to know what the Good Life is, and then impose our subjective preferences on millions of others whose preferences might differ? "If every man be the only judge of his own interest, if we can ascertain what makes him better off *solely* by observations of the *preferences* his actions *reveal*, then however Society develops under free choices, we must assume that whatever is, is the best possible world at the moment."[11]

But moral relativism with regard to public choice is only the first obstacle.

The "happy city" has always been thought of as a small place. The selection from *Sovereignty* which we have chosen for our prologue sets the problem very nicely: the "common good" cannot be sought "in methods which the model of a small, closed society inspires"—and yet these are virtually the only models that our tradition can supply us. The scale of modern life—a scale made possible by economic progress, first in agriculture and then in manufacturing—has permanently and profoundly changed the context of politics. As Pierre Manent has recently observed, human beings have invented only three essential political frameworks beyond the tribe: the city, the nation, and the empire.[12] Empires are still possible, but we do not want them; autonomous city-states are no longer an option; and so the nation is where the Political Good will have to be realized. We must try to imagine the Good Life on a scale that encompasses tens and hundreds of millions, when the whole tradition of political inquiry has held it possible only for the tens of thousands—and possibly not even for that many.

Furthermore, the modern economy changes more than the scale of *politics*. It also transforms *social* life, which is at all times the foundation on which the state is built. The family, the neighborhood, the workplace, the town—all these are changed in obedience to the requirements of economic life. These requirements, de Jouvenel reminds us, are "draconian"; they overturn much of the ancient moral teaching and unsettle all established social relationships. Where morality once urged the moderation of desires, the modern economy must continually awaken new desires so that they can be satisfied by new *goods*. The love of money, instead of being the root of evil, must be seen instead as the spur to all social and economic progress. The old and respected must be replaced by what is new and efficient, whether in matters of morality or in matters of technique. Rootedness and routine—long valued for the stability they bring to human relationships—must give way to mobility, flexibility, even opportunism.

The "payoff" is that modern society can support vastly greater populations, at unprecedented levels of physical comfort, while requiring fewer hours of less physically arduous labor. More of us live longer, and better, in material terms; and since we live longer and retire earlier than previous generations of workers, we work for a smaller fraction of our adult lives, giving more of us than ever before significant amounts of leisure time.

A useful question now makes its awkward appearance upon the stage: Is it not the case that this improvement in the material conditions of life for increasing numbers of people is, *itself*, the Good Life; what else, after all, do we need? And if economists can tell us how to drive this process to ever higher levels, can they not abandon political science altogether and strike off on their own?

IV

To put the answer in classical terms, what the modern economy supplies is *mere* life, while what we require is the *good* life. To achieve the latter it is necessary that citizens *desire* what is good—that is, something to be acquired "because it improves us" (as de Jouvenel puts it), and not simply because it has been made available to us by the market. For that to happen it is necessary that our desires be *educated*. This is not a new idea; both classical and modern authors acknowledge that the desires can be educated, but both make an important qualification: education will succeed only with the few; or it will succeed only under conditions radically different from those that exist in modern times: in a small city, with a homogeneous citizenry, preferably under the influence of common (and powerful) religious institutions.

De Jouvenel acknowledges the force of these arguments, and accepts the general conclusion that the finest things will never be desired by the many. But he insists that *better* things can be desired by *more* and possibly by *most* citizens—an important enough departure from the classical doctrine to be considered radical. But it is a departure imposed by a grim necessity: "We live in majority societies where beautiful things will be wiped out unless the majority appreciates them."[13] Despite our great economic achievements, modern life is, in the main, ugly, dreary, and dispiriting: there is an enormous gap between what our resources make it possible for us to have, on the one hand, and what we have chosen to have, on the other. This would be a matter of merely aristocratic regret, were it not for the reality that a dispirited and demoralized civilization is incapable, first, of excellence, then of self-awareness, and finally of self-government.

V

The essays in part one of this collection—"The Elements of Political Economy"—provide a masterful exploration of the problem of conceptualizing the Good under modern conditions, in a language that borrows from both economics and political science. Beginning with the traditional conceptions of welfare economics, de Jouvenel raises immediately the political problem. Can welfare economics supply criteria for political choice?

The traditional answer is that governments should choose policies that maximize welfare, defined, first, as increasing national income and second, as distributing that income in whatever way leads to a "greater sum of satisfactions than dissatisfactions." This framework is much clearer, firmer, more objective than anything supplied by contemporary political science, and for this reason economists have moved into the first ranks of the advisors of the modern state. But in fact, de Jouvenel argues, the framework has significant limitations. The first limitation is that the "ontology" of welfare economics is itself political; that is, it is borrowed from Hobbes (although few economists are aware of their debt): human nature is the seat of unending desires, and the objects of these desires are goods, "worth precisely what the desirer is willing to give for them. Therefore various goods can be compared and added up, however different in nature, because they have this in common that they are desired, and can be compared because they are more or less desired."[14]

What all the consumers together desire is, perforce, the *collective,* or common good. But it is obvious that what all consumers together desire might *not* be all there is to the social good; consumers might not want schools, or national defense, or breathable air—things which are nevertheless necessary to the survival of the society or the regime. The sum of individual choices might be different from the best *collective* choice. Furthermore, consumer/citizens cannot be asked to offer a price for items that are not actually for sale, such as social order itself—without which there could not be other satisfactions.

That the sum of individual preferences does not necessarily add up to the common good is a phenomenon that American political scientists have not been eager to puzzle over. One reason for this perhaps is that in the United States, the relationship between the "general will" and the "will of all" has been, for the most part, tolerably close: the various goods that consumers, in their private capacities, have desired have not, usually, been inconsistent with the requirements of social order and republican self-government. Furthermore, civic education, at least in the past, placed a very high value upon constitutional government, civility, disinterested public service, and other requirements of a healthy democratic state. But it is precisely the tendency of welfare economics and political science to take such *conditions* as *givens* that proves so dangerous, because it encourages us to forget that they are not givens at all, but the products of statemanship and political art of a very high order. The farther away we are from the origins of this art the more likely we are to take it for granted.

To the extent, therefore, that both political science and economics lack an adequate framework for *public choice* (to use a contemporary phrase with a controversial meaning), to that extent we are in danger of creating governments that can give people what they *want* but not what they *need*[15]—and that "first things therefore may come to be lost in the pursuit of last things."[16]

VI

But the Good, whatever we decide that it is, or whatever it requires us to choose, cannot simply be imposed from above; it is not a *government program*. In *Sovereignty*, de Jouvenel provides a powerful discussion of why all efforts to conceive and then institute intricately contrived schemes for public happiness have disastrous consequences. Having done that much, de Jouvenel might have stopped where so many others have stopped, and simply embraced the "market" as the source of all that we can identify as good.[17] This he does not do; de Jouvenel is a liberal but not a libertarian. The problem of the public good cannot be *solved* by the state; but the state has a role to play in its solution, nonetheless.

It is the responsibility of the public authorities (although not theirs exclusively) to foster the *conditions* under which the common good can emerge. (In a democratic state, this is also the responsibility of citizens in both their private and public capacities.) One of those conditions, for example—in some ways the centerpiece of his argument in *Sovereignty*—is "reciprocal trustfulness". Citizens must be able to trust one another before they can engage in *any* meaningful social activity, including, most importantly, *economic* activity. (We have seen, in the former Soviet Union, what the absence of trust does to economic progress.)

The concept of *amenity* is the core of de Jouvenel's discussion of the good. An "amenity" is a condition which makes life pleasant. Human beings are "sensitive" creatures; we are powerfully effected by what we see, hear, smell—by our surroundings, both physical, social, and moral. The improvement of those surroundings is properly, therefore, part of the study of political economy. Economists (and the statesmen they advise) must learn how to incorporate amenities into a system of national accounting, so that we will be aware of their increase and decrease over time. Furthermore, to the extent that a normal marketplace fails to supply such amenities, or actually contributes to their disappearance (through such externalities as environmental pollution, or the excessive mobility imposed by national labor markets)—to that extent public authority must intervene to supply what is missing. And that, of course, brings us back to the original problem: to supply what is missing we must be able to *name* it; we must have a theory of public amenity, or at least a general picture of the circumstances in which *Homo Felix* lives and works.

De Jouvenel's theory of amenity begins where the ancients began: human happiness is the fulfillment of a potential; it consists of growth *toward*, rather than possession *of*. The greatest boon of the modern economy is not, therefore, the "things" it gives us—the movies and bicycles and electronic gadgets—but the leisure and comfort that it makes possible, for the first time, for the majority. What a revolution the forty-hour week is! And what a revolution also is the application of machinery to labor, and the extraordinary reduction in the physical effort involved even in such occupations as mining and agriculture. The shortening of the workweek and the reduction in the physical rigors of labor have provided humankind with an extraordinary opportunity. How have we used it?

> Imagine that an eighteenth century philanthropist, say the Marquis de Mirabeau or Thomas Jefferson, were resurrected and briefed as to the increase in labor productivity and wealth which has occurred since his day. He would certainly imagine a world where beauty and culture prevailed, where the setting of life would immediately manifest the social wealth.[18]

Who could doubt the disappointment of our ancestors at the dreariness and coarseness of modern life, despite such enormous wealth and opportunity? "I would deem myself fortunate indeed," de Jouvenel concludes, "if I had found it possible to contribute towards the [induction of] our increasing wealth in the service of a greater amenity of life."[19]

If happiness is the fulfillment of potential, then education, as well as work, must enter the welfare calculus. De Jouvenel believed that the emphasis economists placed on education for the workplace and for increased productivity (what would nowadays be called "preparation for the global economy of the 21st century") was too narrow, and he made a straightforward case for liberal education as "an education for those who may look forward to a life free from pressing cares."[20] Because modern workers will have more leisure than their ancestors, the aims of a liberal education are now relevant for a much wider section of the population than ever before in our history.[21]

> The case for developing the average man's skill as a laborer is unaswerable, since among the benefits procured, despite the loss of work time, is the progressive enlargement of that share of time during which he is a freeman, a "gentleman." [B]ut the greater the share thus liberated, the more pressing it becomes to educate man for the fruitful use of this free time.... In short, future generations, which can look forward to an increasingly lighter burden of work, and to an increasing share of free time, require a liberal education.... Education then has a dual purpose: to make man's labor more productive, and his leisure more fruitful. And the greater the gains in one direction, the more necessary is progress in the other."[22]

Necessary—because the market can only supply goods which citizens desire, or can be induced to desire. Advertising can persuade consumers to want the new goods that the economy is capable of producing; but only education can teach citizens to place a high value on the *conditions* which make public happiness possible, and which are not the products of the market but of statesmanship.

VII

The selections in part two—"Problems of Post-War Reconstruction"—concern a variety of problems for which political economy supplies useful insights: international monetary reform; democracy in former colonies; Soviet economic planning; and others. Even though some of these essays deal with controversies long settled, their qualities are worth savoring, nonetheless. There has never been a clearer indictment of rent control and its consequences than de Jouvenel's discussion of "dollar-a-month rents" in Paris in the late 1940s.[23] And while Algeria is no longer a "pluri-communal" state, what de Jouvenel has to say about the problem of "two nations in one" is relevant to more than one country in the modern world—and is far more sobering than much contemporary analysis of communal conflict.[24]

Two essays in this section, however, are of direct and prophetic relevance to contemporary problems. The first is "Money in the Market," which was written in 1955, before the relaxation of exchange controls in Western Europe; it anticipates a time when national currencies will be freely traded against one another, and outlines the challenge of interdependence that such trading will impose on all countries who seek to join the international economy. "The Political Consequences of the Rise of Science" offers a dissent from the widespread view among intellectuals that science and democracy are natural allies. ("Unwittingly and indirectly, the scientist undermines the juristic order.... science, far from providing automatic support to democracy, constitutes a challenge to it, which we must find ways of meeting.") The picture de Jouvenel paints of an increasingly befuddled citizenry, looking to science as the source of ever greater boons while growing increasingly doubtful about its own capacity to make judgments, is painfully close to our contemporary reality.

The selections in part three—"The Political Economy of Natural Resources"—display an aspect of de Jouvenel's work already present in the 1950s, and that grew more important during the last two decades of his life. The conventional word for this theme is "environmentalism," but de Jouvenel's approach to the environment borrows from an older tradition—"conservation"—to which he has added the economist's interest in "amenity." The result is something very different, in interesting and instructive ways, from the dominant modes of contemporary environmental writing.

First, de Jouvenel acknowledges that the environment is a *resource*— it is there to be used, but not wasted. The economic problem is to find a method of forcing human users to pay an accurate price for what they take from nature; otherwise, our uses will be profligate rather than prudent. Taking care of what has been given us is called "stewardship"; the virtue of the steward is "husbandry," a word which encourages us to think of the earth as a garden, rather than as a wilderness (where we do not belong) or a mine (from which we can simply extract without limit). "We esteem ourselves masters of the Earth. But should not an owner be the husbandman of his land? Must he not tend it as he uses it? Shall he not indeed delight in its beauty as well as enjoy its fruit?"[25] The value of this approach is that all who use a garden can be required

to bear their share of responsibility for it, a process to which economists could make greater contributions if they paid more attention to
natural resources.[26]

But while the environment is a resource, it is also our *home*; the
efficient use of resources need not prevent us from making our immediate surroundings more pleasant. Here de Jouvenel's work is reminis-
cent of an older American tradition exemplified by Frederick Law
Olmsted, and other architects and designers who hoped to merge Nature and City into one felicitous human environment. What a refresh-
ing surprise it is to encounter a paragraph such as this (from "Efficiency
and Amenity"):

> In writing and image, many glimpses of the Golden Age have been vouchsafed to
> us; they concur quite remarkably. *Homo Felix* moves against a background of
> beauty, delights in his workmanship, is benefited by the company he keeps, and
> his song of joy praises his Creator. Most often he is shown in a landscape mel-
> lowed by the human hand, with a nice balance of trees, meadows and stream; a
> graceful temple however testifies to urbanity. Contrariwise, if *Homo Felix* hap-
> pens to be painted in a public place, then the greenery of the surroundings shows
> through the monuments of the town. The latter is no more than a meeting place for
> worship and conviviality. *Homo Felix* is not idle, but the enjoyment of doing things
> so overcomes the awareness that they must be done as to exclude any sense of
> drudgery. His associates move his heart and quicken his wit; expecting the best of
> him, they help him to achieve it. He opens his eyes at dawn, eager for the activi-
> ties of the day, and closes them at dusk; free from worry he exerts no pressure on
> any other man nor does he endure any.

A "background of beauty," good work and good company: this is no
elaborate Utopian fantasy, or the beginning of a complex national administrative program; it is only a picture meant to entice us by its charm
and its simplicity, and to suggest the *conditions* under which the good
life might be pursued. We cannot, after all, find what we are seeking
unless we have a picture, however sketchy, of what it looks like. The
great virtue of de Jouvenel's vision of the Good Life is that it embraces
nature, economy, and polity in a single frame; and if we can agree with
his qualification ("maybe the picture drawn thereof was a fanciful one")
we must also agree with his conclusion: "But surely there is some way
of life which would be an improvement upon that which we find."[27]

A second aspect of de Jouvenel's discussion of natural resources is
his awareness that economic interdependence and the increased ease
and speed of transportation and communication, all make the world an
apparently smaller place—without making it more peaceful or easier
to manage. We are not yet, he says, "one World"; but we are increas-

ingly conscious of the earth as "one place." The famous photograph of the earth in space (which "I can now hang upon my wall, just as easily as a picture of my own house") should not fool us into thinking that the world has become a small town (or worse, a "spaceship"), easily governed (or "operated") if only we "mingle" and get to know one another. International interdependence will, for one thing, expose the radical *inequality* of nations: some have more natural resources than others, a fact of geography about which policy can do very little.[28] Because some nations have much and others little, the conservation of natural resources will soon run up against an increased competition for their more vigorous exploitation, more chaotic because it will involve many more players than ever before.[29] And for a long time to come, the ease of transportation will mean simply that refugees can move more readily across borders, spreading political instability and other forms of disturbance.

Finally, de Jouvenel's interest in conservation is folded within his larger aim, which is to focus our attention on the Good Life as the guide to public choice. There has long been a tendency among environmentalists to segregate a concern for (say) habitat preservation or clean air from other concerns, on the grounds, perhaps, that distraction will dilute the energies of a "movement" that considers itself embattled. But political economy tries to connect the pieces: to link economic growth with a more prudent use of natural resources, or the preservation of "natural" beauty with the better design of urban spaces. There is great wisdom, we are convinced, in de Jouvenel's clarity about the importance of such balancing.

There is great wisdom also in his sense of historical perspective. The last decades of the twentieth century have been a fertile breeding ground for multiple forms of hysteria, and it is often hard not to get the sense from our current intellectual debates that the End is Near. By contrast, de Jouvenel is aware of how much has improved—even apparently small things to which most citizens give little thought, such as the disappearance of class distinctions in dress, which has been made possible by the growth of mass-produced clothing. When we become more conscious of how difficult life was for most of our ancestors, even as recently as two generations back—longer hours, harder work, less food, and shorter lifespans—we become more conscious of the opportunities the modern economy presents, and less preoccupied with what seem like catastrophic problems. But at the same time we should be equally conscious of how we have wasted our opportunities by letting what is last take precedence over what is first. It is de Jouvenel's ability to expose the pettiness of our public ambitions that is among his greatest strengths as a teacher.

—Dennis Hale and Marc Landy
Department of Political Science
Boston College
Chestnut Hill, Massachusetts
November, 1997

Notes

1. For a discussion of de Jouvenel's contribution to political science, see our earlier collection, *The Nature of Politics: Selected Essays of Bertrand de Jouvenel* (Transaction Books, 1992).
2. The Society for Economic, Industrial, and Social Research.
3. Published as *Vers la forêt du XXIe siècle* (1978).
4. See, for example, *L'économie dirigée* (1928); *La crise du capitalisme américain* (1933); *Napoleon et l'économie dirigeée* (1942); *L'économie mondiale au XXe siècle* (1944); *Problems of Socialist England* (1946); *L'Amérique en Europe: le plan Marshall et la coopération intercontinentale* (1948); *The Ethics of Redistribution* (1951); *Problèmes économique de notre temps* (1966); and *Arcadie, essais sur le mieux-vivre* (1968).
5. "Back to Basics: The Concrete Economy," in this volume.
6. Wilson C. McWilliams, "Foreword" to *The Nature of Politics*, p. 38.
7. See also *La décomposition de l'Europe libérale: Oct. 24–Jan. 1932* (1941). *On Power* was followed in 1955 by *Sovereignty: An Inquiry into the Political Good* and *The Pure Theory of Politics* (1963). *On Power* was first published by Viking Press, in 1948, in a translation by J. F. Huntington. The Viking edition was reissued in 1995 by the Liberty Fund, which published a new edition of *Sovereignty* in 1998, with an introduction by Daniel Mahoney.
8. De Jouvenel visited the United States for the first time in the 1930s, as a correspondent for French newspapers. His private aim was to study the Roosevelt administration's approach to economic reform.
9. "A Better Life in an Affluent Society," this volume.
10. It is a recurring observation in de Jouvenel's work on America that the most progressive intellectuals failed to appreciate the stubborn independence of the United States Congress, and were constantly embracing schemes to "discipline" the legislature to the will of the executive. Americans, de Jouvenel believed, should learn to cherish the independent legislature as they cherish the independent university.
11. "Efficiency and Amenity," this volume.
12. Pierre Manent, "Democracy without Nations?" *Journal of Democracy* 8 (April, 1997): 92–102.
13. "Toward a Political Theory of Education," this volume.
14. "The Idea of Welfare," this volume.
15. That many citizens–and many scholars as well–will find this distinction paradoxical is a sign that the phenomenon is already well advanced.
16. "The Idea of Welfare."

17. De Jouvenel had a great admiration for both F. A. Hayek and Ludwig von Mises; yet his understanding of political economy differs from theirs in significant ways.
18. "Efficiency and Amenity," this volume.
19. Ibid.
20. "Toward a Political Theory of Education," op. cit.
21. Liberal education is not suited to everyone, however, which raises the difficult question of what those who do not learn better uses of their leisure will do in their spare time.
22. Ibid.
23. "No Vacancies," this volume.
24. "Reflections on Colonialism," this volume.
25. "The Stewardship of the Earth," this volume.
26. Another virtue of this approach is its acceptance of human beings as rightful proprietors of the garden. Much of contemporary environmentalism is frankly antihuman in its implications—the school known as "deep ecology", for example, which asserts without apology that man is an intruder in the wilderness. It is not irrelevant in this context that de Jouvenel saw a Christian imperative to conservation.
27. "Effiency and Amenity."
28. See "From Political Economy to Political Ecology," this volume.
29. See, for example, the discussion in "An Economic View of Marine Problems," this volume, which anticipates some of the problems of enforcing an "international regime of the oceans"—including the possibible exhaustion of fish stocks through harshly competitive over-fishing.

Prologue

*"The very varied benefits which men can in course of time
confer on one another by mutual intercourse do not resemble....
a convergent series of which the formula can be found, but a
divergent series which cannot be totaled. And the common good
has seemed to us to consist in conditions which make possible
the development of this indefinite series. Trustfulness between
partners struck us as the most obvious of these conditions....
What we have met with is a contradiction between, on the one
hand, the growth of this state of trustfulness and, on the other,
the indefinite development of the relations between men, the
enlargement of the area which they cover and the diversifica-
tion of their content. The contradiction is one, clearly, between
the effects sought and the condition necessary to their achievement. This contradiction has become steadily clearer; the quest
for the climate of trustfulness raises in the mind the picture of a
closed, narrow circle of neighbors who are very much alike,
who value highly a type which each strives to realize and who
are very proud of a common denominator which all wish to
maintain. This picture.... strikes our minds with extraordinary
vividness.... [A]lmost everyone subconsciously wishes to
recover the warmth of the...small, closely-knit society which
was the school of the species. This unavowed regret is the root
of nearly all utopias, both revolutionary and reactionary, and
every political heresy, left or right...[T]he small society, as the
milieu in which man is first bound, retains for him an infinite
attraction; but...any attempt to graft the same features on a
large society is Utopian and leads to tyranny. With that
admitted, it is clear that as social relations become wider and
more various, the common good conceived as reciprocal
trustfulness cannot be sought in methods which the model of a
small, closed society inspires; such a model is, on the contrary,
entirely misleading."*

—Bertrand de Jouvenel,
Sovereignty: An Inquiry Into the Political Good

Part One:

The Elements of Political Economy

*"So it seems that individuals as such are quite
incapable of weighing rightly or meaningfully the
value of government activities. And if the public
authority seeks to rest its own appreciation of its
service as against others which might be provided
out of the same resources, or its appreciation of
some of its services as against others, on some
form* of subjective appreciation by consumers as
such, *it must go terribly astray. In other words
it seems that public policies cannot be made to
rest upon what people desire* in their private
capacities. *"*
—"The Idea of Welfare," 1952

1

The Idea of Welfare

I

Last winter I was in America attending "The Great Debate" [on U.S. troop commitments in Europe—Eds.]. During the extended hearings held by the four assembled committees on Armed Services and Foreign Affairs of the two Houses, two different points were dealt with: there was the constitutional or formal issue: did the President have the right to commit troops to Europe on his own, without the consent of Congress? And there was the substantial issue: should troops be sent?

In short *who* was to decide and *what* was to be done? All of political theory can, in my view, be ranged under these two headings of *who* and *what*.

Who is the legitimate authority? To whom does Imperium *sive* Sovereignty belong, and by whom is it to be exercised? How is this exercise conferred? How is it partitioned out into *potestates*? What is the legitimate province of the several *potestates*? All this, and much more, constitutes the realm of *who*: a major sector of political science.

But surely not a more important one than the realm of *what*. *What* is the proper decision? By what standards appraised? Based on what assumptions as to man's nature and *summum bonum*, as to the final cause of society and the proper purposes of government?

My interest lies with the second sector. This can be designated as the theory of political choice or the theory of the best decision. We may indeed name it at will, as explorers do of uncharted lands, for, to my limited knowledge, very little work has been done in that field for a very long time. The problem of *who* has held sway. Why this predominance of the problem of *who*?

From *Cambridge Journal* 5, No. 11 (August 1952). Reprinted by permission of the author.

Three reasons may be propounded. First, it is the problem of attribution of power, a thing which men covet. Competition for power communicates its warmth to discussions about titles to power. Secondly, when the attribution of power is in doubt, the legitimacy of authority in question, such disorders follow that the problem of the best measures becomes academic, and the first need of society is for a recognized authority. Thus it is in fact necessary to begin chronologically with the problem of the legitimate authority. Whenever that has been in dispute—as in France it was during the delphinian stage of the Hundred Years War, or indeed more recently with the duality of Vichy and London or Algiers, terrible consequences follow. It was of course the great achievement of Ancien Régime Europe to settle the problem of *who* by monarchic succession. (This, however, left the vexatious problem of the passing of the crown into foreign hands.) And politics has of course been mainly concerned during almost the last three centuries with shifting the notion of legitimacy which now applies to the team emerging out of a periodic auctioning of political leadership.

The third reason for the major importance assigned to the problem of *who* is that men are very prone to think that the proper decision follows *ipso facto* from the choice of the proper ruler. The candidates for office certainly seem to think so. The whole faction which surrounds and supports pretenders thinks so.

This linking of the "proper decision" with the "proper ruler" can be regarded in two ways. It can be maintained that anything he-who-is-entitled-to-command, *does command*, is therefore right. This is arbitrary government. Such theory is the theory of despotism, whether it applies to the anointed or to the elected, to any individual or group of people. It seems incredible that the theory of despotism should ever have been held, and even more so that it should be held today by a great many people quite unconscious that they do. That has been and is possible because the relationship between the "proper ruler" and the "proper decision" is more often regarded the other side up.

The proper ruler shall take the proper decision *because* we have recognized *before* adjudging him the proper ruler that his future decisions shall be proper, either because generally speaking he has been rightly equipped morally and intellectually to take the right decisions, or because, more definitely, we have chosen him on the *strength of the decisions* he proposed to take on his program.

Choosing rulers on the strength of a judgment of character was of course the principle of the representative system, which has now been discarded: the choice is based on the program. Therefore it can be said that there is no point in discussing what those who govern should do since they are enabled to govern only in consideration of the decisions they in advance promised to make.

To this there are two answers. It may be observed that in fact the commitments are very vague and general. A government arising out of an election takes its promises only as a limiting factor of its decisions. But it is more meaningful and fertile to make another answer. Assuming, against evidence but for logical purposes, that decisions in democracy are not made by those in power but by the *people themselves,* then indeed for those in power there is no problem of what to do; what to do is for them "given"; but in that view of things "the people" make the decisions. Then *for them* there is a problem of *what.*

There is a problem of *what* for you and for me. Assume that on the morrow of a popular referendum offering the choice of measures A and B, we agree that A is the "right" measure *since* it has been chosen, yet on the eve of the referendum we can make no such abandon of our own judgment to that of the community, as we do not know what the community prefer. We have to vote in order to know which *we ourselves* think best of A or B.

However eager modern political science shows itself to take choices as given, these must in fact, at some stage or other, be *made.* Indeed a democracy is by definition a regime where every individual, *qua* citizen, is supposed to be choosing for the community the decisions it should take through the proper agencies. This is a continuous process known as the movement of opinion. The choice may be, at some moments merely a "paper choice," we would rather have this decision than that, but these paper choices do weigh or are supposed to. For the man in office, it is a continuous process of effective choices.

Are these choices of what should or should not be done entirely irrational? Who would go so far? Yet sociologists are prone to treat them as irrational. This is regrettably implied in the focusing of interest upon the evolution of such choices (for instance in dynamic pollstering) *rather* than upon the act of choice itself. If this act is at all rational, made by reasoning with the help of criteria and with the use of assumptions, then the choice of criteria and of assumptions are of the utmost interest to the political theorist. And if the process is rational it follows that the reasoning can be improved, the method of choice perfected. Which is surely something worth our labor.

It is difficult to deny at least that *some* people use *some* apparatus of thought to make *some* decisions. As soon as this is granted it becomes important to study and improve this apparatus. This seems to evoke the opposition of many political scientists. They feel on safely scientific ground only as long as they study opinion as given. I wonder whether here the urge to be scientific does not constitute an obstacle to science. A physicist does not feel at his most scientific when he asks people to give him their impression as to the relative weights of different items and classifies the replies. He deems it his office to provide these people with *means* of *actually comparing* the weights. In the same manner I think political science should not shirk the task of elaborating a method whereby a *better* political decision may be known from a *worse*.

Political decisions are sometimes called "courses," which is a good enough word because it evokes their execution *over time* and the deployment of their effects over time. Obviously to know a *better decision* from a *worse* you must have some view of these effects, that is some understanding of social mechanisms, and some means of appraising the value of effects.

If for instance the question at stake be the suppression of gambling, you may adjudge this a good decision on the grounds that gambling is morally bad, and then you may contemplate the execution of this decision over time, foresee that it will not be executed, that it will tend to increase disobedience to law, perhaps corruption of the repressive force, and you will have to weigh these disadvantages.

This is just an instance of a simple political problem. It involves *values* and *assumptions*, but these do not make the problem unmanageable. The values will be given different weights by different people. And it is interesting to know why. Assumptions may be different, and it may be possible to test their relative adequacies. To say that this makes the problem incapable of being stated with precision is equivalent to denying the possibility of algebra.

The importance of stating the problem and then inducing individuals to state their values and assumptions lies to a great part in the consequence of tying them down to values and assumptions which they must then carry over to other problems. It is already a great thing to get a given individual to use throughout the political field the same values and assumptions, a consistency he often fails to observe. But also the bringing of values and assumptions to bear on several different problems must lead him to reject certain assumptions which he is not willing to accept in all cases and to redress some estimations of values, which he is not willing to adhere to throughout.

Should political science do this sort of thing, that is, work towards a methodology of political choice? I think it should, but it is a fact that it does not.

II

In the meantime economists put us to shame because they have courageously embarked upon a job which really lies in our province. I am of course alluding to those two important segments of economics known as national income accounting and the new welfare economics. Such work bears a direct relation to the preoccupations of those who govern. If the politician asks the political scientist: "What should I do?" there is either no reply, or a purely formal one ("Execute the will of the people" but that tells me nothing as to what I myself should will), or again it may be: "Attend to *Bonum Commune.*" This looks more promising. But unfortunately no criteria are provided by which I may tell how to maximize *Bonum Commune.*

The economist on the other hand does offer something more concrete. He states that it is good to increase the National Income and offers means to measure its increase. He also states that it is good to alter the distribution of personal incomes in any way that causes a greater sum of satisfactions than dissatisfactions. It is the fashion among welfare economists to deny that they are comparing satisfactions. But "the lady doth protest too much". That is in fact what they do. Professor Pigou insists upon it with vigorous honesty. "Welfare relates to satisfactions."[1]

The politician uses the language of welfare economics: he expounds his achievements in terms of increases of the national income; and he justifies measures hurtful to some by claiming that others have so profited as to make the balance of alterations favorable. While it can be said that politicians are indebted for their mode of thought to the disciplines mentioned—and that is most apparent in the use of national income accounting—it can also be said that these disciplines refine the actual attitude of politicians, and this is most apparent in the attitude to distribution of incomes or satisfaction.

Anyhow the close relationship between live politics and academic work is precisely *that which one would reasonably expect between politics and political science*, and which in fact is not to be found. Such a connection did exist in the days of Hobbes, Locke, Burke, Siéyes, Benjamin Constant, in fact up to say the eighties of the last century. Actual political discussions drew largely upon doctrinal discussions on the form of government. Today they draw upon the contributions of economics. This one tends to explain in what seems to me a facile manner by saying that now problems are mainly economic. What this means really is that problems are *appraised* in the language of economics. Take for instance the problem of "how much rearmament Europe can stand." This is discussed in terms of allocation of national product, but what is really at issue is not that national incomes cannot stand more than so much rearmament, it is in fact that European opinion is not so conscious and convinced of its military peril as to be willing to accept a substantial (or indeed any) compression of its way of life: that is a *political* situation; *economics* provides a *language*.

The present glaring precedence of economics over political science in the counsels of government does not seem to me due so much to the nature of the problems as to the attitude of economists as against that of political scientists. The economists have been more daring. They have forged ahead because they have wanted to be effective and have to that end ventured assumptions. The purpose of this lecture is to investigate these assumptions and to find how far we can trust a language which is being widely used, and is providing an inspiration to those in responsible positions. It is stretched even to provide comparisons of the welfare of different societies, even the welfare of different civilizations in different centuries. It is currently invoked to find what contribution different nations should fairly make to a common purpose, such as Western defense. These are very delicate problems. Have we indeed got an instrument of measurement allowing us to do all these things? If we have, this effects a major revolution in political science, of which we must take cognizance and to which we must gear our thoughts. If we have *not* such an instrument while it is commonly thought that we have, then there is a potential *danger* of major mistakes being made. Finally it may be that there is an apparatus of thought which can be used for some purposes and not for some others, under some assumptions and not under some others, which we should seek to define in cooperation with economists.

III

In the dismal days of equilibrium theories, which showed that under frictionless conditions, not to be found in reality, a general equilibrium would result about which nothing much could be said, the Western mania for measuring stood economics in good stead. Estimates of wealth or of national income were made at various times by adding up monetary values. These estimates came to be lined up by people who were not regarded as real economists, such people as Mulhall or Webb. It seemed interesting to try and make them comparable by eliminating the influence of price changes. It then appeared that this wealth or this national income moved up with greater or lesser speed in different periods and that it was best to have it move up as rapidly as possible. It came to be regarded as a rough "measure" of the common good, though the word was never pronounced.

In the meantime, preoccupation with poverty made it of major interest to find whether the standard of life of the least favored was being satisfactorily improved. It came to be adjudged a chief concern of the state to improve it, if necessary at the expense of the better placed. The idea of welfare thus took some shape as the idea of an increase in the national income coupled with a redistribution among individuals to the benefit of the least favored. After various tentative formulations, finally the idea was fully and coherently set forth in that famous book: Professor Pigou's *Economics of Welfare*. This can be said to have opened an era of fruitful thinking for economists, in the sense that henceforth they had criteria for advising this or that policy.

Let me here stress that the setting up of criteria for government action was made possible to economists by their implied philosophy. They will of course insist that they have no metaphysics and pass no value judgments. But that is quite false. Whatever else they may think outside their department, as economists they have a view of man, and derive from it value judgments. To the economist as such, man is essentially a consumer. Therefore, whatever ontological views the economist may hold in his private capacity, as an economist he adopts the Hobbesian view of human nature as a seat of desires; man desires, the things he desires are to him good, they are *goods* in the economic language. And they are worth precisely what the desirer is willing to give for them. Therefore various goods can be compared and added up, however different in nature, because they have this in common that they are desired, and can be compared because they are more or less desired. This comparing and adding up is valid in the case of one man choosing the parcel of goods most agreeable to him within the ambit of his resources. And this validity may be carried over to the case of a great number of men exercising their choices simultaneously on the market. They are regarded as one consumer; though of course the choices here are weighted by the distribution of incomes. But this being given, at a given moment it is fair to say that the values of the various categories of goods on the market reflect the desires of the consumer body, such as it is at this moment.

Now two things emerge clearly from this very rough picture. One is that it can take into account only those goods which are at this moment to be had for money. Welfare economists state, with all the desirable clarity, that they can only deal with economic welfare, that other elements of overall welfare must remain out of their ambit. The second is that the whole validity of measuring with the same rod things different in species rests upon their appreciation by the same agent: the sum of individual consumers.

Welfare economists are well aware that there is a jump involved in passing over from one consumer as judge of values to the whole body of consumers. All the more so while individual consumers are unequally endowed with the "economic vote." Unease about this inclines them, short of political or sentimental preference, to regard *even* distribution of incomes as desirable for purely methodological purposes. It is easier to treat as a single consumer a number of consumers equally endowed, than a number of consumers unequally endowed.

But if there is a jump involved in passing from one consumer to the whole consumer body, there is another and steeper one involved in adding to the values set by the consumer body those which are set by a different judge of values, that is, government.

To the movie shows, bicycles, and other innumerable things called forth by consumer demands, government adds, say, battleships. Battleships can be compared in monetary value to bicycles because their production calls for materials and labor which are appreciated in money, an appreciation which rests primarily upon the workings of the consumer economy. But can battleships be said to add to the subjective economic welfare of consumers? If then the national product comprises these battleships, does it not cease to be a fair measure of total consumer welfare, as appreciated by them?

The great pioneer of national income accounting, Simon Kuznets, has made this point with the utmost vigor in a fundamental article, published in the *Harvard Review of Economics and Statistics* (August 1948, no. 107) that "the final goal of economic activity is provision of goods to consumers and that everything else, by the nature of the case, is intermediate product." Governmental activities in that view should be appraised as costs incident to the ultimate satisfaction of the consumer, the final judge. This seems consistent as against what Kuznets calls "the fetishism of conceiving the government as an ultimate consumer itself, given a corporeal entity the satisfaction of whose needs is raised to the same status of finality as the satisfaction of the needs of the men and women who comprise the community."

IV

However admirably careful the pioneers in this work have shown themselves in indicating what they do measure and in excluding what they do not, the abundant evidence provided about something as against the total lack of evidence about the other things involved in the prosperity and happiness of a commonwealth, tends to cause *neglect* of these other things.

Let me first attend to the drawback of emphasizing those services obtained for money as against those which are not. Anything people are willing to pay for is an addition to welfare. And things are contributions to welfare only in such proportion as people do pay for them. Stupid moving pictures are an addition to welfare. Those things which are free, such as an excellent climate, are not counted and do not figure in those international comparisons of welfare one ventures upon; while the production of waterproofs in the country where they are necessary *does* figure in welfare. Those things which are provided at a total low cost and of which there is enough (inelastic demand), count very little. For instance in a country where people are very careful that no fires break out few firemen are needed, the fire service is cheap, fire insurance low. Stupid pictures now induce an outbreak of arson. These pictures are none the less an addition to welfare: people have appreciated them. But the fires which break out now call for a vast increase in the number of firemen and the fire machinery: this is also an increase in welfare. Thus an evil and its correction bringing things back to former situation both come out as addition to welfare. It is tempting to stress the neglect of intangibles: to note that total national expenditure on the Established Church of 18 million pounds obviously fails to represent the value really set upon it by the nation, as against other things.

This mode of calculation leads to *underestimation of essentials* of which one stands assured or against an essential which one desires. It also leads to adjudging every complication a gain. As in the following example:

There is a small town whose inhabitants live by serving some local enterprise, let it be a small family factory. This shuts down, bought up by a bigger concern which stands say ten miles away. All the employees are now enrolled in the bigger factory, which runs a bus service to carry the workers to and fro, and they get higher wages to cover the cost of transportation. The new bus service appears in national accounting as an increase of national product, the cost of transportation as an increase of wages, and therefore as an increase of the flow of goods to consumers. Yet all that has happened is that the workers spend more time away from home; their welfare has decreased.

Social phenomena of the highest importance appear in national accounting on what seems to me the wrong side of the ledger. For instance, the break-up of the family. We start with a society of large, well-knit families, the elders being provided for by the adult members and contributing what labor they still feel capable of. We go on to another state of affairs where the elders are shouldered away, and must run their own establishment. To that purpose they get a pittance from government. Affectively they are isolated, physically they are idle, and if they forgo this idleness they forgo their state grant; economically they are useless on the productive side, and less well provided for on the consumer side than they were before. Yet their now having individual incomes comes out as social improvement.

Then again let me suppose that a population of mountain inhabitants engaged in watchmaking, such as the Chaux de Fonds population in Switzerland, finds its business going to larger town factories: these people move down to the factory and get bigger wages: town costs also are higher. Nonetheless the flow of goods to them has increased. In the meantime they have sold their mountain homes. Now it turns out that the town air, laden with fumes, is not good for their children. So they get a yearly holiday of a month, during which they rent their former houses, now paying for the benefits of the open air, formerly free to them: this is again an increase in welfare. Yet they have only in part reverted to their former position.

The last example throws the door wide open to the retort, that in both cases there has been a true increase in welfare: the people moved down of their own free will, didn't they? This means that the down position was a chosen one. Then they moved up for a month again of their own will: and that was again a chosen position. I laid myself open to this retort because it seems to me to bring out clearly what has to be considered. Any change which people make is to be accounted a betterment, since they do make it. They are assumed to be the best judges of their own interest, and indeed they are *within their own behavioral world*.

Now insofar as this viewpoint reigns over the whole field of study, no criticism can be made. Let me for instance revert to the well-known joking objection made to income calculus. Assume that all married couples divorce, and that every husband must pay his former wife for her housekeeping services: nothing really is changed and the national income goes up by the whole value of these services. But the objection can be dispelled by resort to the notion of "chosen position": if this has happened, it is presumably that married couples have preferred this arrangement to the former: they have then moved from one position to another they preferred, and there is an increase in welfare. This is the very solid position, in my judgment, adopted by Dr. Little in his remarkable study. It is fully in keeping with our ideas of freedom that the position of individuals is improved every time they willingly alter it: doing the best for themselves in their behavioral world.

That viewpoint, however, is wholly abandoned when the state contribution to welfare is appraised. The state does prevent people from doing things they want to do, makes them do things they did not wish to do, and applies resources of considerable volume to tasks which individuals would be unwilling to finance to that extent out of their purses as consumers.

V

It is claimed that welfare calculus can guide political choice. Thus Scitovski: "Welfare economics supplies the economist—and the politician—with standards, at least with some standards, by which to appraise and on the basis of which to formulate policies."[2] And this is certainly so in the case of decisions which have the nature of adjudications, involving no consumption of resources by the government. Thus the government changes tariffs and thereby the relative positions of producers within the country. This is good if the total supply of goods is increased and their repartition not worsened, or if their repartition is improved. In the same manner changes in taxation can be appraised good if they alter the distribution of incomes in a way which we hold desirable without decreasing or while increasing the total flow of goods to consumers.

But political decisions involving only a change in the flow of goods are very far from exhausting the range of political decisions. There are some which involve the provision of goods or services to consumers at the cost of consumption of resources by the government. And others again which involve restraints upon individual actions.

Let us consider the class of decisions involving provision of services to consumers at the cost of consumption by government, say education. Can we really appraise the desirability of state-supported education in terms of welfare calculations? That is, can we say how much of it there should be and how its utility compares with other things?

Let us make the simplifying assumption that incomes are distributed in the most desirable manner, each having a share estimated just by all and himself, in order to move the issue of distribution out of the way. Now under this ideal distribution, individuals so apply their incomes that each obtains within the limits of his fairly apportioned income his maximum satisfaction or in other terms he does the best for himself within his own behavioral world. In such conditions (assuming for the moment no state expenditure) all the resources of society are allocated to produce maximum satisfaction of individuals under the fairest conditions of repartition. Say that this society spends so much on education. Now its government deems this not enough and increases expenditure on education, obviously through taxes. The previously ideal distribution of resources is thereby *distorted*. There is *more* of education than the people had chosen and *less* of something else. If we adhere to the subjective conception of welfare, we must maintain that welfare has decreased. Consumers have been moved away from their chosen position.

Some things such as education have to be provided to consumers in greater quantity than they had chosen as individual consumers, that is against their preferences as consumers. That the value of national education to consumers as such is less than its national cost is brought out forcibly by their failure to cover its expenditure by voluntary payments. Again we can imagine battleships being built by voluntary subscriptions. No doubt everybody would give something. The subjective appreciation of battleships is not nil. But it would not amount to anywhere near the value of the British fleet.

Pigou meets this very squarely: a situation containing more satisfaction is not necessarily better than one containing less...it is possible that under certain circumstances a government ought to foster a situation embodying less welfare.

Yes, but what then is the criterion of choice? Government activities are entered in the national product at whatever their cost is. When taken simultaneously with consumer appraisal of other goods this is seen to assume that whatever the allocation of resources to government and whatever the affectation of these resources, it is precisely the right allocation and the right affectation. This in fact marks the giving up of choice criteria. It is assumed that whatever the government does it adds to welfare and is the best use of available resources.

However the use of resources of the state to provide consumers with services which apparently, in their consumer capacity, they would have used less of as against more of something else, is not the main problem arising out of the attempts at welfare calculation.

The essential office and duty of the state, shorn of the more and more numerous *new functions* it has assumed, is to *restrain* people from doing things they would do and should not do, that is it consists in restraining them from "moving to chosen positions." Can this be put in terms of welfare calculus? It can insofar as A's moving to his chosen position would involve B's not moving to his chosen position, as if A intended to rob B of his economies, wanted to move into B's savings account precluding B from moving into a new house. But it is not in fact true that the preventive actions of a government are restricted to such instances which come under the idea of protecting the liberty of B against the abuse of A's. For instance few satisfactions are increased as against the dissatisfaction caused when the government breaks up drug traffic. This interferes with the satisfactions of the sellers who made money, and of the addicts who must be assumed to have obtained subjective satisfactions from the drug since they chose to consume it at great cost.[3] Governments do not, and we, when we advise them in a public or a private capacity, do not think in terms of subjective satisfaction. They must think in terms of preserving the existence of society. And there is no pointer to this cardinal task in welfare theory.

But may not this be regarded as a cost of maintaining the social field without which no welfare is possible? Something like the relationship between investment and consumption. Investment comes off consumption but is necessary to its reproduction and future expansion. In the same manner state denial of satisfaction is the condition of satisfaction. You will note how this welfare formulation resembles the old political formulation: to sacrifice a portion of liberty in order to ensure the rest. Thus while government decisions deny individual wishes they are yet ultimately subservient to the needs of individuals. To the needs, yes; but to the satisfactions?

The whole edifice gains coherence if the Kuznets' assumption is accepted that the resource-consuming acts of the government are to be treated as intermediate products in the process of the satisfaction of the consumers. This, however, supposes that the causal relationship somehow enters the minds of the consumers; an assumption necessary in order to relate these activities to the *final appreciator*, the consumer appreciating on behalf of himself. But this is equivalent to the old political assumption that the individual could appreciate the value to his own interest of the general interest. Hume showed long ago that it is not so. Economics indeed can adduce a new demonstration, or a demonstration in new form that it is not so. When order reigns, its marginal value is very small. The citizen obtains what might be called a formidable consumer's surplus in the maintenance of order at a far lower cost than he would give for it, if threatened. Consequently actual individuals are quite incapable of assigning due value to the activities that do preserve them.

Suppose that in Ruritania which has lived quite peacefully up to now, moral disruption occurs demanding a great police force. And that a number of young men are drawn from the farms to serve at much higher rewards in this police force. This expenditure appears as an increase in the national product, and yet it merely reflects a worsening of the national situation. The underestimation of values which seem assured indeed runs right through welfare economics which are so to speak a socialization of a radically individualistic psychology. Values of Satisfaction are emphasized as against the values of social survival which imply utilities and ethics of another order. While individuals must by psychological necessity make this error of understatement of the values which are most fundamental, because they are taken for granted, on the other hand they may commit an error of overstatement of service-consuming resources whose potentiality they do not well realize because these resources have never or have for a long time been open to alternative uses.

So it seems that individuals *as such* are quite incapable of weighing rightly or meaningfully the value of government activities. And if the public authority seeks to rest its own appreciation of its service as against others which might be provided out of the same resources, or its appreciation of some of its services as against others, on some form of *subjective appreciation by consumers as such*, it must go terribly astray. In other words it seems that public policies cannot be made to rest upon what people desire *in their private capacities*.

Now this is again a political truth of long standing. When Rousseau wished the whole body of citizens to decide the measures affecting the whole body, he made it quite clear that, while participating in this decision, the individual citizen was to have in mind not his private advantage, but that of the whole. Nor can this mean a mere summation of the private advantages of *others*. What A desires for himself in his private capacity is conditioned by his behavioral world which entirely rests upon the certitudes factual, legal, moral, given to him by society as it is. The value to him of these certitudes is incommensurable to the values he, within this framework, sets upon those things which he "from time to time desireth" in Hobbes' words. The greatest possible success in obtaining those things, which constitute "Felicity of this world" *sive* subjective economic welfare, can be a goal only if other things being equal, the solidity of the commonwealth maintained, the moral attitude of men maintained, the social affections maintained, all those things which go to making a society and the best possible society are taken care of.

VI

Other things being equal, it is undoubtedly legitimate to base a decision of policy upon the positive sum of advantages accruing to the sum of individuals composing the community (assuming that we have some means of summation of positive and negative results accruing to and appreciated by the several individuals). But the question raised here is precisely whether it is legitimate to assume that "other things are equal," whether policies can affect merely the situations and satisfactions of individuals without affecting the structure and working of society. It seems safe to state that some measures, class X, are in that case, and that other measures, class Y, are in another class and do affect the structure and workings of society. The distinction is easily drawn. If I am in charge of children for a day and have no other purpose than to amuse them, it will be good policy on my part to see that the games I organize result in every child getting some prize or other: thus will satisfaction be maximized. This policy will not, however, work well if I am in charge of these children for a season or a number of years as their trainer or teacher. My policies X shall then come under class Y.

It seems that the measures which result only in alterations *for* individuals, without alterations *of* society are very few. In those cases it is not legitimate to assume "other things equal," other things are being altered: they may be altered favorably or unfavorably—we cannot say, because we have no criteria for appreciating the value of these changes. We cannot use here the criteria of welfare because the legitimate use of the criteria of welfare rests precisely upon the nonalteration of the framework which is in fact being altered.

If we want a rough pictorial representation of the situation we may say that the maximization of welfare aboard a ship is a clear benefit if X (the ship) proceeds safely on its way. It is clear that the criterion of maximizing welfare provides no guidance to those responsible for keeping the ship safely on its way. Providing this is not affected, then welfare is to be maximized. It has been shown, I believe, that the incorporation of the factor "safe progress of the XX ship" into the individual welfares is unmanageable: because these individuals have no means of comparing this basic advantage with others in subjective terms.

What follows from the foregoing reasoning is not that welfare theories are valueless to the political scientist, but that their proper use depends upon the previous formulation of the objective conditions of social survival. It is only within a framework that they can be used validly. This framework political scientists have not delineated. The conditioning values upon which the conditioned values of individual welfare are based have not been set forth systematically. It may be that this is an impossible: it has certainly been treated as if it were. But the danger attending this situation is that conditioned values, because they have been made the subject of attentive study, may come to be relatively overstated, due to lack of statement of the conditioning values; and first things therefore may come to be lost in the pursuit of last things.

Notes

1. [A. C.] Pigou, "Some Aspects of Welfare Economics," *American Economic Review* (June, 1951).
2. Tibor Scitovski, "The State of Welfare Economics," *American Economic Review* (June, 1951).
3. Indeed the breaking up of this traffic should be adjudged a decrease of national income, were it not for a polite convention not to treat drugs in the same manner as other merchandise. But this convention is against the whole logic of national accounting based on consumer valuations. This is easily brought out: suppose that we come to look upon spirits with the same horror, then this sector of the economy disappears from our accounts, causing a decrease in national product and income. If the commerce of spirits goes on to the same extent, our accounts are stultified to that extent. If strong action is taken against it, then the repressive services become a positive factor in national accounting: we are "richer" by the efforts made not to have something which would give satisfaction to many.

2

Efficiency and Amenity

I

Men have ever desired to improve their material lot. But the idea that year after year the material lot of all or most members of a nation can and should be increased is new. Medieval radicals called for the rejection of the burdens laid upon the workers for the benefit of the privileged classes, but looked no further than the once-for-all improvement procured thereby. The thought that practically everybody can get somewhat richer continuously could not have arisen but for the gradual progress achieved over time and the awareness that it was due to the successive gains in the productivity of labor. Awareness of the process has fostered a demand that it be accelerated. Accountancy has become a major criterion of our judgments.

We find nothing strange in the grading of nations according to their national product per inhabitant, estimated in dollars, never mind how imperfectly. Those which lie in the lower ranges we call "underdeveloped": they are to be pitied, spurred, and helped up. Those which stand on the higher rungs we call "advanced." Such classification is common ground for leaders of opinion in both "capitalist" and "communist" countries. Indeed for more than thirty years, the avowed objective of Soviet planning has been "to overtake the American standard of life." Further, the vast increase in the worldwide prestige of communism is due to the very high rates of growth achieved, and paradoxically enough the poorer countries are tempted to follow the communist path as that which leads fastest to the way of life of the capitalist countries.

Earl Grey Memorial Lecture, King's College, Newcastle-upon-Tyne, 1960. From K. J. Arrow and T. Scitovsky, eds., *Readings in Welfare Economics* (Homewood, IL: Irwin, 1969): 100–112. Reprinted by permission of the Academic Board of Newcastle University.

In the advanced countries themselves the yearly rate of growth is a subject of great interest: if high it redounds to the credit of the government, if low it affords an argument to the opposition. Such focusing of attention upon economic growth should lead to the acceleration of the process.

May I quote just a few figures? The United States have amazed the world by multiplying real product per inhabitant almost sevenfold since 1839, according to the estimate of Raymond W. Goldsmith; that is a pace of 1.64 percent per year; in France during the last decade (i.e., 1949–1959), real product per inhabitant has increased by more than one half, growing at a rate of 3.5 percent a year. If such a rate were sustained, it would *treble* the flow of goods and services per inhabitant in thirty-two years. This would imply a metamorphosis of life in the course of a generation. The British rate of increase has been a good deal lower, about 2.1 percent yearly (1948–1958), which if sustained would imply *doubling* the flow of goods and services per inhabitant within a generation. May I be so indiscreet as to say that I hope to see the British rate of growth increased by British entry into the faster growing Common Market? I must stress that the figures quoted all refer to progress of gross national product per inhabitant, not to the progress of production per man-hour, which is higher.

My figures serve no other purpose than to indicate the magnitude or speed of change. Surely if all the children now being born can, when reaching the age of thirty-two, find themselves two or three times better off than their parents are now, it is worth thinking of what to make of this opportunity. This is the problem I wish to raise. As we shall find, it is by no means an easy one to discuss.

II

The statement of the problem contains by implication two value judgments which should be made explicit. Firstly, I have assumed that people could obtain more and more goods and services and implied that it is a good thing; I so believe. Secondly, I have said that we should think of increasing riches as an increasing opportunity and implied that we can make thereof a better or worse use. These two assumptions may well pass unchallenged because they agree with current common sense. But however trivial the position taken, it has to be noted that it contradicts two strongly entrenched schools of thought, one ancient the other modern. The ancient moralists have all held that man should limit his desires, that the pursuit of ever more goods and services is folly, bound to make men wicked and miserable. By reason of our first premise therefore we run foul of their venerable wisdom, and indeed we shall find that our wealth-mindedness brings us into conflict with many values which deserve respect. The second premise clashes with the relativist school, so powerful nowadays, which holds that there are no values other than subjective. If every man be the only judge of his own interest, if we can ascertain what makes him better off *solely* by observations of the *preferences* his actions *reveal,* then however society develops under free choices, we must assume that whatever is, is the best possible world at the moment.

The position sketched out therefore is *modern* in opposition to the ancient moralists, and if you will it is progressive. It is however *classical* in opposition to the relativists, in its assumption that the judgments we pass upon the quality of life are not mere expressions of individual fancy but tend to objective value, however approximately attained.

III

To approach our problem, let us firstly ask ourselves how much good has come out of the economic progress already achieved and how near it has brought us to a Golden Age. A great deal of good has come out of economic progress up to date. Among these goods some figure in our statistics and some do not—housing does, and so does the labor-saving equipment provided to housewives; in the case of the latter however, mere statistics fail to do justice to a major boon, which has transformed the life of the better part of mankind. The shortening of the work week figures into our statistics as well as the holidays, but what cannot figure is the great lessening of the physical labor involved in work. Indeed if we could draw two curves, one of them describing the shortening of the work-time and the other the lessening of the intensity of muscular effort per hour, we would find the second falling far more than the first.[1] Some changes such as full employment which spares men the anxiety and indignity of being unwanted do not arise directly out of the progress of productivity but are closely linked with it, and so are the social measures for the relief of misery which we could not have afforded but for our enrichment. Some effects figure in statistics but have connotations which do not so figure; for instance the great transformation of workers' clothing has erased a visible distinction. If I may add a light note, when I see two drivers locked in conflict, I reflect that but for the automobile, one of them might be on horseback the other on foot, while now they are on the same footing.

It is idle to say that all have benefited from economic progress. Obviously the class which had servants cannot afford them any more due to the up-pricing of labor; and this by itself involves for the class mentioned a great decline in the ease of life; but also it makes for greater similarity of situations, and presumably for readier understanding.

We could of course say more about the benefits of progress but some shall be stressed in due time. On the other hand can we say that our progress has brought us anywhere near the Golden Age? I fear not.

In writing and image, many glimpses of the Golden Age have been vouchsafed to us; they concur quite remarkably. *Homo Felix* moves against a background of beauty, delights in his workmanship, is benefited by the company he keeps, and his song of joy praises his Creator. Most often he is shown in a landscape mellowed by the human hand, with a nice balance of trees, meadows and stream; a graceful temple however testifies to urbanity. Contrariwise, if *Homo Felix* happens to be painted in a public place, then the greenery of the surroundings shows through the monuments of the town. The latter is no more than a meeting place for worship and conviviality. *Homo Felix* is not idle, but the enjoyment of doing things so overcomes the awareness that they must be done as to exclude any sense of drudgery. His associates move his heart and quicken his wit; expecting the best of him, they help him to achieve it. He opens his eyes at dawn, eager for the activities of the day, and closes them at dusk; free from worry he exerts no pressure on any other man nor does he endure any.

Such, in brief, is the picture of *Homo Felix*. As against it the man of our day lives steeped in ugliness, injured, whether he be aware of it or not, by ugly sights, ugly sounds, ugly smells. His labors, in the great majority of cases, give little scope for his talents, and he can seldom forget that they are done solely for the sake of the reward. He is exceptionally fortunate if the company he keeps induces him to reach the excellence of which he is inherently capable.

It is a long way indeed to the Golden Age. Maybe the picture drawn thereof was a fanciful one. But surely there is some way of life which would be an improvement upon that which we find.

IV

An opinion which enjoys great currency is that the productivity gains we may look to, will for the greater part, translate themselves into a very rapid shortening of the time of work, so that we may expect in a few years the thirty-hour week or even the twenty-eight-hour week, i.e., three days and a half. Minds which start with this assumption then find themselves faced with the "problem of leisure "; what shall the people do, with all that spare time? They will be half workers, half gentlemen of leisure. Now it is no easy thing to be a gentleman of leisure, and not so many gentlemen have made a good showing at it. So runs the argument.

I happen to doubt very strongly that the working-week shall be shortened as much or as fast as people imagine. A lot of things can be reckoned out on paper which can not happen in reality. For instance, we may picture, say a 3.5 percent increase in production per man hour, of which 2 percent would be taken out in the shortening of the time of work and 1.5 percent in the increase of production per worker. Under such conditions a thirty-hour week could easily be achieved within twenty years, while presumably production per inhabitant would be stable or declining, due to the reduction in the proportion of workers relatively to the population, of which more anon.

This can be worked out with closer arithmetic than mine, but it simply would not work out in life. It is inconceivable that a 3.5 percent increase in productivity per year could occur with a slow expansion of production. High rates of productivity gain are linked to high rates of expansion. High overall rates of expansion are themselves linked with the introduction of new products in the production of which, or thanks to the production of which, the great productivity gains are achieved.

Some people reason as if we could nicely immobilize needs and then take out all our productivity gains in leisure. Let us follow this fancy. Suppose that our needs in lighting had been assessed in 1760, and that the candle industry had been asked to work down the time necessary for the provision of that much amount of lighting. Under such circumstances, the electricity industry could never have appeared as it required a rapidly expanding market. That example has been chosen because lighting is of all goods and services that in which labor-saving has been greatest, but it has also been that for which the expansion of the market has been greatest.

The nature of productivity gains is best grasped if one traces over time the cost in minutes of labor of the several goods and services. Nearly all these costs decline but at very different rates. What makes for a great gain in the collection of goods and services obtained per average hour is the presence, in the "mix," of an increasing variety of products intervening with increasing weights; such presence will be felt the more, the greater the overall expansion. Therefore, if, counting upon a high rate of productivity gains, we proposed to apply them mostly to shortening the time of work, and only to a lesser degree to the increase of production, we might find that the expected productivity gains wither away.

According to Moses Abramovitz, over the last seventy-five years, the productivity increase obtained in the U.S. has been cashed-in to the proportion of three-fourths in the increase of production per man, to the proportion of one-fourth in the decrease of work-time per man. Should we assume that progress continued at just the same rate and was allocated according to the same proportions, it would take another seventy years to bring the U.S. to the thirty-hour week. Now of course one should shun such extrapolations. On the one hand productivity gains can be stepped up considerably. On the other hand we should take into account that cutting down the work week from very high levels certainly does not cut down pro rata the effective input of labor, because the effective input per hour then rises; it is very doubtful whether this same phenomenon would remain operative when cutting down the work-time from lower levels.

I do not pretend to know at what rate through the years the work week can be shortened. But it seems very necessary to point to the demographic phenomena which shall militate against any very great and rapid shortening of the work week. We can easily perceive that the work week of the adult shall have to support an increasing proportion of weeks of existence of nonlaboring population.

We tend to live longer, and every year more that we live beyond working age is an added charge upon the worker. To an increasing degree the poor of an advanced society are its aged, and if we wish, as I feel we should, to pursue our effort for the relief of poverty, we must give to the aged a greater share of the proceeds of our work because of their increasing proportion and in order to raise their relative status. In the same manner, every year more which an adolescent spends at school is an added charge upon the adult workers. And surely nothing is more desirable than the successive prolongation of education. This can endow youths both with a better capacity for production and, what seems to me more important, with a better capacity for the right use of life and leisure, of which more anon.

Indeed I strongly feel that we should think of giving less time to productive work, not in terms of less hours per week but in terms of coming later to gainful employment and remaining longer in existence after retirement. Speaking very roughly, delaying entry into the labor market by one year is the arithmetic equivalent of shortening the work week by two hours for a period of twenty years.[2] Shown that the change in labor input arising from the one or the other change is the same, and given the choice, what father would hesitate to prefer longer schooling for his child to shorter hours for himself? Whatever the choice of the individual, the choice to be made in the name of society can give rise to no hesitation. Our opportunities for labor-saving should be applied by preference to the longer and more elaborate formation of our citizens.

This is not to say that the normal work week shall not be shortened, but the effective work week need not evolve in the same manner except for those who are the least employable. There exists already a clearly marked tendency for the duration of work to be longest for the most able—which is a quite natural feature of an expansive economy, which presses harder upon its most scarce resources, human as well as material.

V

People are apt to confuse the two notions of "time not spent at work" and of "free time"—this is a mistake; it neglects the time spent in getting to the work place and back home. While such time is not spent in productive processes, it is not available to the individual. Such transport time was nil in the case of the artisan, negligible in the case of a factory hand of a nineteenth-century mill-town. Nowadays it is very seldom less than five hours a week, frequently ten, sometimes fifteen. This is a subject which our passion for surveys has left untouched. Yet it would be very interesting to have a distribution of the working population according to the number of hours spent on transport to and from work, and the evolution of this distribution over time. It would not be at all astonishing if we found that in recent times average transport time has risen a good deal more than the average work week has shrunk. Indeed in some countries, such as Britain and France, there has been of late no visible trend towards the reduction of the effective work week while there has been a clear trend towards the rise of transport time. I know quite a few workers to whom it costs twelve hours a day to do an eight-hour spell. This great waste of time, attended by nervous fatigue, does not figure in our statistics. We say that John Smith makes so much for say forty-four hours of presence; in fact he gets so much less fares for forty-four hours of presence involving n hours of transport.

National accounting constitutes a great intellectual advance but its best experts are least prone to believe that it offers a comprehensive picture of the human situation. We know that rapid progress in national income involves a ceaseless process of shifting men from A positions to B positions where they contribute more to overall product and are better rewarded. Talking of such labor mobility, we stress the increase in market power which it brings to the subject, and we are apt to forget the psychological costs which may be incurred in the process. The very fact that labor mobility has to be preached testifies that men are often reluctant to break off their links with a given place, a given job, given work associates. Instances of such reluctance are often enough noted in our newspapers, and testify to psychological costs. Economists will say that when people do move, thereby they reveal a preference for the B position—the gain in market power is subjectively superior to the cost of uprooting. True enough if the man has the choice of remaining in the A position or of moving to the B position; but such is not always the case; it may well be that the A position folds up and that he is left no choice. If a professor of Greek becomes the employee of an advertising firm, it may be by reason of the superior reward offered, and then he has indeed revealed a subjective preference; not so if the teaching of Greek is being discontinued in the institution which employed him.

While taking into account the increase in a man's real earnings we fail to take into account the unpleasantness of his uprooting. Nor is this only a subjective cost. It has ever been accepted that there is value in attachment to a place, a skill, and a fellowship. Indeed, the Good Society as it was traditionally pictured was one in which such loyalties were strong; but they must be weak for the proper working of our Progressive Society. The point deserves to be pondered.

The bias of our accounting is most strikingly reflected in our assessment of what occurs when a tannery or paper factory is set up. Its product—in terms of value added—is registered as a positive increment to national product. But the discharge from the factory pollutes the river. Nobody would deny that this is to be deplored; but such an incidental effect is regarded as alien to the realm which we agree to consider in earnest. Nobody says that on the one hand the factory produces goods, but that on the other, quite as concretely, it produces *bads*. I would argue that this is what we should state: there are two forms of production, one of positive value, the other of negative value. Most economists are very unwilling to speak in this manner; they would say that the positive values produced are proved and measured by the prices paid for them in the open market, while what I call negative values cannot be so proved and measured. True enough, because people can buy leather or paper by the yard, while they can not buy a yard of unpolluted river. The factory produces its *goods* in divisible form; it produces *bads* as indivisible nuisances. There are no economic means of stating their negative value, yet this exists, and it is proved by the fact that we become increasingly disposed to vast public expenditures to remove such nuisances. Incidentally the champions of free private enterprise would be well inspired to force upon firms measures for the prevention of nuisances, for want of which the removal of nuisances must inevitably lead to the development of a great new field of public activities. Indeed in any case, important "utilities" of the future will be the industries designed to remove nuisances.

Looking upon our rivers today one thinks of the times when they were personified into semi-deities. Such pagan fancies can only be allegories to Christians, but not useless allegories. The Renaissance made much of the river figures in poetry and sculpture; what poor bedraggled figures we should paint today if we returned to such allegories! With this suggestion we touch upon the *Amousia* of modern civilization.

VI

In an economic policymaking committee I recently happened to suggest that the Parthenon was an addition to the wealth of Athenians, and its enjoyment an element of their standard of life. This statement was regarded as whimsical. When I made it clear that it was seriously meant, I was told that the standard of life is expressed by per capita private consumption of goods and services acquired on the market. Meekly accepting this correction, I asked my colleague whether when he drove out to the country on weekends, his satisfaction was derived from the costly consumption of gasoline, or from the free sight of trees and possibly the free visit of some cathedral. At this point people are wont to make a distinction between the useful and the pleasant. I would certainly not deny that there is a stark utility in being so clad as to be protected against the cold, but I fail to see any difference in kind between enjoying a variety of clothes and enjoying a variety of flowers, and happen to prefer the latter.

Until quite recently the laborer meant the agricultural laborer. Throughout the millennia, production would be equated with agriculture. The business of procuring food undoubtedly has a prior claim upon our attention, and I feel no doubt that growing food is more important business than art. Strangely enough, while production had this vital character, it was looked down upon. In all the civilizations of the past the producer was a mean person and his concerns mean concerns. Paradoxically production has acquired an unprecedented moral status while less and less of it caters to indispensable needs, to whit the precipitous fall in the agricultural labor force. I have no quarrel with the enhanced status of production; indeed I feel certain that modern society's great success in production is mainly due to our thinking better and thinking more of production. It is not a matter I propose to discuss here but in my view the great contrast offered by our civilization with the civilizations of the past lies in that *their* social leaders would have deemed it *improper* to think of production, a concern of underlings, while *our* social leaders are recruited on the basis of their *interest* in and contribution to the heightening of *efficiency* in production, a change which occurred in our own society within a small number of generations.

But if I do not at all object to the much enhanced status of production, I may point out that production has come to embrace so much that it would be foolish to grant any and every productive activity the moral benefit of an earnestness not to be found in so called "nonproductive activities." When popular newspapers propose to bring out their comic strips in color, I find it hard to regard such "progress in production" as something more earnest than planting flowering shrubs along the highways. I am quite willing to regard poetry as a frivolous occupation as against the tilling of the soil but not as against the composing of advertisements.

When organizers of production have to relieve a situation of hunger, efficiency is the one and only virtue. But when this virtue has been thoroughly developed and comes to be applied to less and less vital objects, the question surely arises of the right choice of objects.

VII

Most economists, among whom the masters of the science, would deny that there is any real problem here. They would stress that individuals, in the handling of their family budgets, display their preferences, and that therefore the allocation of total consumer expenditures, subject to the existing distribution of incomes, reveals the preferences of the public as a whole; that therefore also the collection of goods and services obtained at present is presently the best possible, the right one. They would go on to say: "You personally may think that a different collection would be better, but in so stating all you do is to pit your single subjective preference against the aggregate of individual subjective preferences."

However powerful this argument, it is not decisive. We can point out, firstly, that current choices are made between currently available goods and services, secondly, that they are a function of the consumer's own past.

Speaking to the first point, it is not true that the buyer is the sole author of his choices. These of course depend upon what is offered. Let us turn our minds, not without shame, to the goods which were first offered by colonial traders to American Indians and African negroes. What were they? Trinkets and liquor, objects useless or harmful, the market for which could be rapidly expanded because emulation fostered the demand for baubles and habit the demand for liquor. In the case of our own laboring populations the initial exploitation of the popular market was little better. The first industries which really benefited the people were the cotton and glass industries, both conducive to neatness and hygiene.

As our working classes got richer, a greater obstacle stood in the way of selling them anything worthwhile. There was a fatter weekly pay envelope, but accumulating out of this weekly pay the wherewithal to acquire, say, a house required an inordinate strength of character. In my own country the point was made *ad nauseum* that people would rather spend on drink, the movies, and other evanescent goods and services than upon getting a proper home. This was a most unfair judgment; the situation altered radically as soon as housing could be made available, to be paid consecutively out of incoming pay.

The order in which goods come to be offered is also important. The American economy was characterized after World War I by the great upsurge of the motor car and the movie, after World War II by the comparable upsurge of household equipment and the television. It is at least plausible that if the second set of goods had become available before the first, their home-binding influence would have colored the American way of life.

The second point is of course that consumer choices are a function of the consumer's own past. For instance, in my library there is not a single book in Russian; this of course is because I cannot read the Russian language. Now suppose that there were no books left or published in any other language than Russian. Then I would have no books at all, which, by the reasoning which is now current, would establish that I do not like reading. Presumably I would take pains to learn Russian, but, starting at my time of life, I would not become proficient at it; it would take me a great deal of time to work through a book; possibly I would then turn to comic strips; this would triumphantly reinforce the proof that "people prefer" comic strips. Revealed preferences in fact reveal *ignorances*, the lack of intellectual and aesthetic formation.

VIII

I suspect that our society is the most deficient in culture which has ever been seen. It is a natural need of man to express himself in oratory, poetry, song, dance, music, sketching, sculpture, and painting. If culture has any meaning, it means that the aptitudes which all children have, in diverse degrees, for some or other of these pleasurable activities should be cultivated. This can not harm the development of another and more scarce aptitude, that for understanding and conveying such understanding in the language either of philosophy or of mathematics. But the aesthetic pleasures should naturally be the most common. Their lack makes us properly barbarians, if the barbarian be the man without powers of appreciation or expression.

Strangely enough anything which lies in the realm of aesthetic enjoyment is regarded in our wealthy society as nonessential. Nonessential and "distinguished"; no doubt we think highly of "works of art" which the rich may possess and which the poor are invited to admire in a museum. But this treatment of works of art by itself displays their "eccentricity" in the literal sense of the word, with regard to our civilization.

In my opinion, it is the very definition of philistinism to think of art with a capital A, no matter indeed whether this way of thinking is that of the much blamed bourgeois or of the artist himself. In the epochs of culture, the term "the arts" corresponded to our present notion of "the industries." Thus in Florence the "arte di la lana" meant the industry of woolens. One did not think that turning out woolens was one thing, concerning oneself with beauty another. One did not think that building edifices of worship, or public edifices, or private houses was one thing entirely distinct from any preoccupation for beauty. The nineteenth century, which was basically philistine, developed the notion of the "objet d'art," the small thing of beauty which the rich, having turned out goods without beauty, could thus afford to lodge in their houses built without beauty.

The dizzying height of prestige to which painting has risen in the last two generations is, I feel, the true index to the philistinism of our society. In an age of culture, painting is not a thing in itself, it is an element of decoration fitting into a pattern of beauty.

The fact that there are objects of beauty in the museums of London and Paris does not acquit us of the fact that London and Paris are not beautiful; within them any combination of buildings we can point to with pride is at least a century and a half old. Since then we have done nothing to improve; everything which has been done has tended to degrade.

It is claimed that people do not care. It seems to me that their behavior testifies to the contrary. How do people spend their holiday? In escaping from the setting in which they are forced to live; they go to the country to see what the world was meant to look like, and they go to ancient cities whose inhabitants were concerned, however poor, to achieve a beauty which in our wealth we neglect. Indeed when on weekends one sees people teeming out of London one is tempted to think that the word "Sunday" has been restored to its primitive meaning: it is now the day without smog.

From people's behavior it seems apparent that as individuals we attach far more importance to beauty than we do collectively as a society. Why do we, as a society, set so little importance upon it? My own feeling is that the preoccupation with beauty is always associated with the feeling that life centers upon singing the glory of God; were I to discuss how Puritanism has divorced the good from the beautiful, and how the secularist concern for man alone has become a concern for "functional," I would be treading upon ground which would be controversial and moreover using big words in an elliptic manner which is apt not only to mislead the audience but to muddle the speaker. Such investigation of causes is indeed not relevant at this time and for the purpose on hand.

IX

I find it hard to agree that the man of our society has a high standard of life. The life of modern man seems to me unstructured; it flexes to embrace the new good which is offered; possession thereof alters the shape of life which is therefore a function of what happens to be put on the market. This is an invertebrate, amoebae-like progress of the way of life. If anyone were to furnish a house by accumulating "good buys" wherever and whenever encountered, that house would be a meaningless clutter, without style or personality. This is to me the aspect offered by our life.

Imagine that an eighteenth-century philanthropist, say the Marquis de Mirabeau or Thomas Jefferson, were resurrected and briefed as to the increase in labor productivity and wealth which has occurred since his day. He would certainly imagine a world where beauty and culture prevailed, where the setting of life would immediately manifest the social wealth; in poorer societies the edifices of God, the palaces of rulers, and the mansions of the rich had been made beautiful. An epoch of general wealth would surely be one where the houses of the people and their work places would be built with the same loving care; that we were on the threshold of such an age was assumed already by Ledoux (1736–1806) in the last third of the eighteenth century.[3] Also it had previously been the good fortune of the artisans serving a rich market that they could work with delight. When the mass market had become a rich market this would seem destined to be the lot of all workers; finally it had been the privilege of the well-to-do that they could enjoy good company, with pleasant manners and interesting topics. Presumably, with a society wealthy throughout, this sort of company would be that of Everyman.

Now of these three goals relating to the setting, the work, and the company, which seemed natural outcomes of growing wealth, the first—setting—and the last—good company—have not been achieved merely, as it seems to me, through an inexplicable lack of attention to them; the second, which is possibly the most important, deserves special attention.

It does seem true, up to date, that we have had to pay a price for the increasing productivity of labor in the sense that the Industrial Revolution from its very beginning has created a new phenomenon which I would call "pure labor." In order to live, men have ever needed to perform certain activities, be it hunting, fishing, tilling, building, weaving, etc. It seems to me however that in the case of those folk we call "primitive" the activities devoted to the material substances of life have been admixed with play, sport, devotion, as we can still see it in the case of vine harvesting, which is all suffused with joking, laughing, its brief spells of matching speeds interspersed with episodes of bantering and courting. As against this, modern work has become an altogether bleaker thing, purely a task to be performed for the result, under the sign of efficiency alone. It is by no means different in the so-called socialist countries where "norms" of work are successively raised. I have noted that work has become in the last generations very much less exacting in a physical sense, but as against this we must set, I think, the bleakness of work. The lessening of the physical strain of work is a recent phenomenon, its bleakness is an altogether more ancient phenomenon. It is probably as old as the regimentation of work, which has existed for a long time (think of the galley slaves) but which has become a far more widespread phenomenon.

It is, I think, the bleakness of work which has led to our current dichotomy of man, of whom it is expected that he be purely efficient in his hours of work, while he is allowed, nay encouraged, to satisfy his wants in his hours of leisure. From which it naturally follows that nothing seems more important than to successively whittle down the hours of work. But work is so essential that the psychological deprivation experienced by man at work colors, I believe, his whole life. It can be observed that the men who in fact seem to have a good life are not those who work few hours (in which case the good life would have been that of the rentier who had no hours of work at all) but those who can take pleasure in their work. And therefore I believe that we should regard the amenity of work as a much more interesting goal than the shortening of work hours.

X

There are many other points I would like to touch upon, one of them is the following. Those out of work on a pension by reason of age shall form an increasing proportion of our population. This shall constitute a very large "leisure class" of a very different complexion from the "leisure class" of the nineteenth century; much more numerous, on the one hand, and on the other, distinguished from the working class to which all adults now belong, not by *greater* incomes but by *smaller* incomes. Our society now comprises no "leisure class" at the top of the income ladder, but a large "leisure class" at the bottom of the income ladder: the aged.

This phenomenon of a very large population combining a great deal of leisure with very little money poses the problem of its way of life. I think it is very miserable in the present day. Surely it deserves to be given some thought, and the problem is not insoluble since the combination new to us of a great deal of leisure with scant material means is the very condition under which Greek culture flourished. The aged may be the Greek among us, if we attack the problem in that way.

This is but one of the points I wished to raise. I would deem myself fortunate indeed if I had found it possible to contribute towards the crystallization of a concern to induct our increasing wealth in the service of a greater amenity of life.

Notes

1. Note that I speak of muscular effort; nervous fatigue is quite a different business.
2. Assuming a typical year of forty-eight weeks of forty-four hours, it shall take twenty-two years at a rate of two hours per week to retrieve one year of delay in entry.
3. The industrial city of Chaux, then designed and built by Ledoux, testifies to the preoccupation.

3

The Political Economy of Gratuity

I

A general investigation of all the groups of causes by which welfare...may be affected would constitute a task so enormous and complicated as to be quite impractical. It is, therefore, necessary to limit our subject-matter. In doing this we are naturally attracted towards that portion of the field in which the methods of science seem likely to work at best advantage. This they can clearly do when there is present *something measurable*, on which analytical machinery can get a firm grip. The one obvious instrument of measurement available in social life is *money*. Hence the range of inquiry becomes *restricted* to that part of social welfare that can be brought directly or indirectly into relation with the *measuring-rod* of money.

This is a famous statement by a famous author, Professor A.C. Pigou. It acknowledges that economics excludes from consideration many factors of welfare, and gives good reason for such an exclusion. It is not my purpose here to criticize economists for a restriction of their field of interest which was necessary to the development of their science. It is my purpose to ask whether certain factors, which it was formerly wise to leave out, should now be taken into account.

Economists are heavily indebted to the antique institution of "money": universal familiarity with this "rod" enabled them from the outset to involve in homogeneous arithmetic operations objects heterogeneous in kind. Indeed, money does a great deal more than permit a quantitative comparison of different commodities; if one concentrates upon an individual "purse," and if the acquisition by its holder of a certain collection of objects requires a certain "outgo" from this purse, and if one then finds that a given exertion by the holder of the purse is necessary to obtain an "ingo" exactly remedying the depletion of the purse, it

Reprinted from *Virginia Quarterly Review* 35 (Autumn, 1959): 513–26. Used by permission of the publisher.

becomes possible to state that this given exertion by the individual considered is "equivalent" to the collection of the commodities acquired. Therefore, "toil" and "labor," those exertions which replenish "the purse," are integrated within the same quantitative framework with "goods," those objects of desire for the acquisition of which one empties the purse.

The possibility of submitting many kinds of things and actions to a single instrument of measure has served economics well, and it is understandable that those elements which could not be processed through the monetary mill should have been rejected. This rejection did not imply that those elements were regarded as unworthy of notice but only that they were regarded as unfit to be handled by the intellectual plant set up by economists. While there was no intention of slight in such exclusion, the growing prestige of economists naturally emphasized the importance of things economists talked about, to the detriment of those things they did not mention.

In our day economic science (entirely superseding political science) has become the statesman's guide to popular welfare. In this exalted role, it must paint a fuller picture, and it then seems that it has to reintegrate those factors which it formerly omitted. I propose to mention here three adjacent fields into which economists should, I believe, extend their inquiry, i.e., free services, free goods, and negative goods or nuisances.

II

> On the other occasion, Antipho, in a conversation with Socrates, said: "I consider you indeed to be a just man, Socrates, but by no means a wise one; and you appear to me yourself to be conscious of this; for you ask money from no one for the privilege of associating with you; although, if you considered a garment of yours, or a house, or any other thing that you possess, to be worth money, you would not only not give it to anybody for nothing but you would not take less than its full value for it. It is evident, therefore, that if you thought your conversation to be worth anything, you would demand for it no less remuneration than it is worth. You may, accordingly, be a just man, because you deceive nobody from covetousness, but wise you cannot be, as you have no knowledge that is of any value."

Antipho's argument, as recorded in Xenophon's "Memorabilia of Socrates," is quite clear and has a modern ring. The fact that one man's exertions provide "goods" to other men is witnessed and measured by the price which the latter pay the former; and where there is no price, there is no tangible trace of the service rendered, of the advantage ob-

tained, nothing "on which analytical machinery can get a firm grip."
Antipho was by profession a Sophist, i.e., he sold lessons of wisdom;
his getting a price for his lessons he used as proof that they were of
value to his customers, while Socrates, so the reasoning runs, admitted
the lack of value of his own lessons since he demanded no payment. A
modern economist might reject Antipho's "proof," but nonetheless he
would accept its implications: in reckoning up the "national product"
of Athens, our economists would include the services of the Sophists,
and would not enter the services of Socrates. Services which are sold
count as "production," services which are given do not.

The fact that Antipho enters the picture while Socrates does not becomes of great importance when the picture drawn by the economists
serves as a guide for policy. The name of Socrates should not lead us
astray: our criticism is not that the economist fails to set the "right price"
upon the incomparable services of Socrates: there is no right price for the
incomparable. Our complaint is that free services are omitted by reason
of their gratuity, which tends to bias the picture of society.

The very existence of society rests upon the care lavished by mothers
upon their children. There is no financial reward for this activity; consequently it does not figure in the assessment of national product. Thus, if
we have two sisters, Mary and Edith, the first of whom bears and raises
children while the second becomes a film actress, the latter, being paid,
counts as a "worker" and "producer" while the former does not. Thus,
whenever a potential Mary becomes an actual Edith, the national product
is raised. Let us now imagine a third sister, Ruth, who is appointed a
government inspector of child care: being paid, Ruth is a "producer"; her
whole occupation, however, is to inspect Mary, the mother, who is not
accounted productive. Surely we have here a biased picture.

A pioneer in the national income field, Professor Colin Clark, has
attempted to measure this bias. He has sought to place a financial valuation upon the services provided within the home. In order to place a
price upon unpaid services, it is necessary to equate them with similar
services performed by paid agents. The procedure adopted can be
roughly summarized as follows. There is a population which is served
by paid agents, i.e., the population of welfare institutions. The cost per
head, within each age-group, of the services afforded within these institutions, can be found by deducting from the cost of upkeep that of
accommodation and of the purchases of goods and services from outside the institution: this gives the bare cost of services. These costs are
then applied, per head of each age group, to the population of private

homes, according to the assumption that the average consumption of services for each age-group is the same in the home as in the institution. Having followed this procedure, Colin Clark reached a conclusion which he thus summarizes:

> The order of magnitude of these services, which we have up to now excluded from all our estimates of national product, is found to be very much larger than is generally supposed. With money value of net national product (as at present recorded) of some £16 billion per year, the value of house-work, nearly all unpaid, should be reckoned, at present day prices, at about £7 billion per year. This consideration will upset many of the ideas about national product which we have held hitherto; particularly if we include this large additional item, we find the rate of growth of overall national product to have been much slower than we generally suppose.

The point raised is of great importance, especially in view of the interest we bear in "underdeveloped" economies. In the latter, the individual benefits from a network of noncommercialized services which extends far beyond the confines of our modern "rump family." The volume of monetary commerce is then low and if national accounting seizes only the latter it gives an inadequately low figure for national product. The figure can more easily be corrected for the inclusion on noncommercialized goods than for that of non-commercialized services. Economic accounting will grossly overstate the gains of economic evolution percentage-wise, because it will relate gains in commercialized values to an underestimated initial position; but also it will exaggerate the gains in absolute terms, as it will take into account every gain in the values traded, while omitting from consideration the losses of free services which will attend the breakdown of preexisting noncommercial circuits. For instance, a man who moves, say, in an Arab country, from a traditional way of life to urban employment no doubt gains in command over market goods; at the same time he loses in the services tangible or intangible afforded by kinship links. It is perhaps an excessive division of labor that the economist should take notice only of the former phenomenon, and the sociologist mainly of the latter. No doubt insofar as such transformations occur through the voluntary movements of individuals, they are to be accounted a gain, since the movements testify to preferences. But when it comes to planned changes, attention must be paid to the losses of free services involved in the transformation.

While the neglect of free services leads to overestimating the gains involved in early phases of economic development, conversely it may lead to underestimating the gains involved in phases of advanced development. A dwindling practice in early development, free services are an increasing possibility in late development. Over a long period of time Western man has received an increasing collection of commercialized goods and services in exchange for decreasing hours of less strenuous toil: consequently he enjoys an increasing reserve of time and energy available over and above that which is expended on his income-obtaining occupation. He may spend his free time in consuming amusement services provided by the "work" of others; or he may invest his free energy in services provided to himself (e.g., learning), to his family (e.g., housework), and to his fellow citizens (e.g., civic activities). National income computation fails to include such values.

An interesting point, the treatment of which I must here abridge, is that free services are valuable not only by reason of their being services, but because they are free. It used to be regarded as a hallmark of the freeman that his endeavors were not addressed to material rewards, but to the achievement of personal excellence, displayed in the granting of boons to others; the latter term was stressed by Christianity. Utopian socialism was unquestionably mistaken in assuming that a society could be run on the basis of such motivations alone. More efficient proved the idea of the economists, that the individual should not only be allowed but even encouraged to sell his labor as dearly and buy his goods as cheaply as possible, i.e., to drive, on both scores, hard bargains with his fellows. But the more successful the outcome of such attitudes, the more room there is for a sector of free services which may then be regarded as a precious "outcome" of economic transactions.

III

Man's life cannot endure beyond a minute or two without air, or beyond a day or two without water. We are utterly dependent upon what our forefathers called "the gifts of the Creator" or "the bounty of Nature." However vital these natural goods, they have not, with one notable exception, come within the purview of economists, a fact which Ricardo explained as follows:

> [T]he brewer, the distiller, the dyer make incessant use of the air and water for production of their commodities; but as the supply is boundless, they bear no price. If all land had the same properties, if it were unlimited in quantity, and uniform in quality, no charge could be made for its use.

If extreme abundance makes these "free goods," it follows that changed conditions can shift them to the class of "economic goods."

"Let me sell you a pound of ice" is a dreary joke from one Eskimo to another, but a reasonable proposition addressed to a man at the equator. Within the historic memory of our Western societies we have seen standing timber shifted from the class of free goods to that of economic goods. Delivered lumber had a price, derived from the labor involved, but standing timber was freely available. Note that demanding a price for the standing tree, before it could be felled, proved a condition which was met with astonishment and reluctance.

There is something more than abundance which has militated against the "pricing" of natural goods, i.e., the feeling that while a man may legitimately demand payment for his "toil and trouble," he may not exact payment for a gift of God. This feeling is strongly displayed in Moslem laws relating to water: while this is an unmistakably scarce commodity in most Moslem countries, nonetheless legislation adhered to the principle, derived from the Koran, that water may not be sold. In the West, there has been an ever-recurring propensity to contrast the validity of proprietary rights in artifacts and the "artificiality" of proprietary rights in natural assets. So staunch an apologist of private property as J.B. Say wrote as follows:

> The earth…is not the only agent of nature which has a productive power; but it is the only one, or nearly so, that one set of men take to themselves, to the exclusion of others, and of which, consequently, they can appropriate the benefits. The waters of rivers, and of the sea, by the power which they have of giving movement to our machines, carrying our boats, nourishing our fish, have also a productive power; the wind which turns our mills, and even the heat of sun, work for us; but happily no one yet has been able to say: "the wind and the sun are mine, and the services which they render must be paid for."

Ricardo comments upon this:

> Can any one doubt that if a person could appropriate to himself the wind and the sun, he would be able to command a rent for the uses to be derived from them?

Here "appropriation" is represented as the condition giving rise to payments for the services of natural assets. This is a good point for which we can provide a homely illustration. When motor circulation so increased in our towns as to cause a daily scramble for curb parking places, such increasing pressure upon a limited supply, uneven in quality, failed to occasion the phenomenon of rent, with higher prices ruling for the occupation of the most convenient stands. This did not occur because there were no sharp-eyed owners of curb space. This shows that "pricing" is not an automatic outcome of scarcity. In the example quoted, it seems clear that if the institutional setup had been favorable to "pricing," curb owners would have made large gains which would have induced the early development of parking facilities.

It seems unfair that anyone should idly benefit from the scarcity rent of a natural resource increasingly called for. On the other hand, however, the persistent gratuitousness of the resource is a socially unwholesome phenomenon. Men (whether acting as individuals or as firms) use services sparingly insofar as they are costly, and wantonly when they are "free." If the supply is limited, the race to be first served is morally worse than the process of auction. If the resource is in any way exhaustible, its gratuitousness hastens its depletion. A price therefore must be put upon the services of the natural asset, to discourage its abuse, to finance its replenishment, and to stimulate its development, if feasible. Such is the practice in the case of so minor an asset as "a shoot"; however, it is not the practice in the case of incomparably more important assets.

We would regard it as unfair to enjoy the services of a man-made structure without paying at least the cost of maintaining the asset's ability to maintain that flow of services. But we are aware of no such obligation in the case of natural assets. Of course the man-made asset is held by someone who claims compensation from us. Not so the natural asset, and therefore no compensation is exacted. Economics retraces transactions between men, and no such transaction occurs in respect of the wear-and-tear of a natural asset unless a human claimant appears and obtains acknowledgment of his claim, in which case the damage figures, measured by the compensation granted, on the books of the acting individual or firms as a part of its costs of production: therefrom it passes in that guise into national accounts. But, in the absence of such compensation, the injury caused does not figure at all in the national accounts, an omission which leads to an unconscious falsification.

Let me offer an example. In a neighborhood well known to me, a river ran, clean and pleasant, affording to the riparians drinking water and a swimming pool. A tannery was set up on the river, making it unfit for drinking and sport. The contamination of the river required the building of a costly aqueduct to bring pure water from a distant source. Now, in national accounting, the services afforded by the tannery and those afforded by the aqueduct are added together as two distinct gains. But surely this is wrong. The building of the water-pipe proved necessary only in order to restore the situation obtaining before the building of the tannery; and in fact restored it only in part, for the people are still short of a swimming pool. The water-work therefore should be regarded as repairing a loss inflicted by the tannery, which was not charged to it, and which figures nowhere in national accounts.

Such losses have not gone quite unnoticed by economists; to reflect the fact that the harm caused occasions no cost to its author, the phenomenon is called "external costs." But since it enters the definition of external costs that no compensation is paid by the author, it follows that the damage remains undefined and unmeasured, is not an economic quantity, and thus eludes the grip of analytical machinery. Let me offer an instance which displays the difficulty of measurement. A village is strung along a "broad street." In the days of coaches and in the subsequent days of sparse motor circulation, the street was a playground for children. In the course of time, traffic has acquired such intensity that parents are anxious about the mere use of the front door by the children. Now it is proposed to establish a costly playground. This will constitute a net gain as against the present situation, not so as against the situation of fifty years ago; but the intervening loss has occurred over a long period of time, not in such manner as to make its measurement easy: the measurement becomes possible only by reason of the expenditure upon the restoration of the lost facility, a restoration which moreover contains some element of improvement.

We lend a more willing ear to complaints regarding the impairment of earning opportunities than when they refer to the impairment of amenities and pleasures. Thus the shrimp fishermen of the Louisiana gulf obtain a hearing from their legislature relative to the impairment of their catch as a consequence of off-shore oil drilling. By contrast complaints regarding the "spoiling of natural beauties" are shrugged off as dilettantish, and they will acquire respectability only as the consumers increasingly make demands for parks and other such. It may well be an important occupation of the future to recreate what in the meantime has been destroyed for want of a price set upon it.

IV

This brings me to the last part of my subject. The theme can be stated with some sharpness: together with our increased output of goods, comes an increased output of nuisances, or negative goods. The output of a nuisance begins as a mere trickle and goes unnoticed until it becomes a stream, by which time its removal calls for a major operation. Let me quote from the *Wall Street Journal*.

"All signs point to an expanding air pollution," warns Dr. John D. Porterfield, the [United States] Government's deputy surgeon general. "We want our standard of living to rise. Yet, ironically, as it rises, our air will get dirtier, unless we are willing to do something about it." ...Air pollution already costs the United States 4 billion dollars a year, according to the Armour Research Foundation, a private group. This staggering sum includes the cost of cleaning smoke-smudged buildings, the damage to painted and metal surfaces by air-borne corrosives, the losses to farmers whose crops are ruined by foul air, and the decline in property-values in smog-plagued areas. But no dollar-and-cents-figure can measure the health toll on persons who breathe polluted air day after day, nor the mental anguish of the housewife whose laundry comes off the line tattle-tale gray no matter what soap she uses.

It is important and promising that such preoccupations should now be granted considerable and frequent space in the main business organ of the country: a generation ago, such concern would have been mocked as unmanly fastidiousness. How many new entrants in factories have been called "sissies " for their reaction to noise, which medicine now calls an "aggressor" of the organism. In the same manner, no doubt, sensitivity to open sewers in the middle of the street was in the distant past adjudged abnormal.

The latter allusion leads us to stress that whatever the contribution of modern industry to the output of nuisances, it may not be regarded as their exclusive source. The noise, smell, and squalor of this or that Asiatic town reminds us that the output of nuisances is a general feature of human clusters, and the use which our neighbor makes of his radio may suffice to pinpoint the origin of the evil, which lies in man's natural unawareness of the annoyances he inflicts upon his fellows.

Let me toy with a fancy. Suppose that instead of deriding the most sensitive people, we had used them as "sensitive indicators," registering the emergence of a nuisance long before people at large grew conscious of it; suppose that whenever such an indicator reacted, a financial penalty had been imposed upon the author of the nuisance perceived; then presumably the cost of producing nuisances would have inspired efforts to avoid or keep down their output. Emphasis would have been placed at an early date upon the "smokeless" use of coal and so forth. Any industrial use of water would have implied an apparatus to restore its purity. No plant would have been built without devices to abate the noisiness of machinery and without complete equipment for the disposal of refuse. This of course is a fantasy in respect to the past, but it may be more relevant to the future than it seems at first.

We can witness a sharp intensive and extensive rise in human reaction to nuisances. The designers of jet planes and rockets are themselves harassed by the roar of their artifacts, the atomic scientists are anxious about the disposal of atomic refuse, the captains of industry move their headquarters away from their belching chimneys, and their workers flee in their holidays far away from the grime and din of their daily round. Far more constructive, however, than this tendency to "get away" from nuisances, is the increasing propensity to "do away with" them at the source. This attitude is rapidly gaining ground in the United States. The elimination of negative goods is coming to be sensed as a positive good.

When a nuisance has gained considerable volume which is being currently fed by well-established practices, there may be no remedy for it other than its wholesale removal by a public agency at the public cost. This was of course the case for sewage. While this is not a pleasant topic, it is relevant because here we find an increase in the standard of life resulting not from people getting something more but from the removal of a nuisance. It is quite possible that a large part of the gains to be obtained in the future by the most advanced nations in the world will be of that form. We may well see the emergence of a whole class of new "utilities" devoted to the removal of different forms of nuisances. If so, the grandchildren of our statisticians may possibly represent the increase from now to then in the standard of life, not only as an increase in the collection of positive goods but with the due weight given to the removal of negative elements.

But as we become involved in massive action against fully grown nuisances, we must logically become alert to incipient nuisances. The manufacture and employment of atomic energy are attended with such dangers that nobody doubts the necessity of imposing upon the manufacturers and consumers costly precautions. This may well serve as a precedent in cases less manifestly critical. Costs of production in the future will contain an increasing element of "nuisance-prevention." If such precautions come to be very important in one country while they remain insignificant in another, a rough comparison of their outputs may then be misleading, taking into account only positive streams and making no allowance for the fact that an attendant stream of nuisances is produced in one case and avoided in the other.

V

We have glanced at the "frontier territories" of economic science; these are "unsettled" lands from which attacks have often been launched against economists, accused of being "nasty" (because they deal with mercenary relations), "brutish" (because they have no eye for "real" values), and shortsighted (because they think little of the conservation issues). The present paper takes a quite different line: it expresses the hope that economists will "settle" the territories surveyed. This becomes the more necessary as economics increasingly assumes the role of a prescriptive science.

But a difficulty already encountered at various steps must be stressed. Economics is a fundamentally "democratic" science in that the economist takes his valuation from "the public." While the philosopher tells people what they should desire, the economist as such only tells people how they should act, given their manifest desires, expressed in market valuations. Thus tied down, the economist must "underestimate" what his society underestimates. This is not, on his part, a deficiency; it is a rule of his intellectual discipline. His submission to "manifest valuations" is a condition of his rigor, which however implies limitations upon the scope of his preoccupations and their term in years.

A certain economist, say Malthus, may well formulate a guess relative to a distant future, but this guessing is not economic science, and has indeed often been proved wrong, because as the situation foreseen draws nearer, it alters valuations and reverses the trend of actions: economic life is teeming with "feedback" effects.

If the limitations of economic science are a condition of its rigor, an invitation to enlarge its scope may imply some contradiction. Such enlargement is however inevitable in view of the fact that our increasing power and speed and achievement urgently call for some advisory science, and economics is chosen to perform that function.

For this purpose, political economy may well stretch to political ecology, i.e., the "flows" which the economist is wont to consider will be regarded as "derivations" applied to the mighty "flows" of natural processes. This becomes necessary since we cannot think any more of human activities as a puny scrabbling on the skin of the Earth incapable of affecting our abode. As our power over natural agents increases, it becomes prudent to recognize in them the character of assets. In short "economics" is the brightly lit zone lying between the natural resources and processes upon which our existence depends ("free goods") and the supreme achievements of our kind ("free services").

4

Order versus Organization

This paper deals with man's taste in configurations and consequences arising therefrom. "The Problem of the Orchard" may introduce the subject better than any abstract statement.

The Problem of the Orchard

Let there be an apple orchard and two distinct groups of school children. The first group is assembled in class and is asked the following question: "In a given orchard, 100,000 apples are to be picked and collected in heaps. How should the heaps be formed?" No child will regard the problem as indeterminate; most will answer that the apples should be collected in a hundred heaps of a thousand apples each. Possibly some few may give different answers, but always in round numbers of heaps with equal numbers of apples to the heap. In the meantime let us send out the second group of children actually to heap up the 100,000 apples. When their task is completed we will find a varied collection of uneven mounds.

Thus the same problem has been given contrasting solutions: A in the classroom, B in the field; A by a process of thought, B by a process of action. This affords us our first general statement: given a set of factors, there is no necessary coincidence between their arrangement by a process of thought (type A) and their arrangement by a process of action (type B).

After the apples are gathered an observer strolls into the orchard. He beholds the B arrangement, and its irregularity faintly displeases him, while his eye would be gladdened by a more regular distribution of the

From *On Freedom and Free Enterprise: Essays in Honor of Ludwig von Mises*, edited by Mary Sennholtz. (Princeton, N.J.: Van Nostrand, 1956). Used by permission of the publisher.

A type. Indeed the unseemliness of the B arrangement may affect him sufficiently to evoke action—he may apply his own labor or that of others to a rearrangement. This affords us our second and third general statements loosely worded: Man delights in perceived order; he is willing to expend labor on its achievement.

The Feeling of Orderliness

We are enamored of order; this passion runs through all of mankind, from the housewife to Einstein. True enough, but what is "Order"? So Platonic an approach is to be shunned. It is a more sensible and modest course to note that some arrangements evoke an immediate pleasure and approval, while others do not. We shall call the first "seemly" and the second "unseemly," hoping that we thereby emphasize that we start from subjective appreciations. We do not then have to answer the question, "what is Order?" Our concern is merely to detect when the feeling of seemliness is experienced.

Tests of seemliness can easily be devised. On your desk, next to the visitor's chair, place twelve pencils, six blue and six red ones, arranged in two heaps, six red and one blue in one heap and then five blue ones in the other. A visitor will itch to transfer the "mislaid" blue pencil to the blue lot, while he will remain quiescent if two heaps of six each contain three blue and three red pencils. Or again, if the pencils are arranged by size with one discrepancy, the visitor will experience something like relief if you restore the continuity of the series. As one goes on to less naive experiments, it becomes apparent that the feeling of seemliness is experienced when we grasp the law of structure according to which the factors are arrayed. If five beads are presented, three large ones in succession and then two small ones, the individual will want to place each small one between two large beads, but if the pattern of three large ones and then two small ones is frequently repeated, its periodicity will make it acceptable.

An office has a stock of envelopes of various sizes. Their arrangement pleases if they are stacked by sizes in a progression. Let there be two collections on two different shelves, each containing the whole range of sizes. A new secretary undoubtedly will set out to assemble all same-size envelopes, substituting one series for two. She will, however, refrain from this rearrangement when she finds that the envelopes on the first shelf carry an engraved address on their back while those on the second shelf do not. The principle of classification has become clear to her and she now regards as orderly an arrangement which did not seem so at the outset.

We want factors to "obey" some understandable principle by reference to which each has and falls into "its place." The understanding can be either artistic or intellectual. Every eye enjoys the shapes of shells, but few minds could formulate that the shapes are generated from an equi-angular spiral. The eye may thus jump to a conclusion while the mind may recognize an organizing principle which does not jump to the eye as in the foregoing example of the envelopes. Thus there are two modes of understanding; appreciation of seemliness involves one or the other forms of recognition of an organizing principle.

Our desire to find things "obedient" to some principle is the mainspring of intellectual inquiry. We seek "hidden" principles of organization whose discovery reveals the orderliness of phenomena that seem disorderly to us.

Our achievements in so marshaling phenomena have been connected with and are dependent upon the progress of mathematics. Mathematics mainly consist in the thinking out of more complex configurations. When an additional "function" or "series" is studied, one more "shape" is thereby added to our intellectual store of "orderly configurations." Let us take a grossly simplified example. Let us assume that we have been unable to form any idea of a closed curve other than the circle. We are then told that the earth "circles" around the sun. But by some means we find that the earth does not in fact describe a circle around the sun.[1] Its movement therefore does not conform to any model of orderliness held in our mind, ergo we adjudge it disorderly. This is meant to stress that the probability of our experiencing orderliness is a function of the store of configurations worked out in our minds. A log normal distribution[2] may seem orderly to a mathematician but to no one else.[3]

Fitting and Tidying-Up

A scientist may be thought of as having access to a great store of patterns into which he delves to find one that will fit the facts he seeks to integrate into a theory. Such a pattern may not be available to him, in which case he must acknowledge failure. For to him the facts are supreme; the theory must fit them. Success may come later in this field because some mathematician, possibly quite ignorant of his concern, has worked out a pattern[4] which will now suit the phenomena.

The inverse relation holds true in the case of those many diverse human activities which we may blanket under the term "tidying up." Take the simple example of the housewife who holds in her mind a given pattern of arrangement to which the objects of "tidying-up" are made to conform.

In terms of our orchard example, the progress of science depends upon the ability of the mind to move away from the simplest type A arrangements to the conception of more intricate shapes. One of these shapes will bear a great likeness to the B arrangement which actually occurs. This is an achievement of science. On the other hand, tidying-up activities consist in moving objects from B configurations, which just occur, toward type A arrangements which are recognized as orderly and therefore desirable.

We can therefore reformulate our second and third general statements: Men have a tidiness-preference for arrangements of which they grasp the structural law, and they have a tidiness-propensity to recast arrangements in accordance with models held in their minds.

Contrasted Meanings of Rationality

The root of the word "rationality" is ratio, i.e., proportion. Considering a given arrangement of factors, we may call it "rational," because the proportions obtaining between parts are such as to spring immediately to the eye, or to be immediately (or readily) understood by the mind.[5] Our pleasure is then bound up with the assent we grant to existing proportions. But an arrangement may be "rational" in quite another sense: if the proportions between factors are suitable to produce the result at which the arrangement is aimed. We thus find two distinct meanings of "rationality": subjective enjoyment of proportions, and objective adequacy of proportions to the purpose of the arrangement. To be more precise, in the first case the arrangement is judged as "a sight"; in the second case, as "an organization for results."[6]

In everyday language, people tend to call arrangements "rational," "reasonable," and "orderly" if their principle is simple enough to be immediately grasped; conversely, they tend to call them "irrational," "unreasonable" and "disorderly," if the principle is not clear to them. Thus order and reason tend to be identified to seemliness rather than to operativeness.

The Case of the Library

In the course of his life an author has collected a private library attuned to his needs. The volumes he uses least have been relegated to the highest and least accessible tiers, while the works of reference are ready at hand. Regardless of authorship and formal subject manner, those works that hold for him some affinity of significance and that are apt to be used simultaneously are placed together. The owner could not easily account for the distribution of his tools (which indeed shifts over time), but it serves his purpose.[7] While he is on a holiday, a well-meaning daughter decides to tidy up and aligns the volumes according to format and alphabetical order. Having wrought, she feels that "it looks better now"; and so it does, but a working arrangement has been destroyed in the name of seemliness. No doubt, the previous arrangement was imperfect and could have been reformed to serve the author's purpose even better. But such an improvement would have been based on a considered judgment of the operator thinking out his process, or by someone else capable of seeing the problem from the operative angle— an "operator-judgment." The reform affected by the daughter was not "operator-based," if I may so express it.

Thinking in general terms, let us consider an arrangement of factors that serves some purpose and is instrumental to some process. Let us call it an operational arrangement. A mind concerned with this purpose, well aware of the process, dwells upon the operational arrangement and finds that it might be made more effective by certain alterations. We shall call a judgment passed from this angle an O-judgment to denote that the arrangement is appreciated from the operational standpoint. O-judgments are the principle of all technical progress made by mankind. Quite different in kind is the judgment passed upon the same arrangement of factors by a mind that regards it without any intensive interest in or awareness of the process. Such a judgment is then passed as it were from an external, extra-processive standpoint. We shall call it an S-judgment (S for sightseer).

The Genesis of Absurdity

Whenever I recognize that an arrangement of factors is instrumental to an operation, I cannot call this arrangement irrational (this would be saying in the same breath that it is related and unrelated to the same operation). But being concerned *ex hypothesi* with this operation I may well call the arrangement more or less rational. In this case I am really comparing a current method or path which I have explored with another method or path which I have discovered. This is an O-judgment.

Addressing myself to the same arrangement, I may fail to identify it as processive and instrumental to an operation, or I may fail to interest myself in this operation, or again I may fail to sufficiently scrutinize the process and arrangement to recognize their complex connection. If I nonetheless pass a judgment upon what I perceive of the configuration, this must be an S-judgment whose principle is a spontaneous and undeliberate comparison of the shape perceived to simple models of seemliness. If this is my attitude, the more complex the process is to which I have denied my attention, and the more complex the attending configuration, the more unseemly I shall find the latter, and the more unfavorable must be my S-judgment. I shall then call the arrangement disorderly and irrational.

An O-judgment is costly in terms of attention and time. It cannot be formed immediately or without effort; therefore, the number of such judgments which I may form is limited. But while I must focus my attention intensively on the process and arrangement in question, a great number of other shapes float into the field of my attention, and my glimpses at them immediately call forth uncostly S-judgments. The more extensive the field over which I may thus roam effortlessly, the greater the number of my S-judgments. Therefore, my store of judgments will tend to be made up of a small minority of O-judgments and a great majority of S-judgments. But while my O-judgments tend to improve arrangements whose processiveness I have grasped and which I endeavor to make more rational (i.e., effective), my S-judgments tend to impeach arrangements of which I considered only the seemliness and which I therefore pronounce irrational. Therefore the larger the number of arrangements upon which I venture to pass judgments, the higher the proportion of the arrangements examined which I shall pronounce unseemly, and the more the world will seem to me to be made up of "bad" and "wrong" arrangements.

But O-judgments are also in a small minority within every other mind. Moreover, diverse minds do not form O-judgments on the same subject matters. It follows that a summation of individual judgments arrived at independently within a society would show that there is of necessity a huge majority of S-judgments over O-judgments. And second, there must be a majority of S-judgments over O-judgments on every arrangement. S-judgments generally entail a verdict of unseemliness, disorder, and irrationality; therefore, a summation of all judgments must result in a general verdict of unseemliness, disorder, and irrationality. It must result in a condemnation of "the absurdity of the universe," and more specifically of all social arrangements.

We actually find that such a philosophy has arisen in our times possibly because we have overextended the field of individual judgment.

The Case of the Judge

Of course, it runs contrary to the principle of division of labor that I should pass judgment on a great number of arrangements. Take a simple simile. As a judge I have to rule on a number of cases per year. It has never been suggested that every litigation in the country should be submitted to every judge. If this would be the case a great number of minds would be conscripted for each case, but no attention at all could be paid to each. Such a procedure would seem inane, and yet consider how many "cases" the daily paper brings to our private court and tempts us to adjudge.

It takes no great psychological acumen to observe that we enjoy passing judgments on matters of which we know very little. This is bound up with our taste in configurations. Problems to which we have devoted scrupulous scrutiny and arrangements which we have delved into deeply offer no scope for application of the simple models that we inherently prefer. It is a relief to turn to problems of which we are ignorant and to which we therefore may apply our models. Be it noted that the greatest scientists who have mastered prodigious complexities are apt to come out with the most naive views on social problems, for example. Their minds are taking a holiday, reverting to the effortless and invalid judgment of seemliness. We could assume that those who are best aware of the difficulties of grasping a process in their own fields, should be most chary of passing S-judgments on other matters; but this is contrary to reality. Our affection for simple patterns is so basic to our nature that the more we must bow to the actual complexities of organizations we understand, the more we want to find simplicity in other organizations.

The Attraction of Simple Figures

All that is known of man's past is testimony to the fact that he has ever associated the idea of perfection with simple figures, which he therefore used to denote Divinity. Basic to every ritual is the circle in which the eye finds no lack and which thus represents (or indeed suggests) the concept of Wholeness. The circular crown seems to have been invented independently by all human societies; the operations of magic have involved everywhere the tracing of figures within a circle.[8] We are told that primitive places of worship and assemblies of worshippers were circular.[9] Movement forming simple geometric patterns was a form of homage to Divinity. Military parades have also been derived from this, as well as our word "theory," which in barrack language still meant quite recently "training in geometric marching."

The setting of effective values upon the simplest geometric figures is strikingly exemplified in the history of warfare. The Macedonians were so enamored with the squareness of their phalanx that they thoughtlessly adhered to their order of battle even when circumstances made it most inadvisable. Frederick the Great and Napoleon's victories owed much to the aesthetic sense of their opponents who arrayed their troops with an eye for symmetry. Frederick and Napoleon gave themselves the advantage of an operative arrangement over a seemly one.

Complex Structures are Characteristics of Life

"Proteins may well be considered the most important of all the substances present in plants and animals."[10] This induces me to ask for a description of proteins. In answer the chemist must first remind me that he regards as elementary factors the atoms of pure substance, though they themselves display a complex inner architecture. Starting from them as simple, the chemist must draw my attention to amino acids, a family of different compounds constructed by different arrangements of a different kind of atoms. Taking pity upon my ignorance, he may invite me to regard these amino-acids as a varied collection of queerly designed jewels, built by different arrangements of different kinds of precious stones. Then he must tell me about polypeptide chains, the stringing together in and from a line of many such "jewels," with a twisting of the chain and in many cases an inter-twisting of several chains. "Considering their structure, we see that the existence of a great number of different proteins (perhaps 50,000 different proteins in the human body) is not surprising. Protein molecules may differ from one another not only in the number of residues of different amino-acids, but also in the order of the residues in the polypeptide chains, and the way in which the chains are folded."[11]

In order to account for the operative properties of protein, scientists have found themselves compelled to successively work out this extremely complicated picture, which stands in sharp contrast to the simple configurations that haunt our mind.

It is a trite remark that our dead body, regarded as a mine of inorganic chemicals, would not yield more than ten dollars worth of chemicals. And while this makes a pretty poor joke, it can be used to emphasize the value of intricate operative organization. Is it not therefore disquieting that our minds should spontaneously favor the tidiness of crystals over the intricacy of active arrangements?

Nothing is more orderly than a crystal of pure copper; therein we find regularity and symmetry at their best. Nothing is more operative than a gene, of which the intricacy baffles our science. A child can grasp and reproduce the structure of the copper crystal, but no human agency can forge this fantastically complicated signature which the gene repeats all over the body of one specific person. Surely so glaring an opposition should teach us not to confuse order with organization.

The Threat of Orderliness

This train of thought leads us to regard the simplicity-preference and tidiness-propensity of the human mind as potentially destructive. Such tendencies run counter to the diversity and intricacy of operative structures. If I could recast the molecule proteins of my body to give them a simpler and identical structure, I would be committing suicide. Practically all men enjoy the orderliness of a military parade, but they are dangerously prone to mistake this enjoyment for the recognition of a supreme form of organization. In fact, the men assembled on the field achieve no operation whatever beyond offering a sight. The idea of over-all organization is frequently aligned to an image of perceivable regularity in human movements as can be found in a parade. But this is the very opposite of organization.

A parade is costly; equally costly is the parade spirit with which we approach the operations of men in general. We tend to believe that society is at its best when its functioning offers to our minds a clear, distinct, and simple pattern. But the only thing then maximized is our intellectual enjoyment. We are prone to mistake our endeavors to maximize our intellectual enjoyment for the spirit of reform. But we have no warrant for the belief that a simplification of pattern that would please our minds would constitute an improvement of society, unless we define improvement as increasing coincidence of arrangements with the figures held in our mind—an extreme of intellectual pride.

Let us now picture a group of operators, each engaged in a process and therefore prone to arrange factors at hand in a manner suitable to his process. Imagine that they meet at regular intervals to devise a general structure. Now if they all individually and responsibly perform the same operations, we can assume that their general decisions as to the over-all structure will take into account operational needs that are experienced by all participants. This cannot be so, however, if the participants are engaged in very different processes and if only a minority of them are in fact responsible for the performing of operations. Then the common ground for the participants will be provided by those general shapes and figures that inhabit our minds and of which the simplest are the most common to all of us. Agreement shall then most easily be reached on orderly arrangements adverse to operational arrangements in proportion to the intricacy of the latter. The rule of order and the operational urge shall thenceforth be in conflict. This is, of course, in itself a pattern of deceitful simplicity. But it may serve to explain some tensions of contemporary society.[12]

Notes

1. Though in fact we would presumably have no means of establishing this if our geometric knowledge were so restricted.
2. See the notable paper on log normal distributions by Professor J. H. Gaddum (*Nature*, Oct. 20, 1954) to which our attention was drawn by Professor Allais.
3. A collection of phenomena becomes orderly for me if and when I can tersely formulate a law of structure whereby each item is assigned the position which it holds.
4. Consider the number of processes which came to be recognized as orderly when related to the Verhulst-Pearl logistic curve, or even better to Gaston Beckman's more elastic model. For an inspired eulogy of these patterns cf. D'Arcy Thompson: *On Growth and Form* (new. ed. Cambridge, 1942).
5. Let us recall that the eye of an ignorant man may appreciate the harmony of proportions of an arrangement the structural law of which he could not reformulate; conversely, a mathematician may formulate a law of arrangement which cannot be transcribed in a visible form.
6. A third meaning of rationality need not concern us here; any configuration whatever is, of course, the outcome of its causes and therefore may be called "rational." In this sense, everything that is real is rational, but then the term becomes so all-embracing as to be useless.
7. For a striking treatment of the general problem of arrangement of tools around an artisan, see Gerald K. Zipf, *Human Behavior and the Principle of Least Effort* (Cambridge, Mass.: Addison-Wesley Press, 1949).
8. Cf. for instance Robert Ambelin, *La Kabbale Pratique* (Paris, 1951).

9. Cf. among many other sources Louis Hautecoeur, *Mystique et Architecture; Symbolisme du Cercle et de la Coupole* (Paris, 1954).
10. Taken from that admirable introduction to chemistry, *General Chemistry*, by Linus Pauling, 2nd ed. (San Francisco, 1953), pp. 592–600.
11. Ibid.
12. Much more could be said on the subject. It might, for instance, be useful to dwell upon our natural tendency, when sight-judging a mechanism or process, to reform or improve it by breaking down whatever feedback it is provided with. But what use, if any, can be made of the views advanced here must be left to better judgments.

5

Toward a Political Theory of Education

The Fundamental Purpose of Society Is to Rear the Young

It is a tautology that the perpetuation of any living species depends upon the successful rearing of its young. It is an empirical finding that such rearing poses to parents a problem of increasing difficulty as we ascend the ladder from the simplest to the most complex organisms. When we are dealing with the lower forms of life, the adults' perpetuating function is completed in the very moment of germ discharge. Of such germs of life, produced in sufficient quantity, and abandoned to water or air, enough enter a favorable environment in which to develop autonomously. Such autonomy of development is denied to superior animals, which require, for survival and growth, the nurture and care of the mother. The greater the perfection to which they are called, the more pronounced their initial helplessness, the more delayed their ability to fend for themselves. These features so culminate in the case of man that I find it impossible to picture a being deserving the name of man developing without the benefit of already elaborate arrangements for his protection. It seems reasonable to regard the mother's need for help in the nurture and protection of the young as having provided the nexus of society, which sufficiently explains the many matrilineal traits of primitive societies.[1]

We must picture, therefore, some social coalition built around the mother as the necessary precondition for the emergence of man. Some species offer instances of such coalitions which, however, dissolve when the young all reach adulthood at the same time. It could not be so in the case of man or his forerunners, since the period of maturation was much

Reprinted from *Humanistic Education and Western Civilization: Essays for Robert M. Hutchins*, edited by A.A. Cohen (New York: Holt, Rinehart & Winston, 1964): 55–74. Used by permission of the publisher.

longer than the interval between births: the coalition therefore had to be permanent, a requisite condition for the development of language.

We do not have to explain how the forerunners of man came to form permanent associations, but we can safely assert that the biological character of the species made its survival impossible but for such groupings; and that, indeed, only within such groupings could man acquire characteristics such as significant speech, which we regard as defining him. Man was born in and of society.

Have I any justification for so farfetched a beginning? I think so, because it emphasizes that the care of the young is the sufficient reason and fundamental purpose of society.

The Main Social Task Is the Education of the Young

It would be futile to bring the young to physical adulthood without endowing them with competence. It seems true of all creatures that they break away from their protectors as soon as they feel apt to cater for themselves: if that occurs after only one season, the time during which they can learn from their seniors is short. It is a boon to us that our period of inevitable dependence is so long: while this has, on one hand, made society necessary, as a corollary it gives us much time to be taught.

What are children taught everywhere, even in the most primitive groups? Skills, manners, and judgment. I put skills first because the teaching of skills can be observed already in the behavior of animals: we can easily watch birds being taught to fly, kittens being taught to hunt. Manners are those modes of conduct which contribute materially and morally to group cooperation. Judgment is the capacity to make the best decisions for oneself and for the group.

Anthropologists have stressed that, in a primitive group, any child gets attention from his seniors: as his seniors pet him in his infancy, so does every senior chide him for bad manners when the occasion arises. Training in skills is given by all, but it is mainly under the tutelage of the best performers that the child learns to fish or to hunt. As those who have lived longest in a dangerous world are deemed by their success (longevity) to have given positive evidence of their prudence, it falls to them to teach judgment: which these elders do by telling tales which imply a moral, and become "lessons of history." It does seem that more of adult activity is addressed to education in primitive conditions than in our advanced societies. It is understandable: survival is doubtful enough to make it essential that the coming generation should be as well or better endowed than their contemporaries in skills, manners, and judgment.

Education Is the Mirror of Society

The behavior of adults is dependent upon, though not uniquely determined by, the education received. But also the education given reflects the values of society.

However much one would like to think of war as a decreasing function of civilization, the evidence is to the contrary. The primitives seem to have less thought of conflict than societies with an already higher organization. Lacedaemon is the classic example of a society where the training of the young tended to make them battleworthy. It is only fair to point out that the purpose seemed to be defense rather than conquest,[2] and also that their training did more than prepare warriors: it overcame laziness, clumsiness, and selfishness. The founder of anthropology, Father Lafitau, stressed the similarities between the institutions and education of Sparta, and those of the Iroquois Indians.[3]

It is trite to contrast the Athenian education with the Spartan. In Athens we find a "liberal education." In social terms, this means nothing but an education for free men. But I think it may also be taken to mean an education for those who may look forward to a life free from pressing cares. Productive skills have no part in this education because production is entrusted to slaves. War skills have but a subsidiary part because the City glories in a safe hegemony.

"Music" becomes essential in such an education: it includes literature in its many developing forms, and thus corresponds to what will come to be known as attendance upon the Muses. Philosophy is introduced at a later stage of history, and also for students more advanced in years. Thus liberal education takes shape as a quickening of the esthetic and intellectual faculties, as a formation of taste and thought, promising a fruitful use of gentlemanly leisure.

Such education can properly be called "culture" because it causes what Alfieri called the *pianta uomo* to flourish: it was, however, only for a minority. Surprisingly enough, it is Friedrich Engels who argues vigorously that slavery and other forms of subjection of the greater number have been historically necessary to allow minorities the leisure necessary for the development of culture.[4]

It is easy enough to recognize that the great cultures of the past, marked on the one hand by a liberal education for a minority,[5] were marked on the other hand by the subjection of the multitude. Nor does it seem true that, as Engels implied, the favored minority, by its very existence, stimulated the development of productive forces. Its members owed it to their position to turn their backs on sordid pursuits. As Seneca remarks of such devices as central heating or stenography: "These are nothing but the devices of our vilest slaves: wisdom sits higher, and does not educate hands but souls."[6] If, due to the practice and example of the Church, the upper classes of Western Europe were open at all times to those rising from below, such ease of access, however laudable in itself, worked rather against the improvement of the common lot than on its behalf. And this, for a simple reason, which Bonald expounds[7]: as soon as a businessman had done well enough, he hastened to become a nobleman, and this implied "living nobly," that is renouncing all interest in materially productive processes. Thereby the chief talents of the productive multitude were skimmed off, removed, by their own choice, from further contribution to the material progress.

The Coming of "Productivity"

Swift, in his *Voyage to Laputa*, rails against the "projectors" who propose new ways of performing material tasks, "whereby, as they undertake, one man shall do the work of ten."[8] His mockery proves that the state of mind to which we owe so much was then already in vigorous ascent. No political or social reformer could possibly have transformed the condition of the multitude as it has been transformed by the ceaseless introduction of new technological processes. Our age is properly the "Age of Productive Capital," meaning that installations and equipment afford labor a productivity previously inconceivable. And nowhere is this better recognized than in the communist countries, which concentrate on capital building.

We can deem ourselves fortunate to live in times when the material condition of the common man is continually improving, when he obtains an ever-increasing flow of goods and services in exchange for work of shorter duration, exacting far less physical effort. Those who turn up their noses at this technological civilization should see in what misery, and at what cost of labor the masses of the people live in the countries where this great advance has not yet occurred. They would then speak just like that Jesuit missionary to China whose initial admiration for the refined culture of the mandarins turned to angry sorrow when he saw the life of the peasant, toiling throughout the day in water to his knees and fed in the evening on a bowl of rice.[9]

Whatever the indubitable welfare-consciousness of seventeenth-century China, it could not remedy its lack of productivity. This lack is surprising in a country which made major inventions many centuries before they reached Europe or were rediscovered there.[10] Political good will of itself cannot cure economic ills, nor can inventions of themselves procure economic goods: there must be an attitude of mind which turns them to productive purposes. A productivity-conscious society such as ours is without precedent in human history.

Before our times, there have been so-called rich civilizations. In fact, however, the eye was drawn to islands of wealth amid a sea of poverty. Now, for the first time, wealth is general—nothing proves this better than the denunciation of "patches of poverty" which now seem to us to be anomalies.What does this imply for education?

Quantitative Progress in Education

Education is "a good thing," and there should be more of it. On this statement, couched in naive terms, there is pretty unanimous agreement.[11] The rough and common meaning of "more education" is "more years spent at school." This, indeed, is the criterion of "educational attainment" used by the U.S. Bureau of the Census, whose reports rank the adult population according to the number of years of schooling completed. Its reports inform us, for instance, that the median education in 1940 for workers in the age group from 18 to 64 consisted of 9.3 years of schooling, while by 1957 this median had risen to 11.8 years.[12] We are also told that, at a given moment, say 1957, the age group 25 to 34 had a higher "educational attainment" than the 45 to 64 age group, the median of school years completed being 12.1 for the first against 9.5 for those older. The "educational attainment" of the whole adult population is, of course, affected by the continuous addition of generations with a higher educational attainment.

If we turn to what is presently being done for education, still employing a quantitative concept, the best presentation consists in ranking the young population by age, taking the ratio of school attenders for every age class, plotting such ratios on a chart and drawing a curve through these points. The curve stays in the neighborhood of a 100 percent straight line for a period of years, and then falls off. Curves of this kind can be compared for the same country at different times or for different countries. Obviously such a curve begins to fall off later when legal age for leaving school is raised, also its shape beyond that age depends upon the opportunities given and taken for further study.

The surface defined by this curve can be called "the tuition area": it is remarkably large in the United States by comparison with other countries.

The Economist's Plea for More Education

Quite recently, there has been a considerable expression of interest among the economists, for increase in education. It is not suggested that their concern for it, as individuals, is novel! What is new is that their plea for more education should be made in their capacity as economists and be based upon economic considerations. It is supported by three important positive findings.

1. The study of economic growth has gone far beyond any explanation based upon the cumulative increase of fixed capital alone. It is now stressed that such growth also depends upon the development of "the economic capacities" of individuals, capacities which are enhanced by education. Education therefore is "investment in man," deemed no less necessary for growth than investment in capital equipment. Theodore W. Shultz, a pioneer in this area of study, asks us to imagine some low-income country acquiring overnight the set of national resources and means of production possessed by an advanced country. Would not its output fall very far short of that of the advanced country to which it is now materially comparable, for want of comparable skills? Conversely, Shultz feels, that the remarkable rates of growth achieved by some European countries after World War II may be due to their having been "long on human capital relative to their stock of reproducible non-human capital," so that successive increases in the latter paid off startlingly well in terms of output—this, because they remedied an imbalance, because there was an excess of skills available to put the new tools to work.[13]

2. The comparison of individual incomes has brought out that personal income is an increasing function of the number of years of schooling completed.[14]

3. The analysis of the unemployed population has shown a clear correlation between unemployment and inadequate schooling.[15]

Of these findings, the second is, by far, the least novel: parents have always assumed that they improved their child's chances of social advancement by affording him more education. The third is quite alarming: technological progress seems to increase the risk of superfluity for the ill-qualified. It is worth noting how far this new fear belies the old fear, so frequently expressed in the past, that the development of "machinism" would grind down the great majority of workers to the performance of witless tasks! On the contrary, it is now felt that economic development as it were makes more room at the top while leaving less at the bottom of the job structure, tends to manifest itself by excess demand for highly qualified personnel, simultaneous with excess demand for jobs by the least qualified. In other words, the labor market tends to divide itself into "floors" with a possibility of inverse situations at different "floors." Whatever the immediate implications of such a situation—and they are of very great importance, but not our present concern—long-term implications are clear enough: the structure of qualifications should keep pace with the changing structure of jobs.

At the same time that parents may regard the future benefits accruing to their children from more advanced education, their fear of unemployment for lack of sufficient education is an additional negative incentive. For society as a whole, the progress of education seems a condition not only of over-all growth, but of preventing that great evil, unemployment.

Some Implications of More Education

Still thinking in quantitative terms, the progress of education means: (a) that the period of mandatory education is lengthened; or (b) that the ratio of those studying beyond the mandatory period is raised; or—and more probably—(c) that both of these phenomena occur, in whatever mixture. In any case, it means that, besides the general increase which the school population must undergo in coming years for merely demographic reasons, a specific increase (corresponding to the idea of "more education") must considerably swell the school population above the age of seventeen.[16]

Stressing that the problem to be dealt with essentially concerns the population above seventeen immediately implies that the attendant increase in teaching personnel requires people capable of giving junior college, or college, or university tuition. In short the teaching population, which must increase in numbers throughout all grades, must be expanded to a much greater degree at its more advanced levels. This requires that capable people should be tempted away from the competing attractions of the professions, business, public administration, advertising, and, to some degree, research itself. This should accelerate the process, already visible, of heightening the material and moral status of professors. Incidentally it will make the teaching profession a far more influential and powerful group in society.

Securing teachers in adequate quantity and of sufficient quality is no mean task. It is, however, in my view, the only economic problem which results from the lengthening of the educational process.

I have found that the foregoing statement often arouses surprise and incredulity. It can be easily justified. Everybody takes it for granted that continued gains in productivity will permit a progressive shortening of the work week. A general shortening of the work week by one hour deprives the economy of as much labor as the delay by one hour of the commencement of work by all the youth of the nation.[17] Thus if the economy can afford the shortening of the work week, it can just as well afford an *alternative* deprivation of labor by lengthening the required time for study. It must however, be clearly put to public opinion that these are *alternative* benefits accruing from gains in productivity. The shortening of the work week is assuredly the self-regarding alternative.

It is not, however, the economic but the psychological problem which concerns me. It seems the natural bent of physically mature human beings to embark upon the active life—the urge is very strong in the late teens; it is quite easily overcome in the case of those who truly delight in study. But they are a minority. For the majority there is a painful tension—often manifested in disorderly conduct—which makes the task of teaching more difficult. The phenomenon is well known, but it is often said that this phase passes away. True enough, but quite frequently such passing away leaves a certain limpness in the individual. As he has not started "doing" when he first felt impelled to the active life, he may subsequently find himself more phlegmatic and less energetic. Moreover, the life and environment of the student are abnormal, especially in the residential universities of the United States. It is worth remembering in this context that such a life was devised long ago in England for men promised to holy orders, and that those destined to an active life came to Cambridge or Oxford much earlier and left much earlier than is the case in the American universities.

Undoubtedly this is a real problem, one, however, which I do not feel experienced enough to discuss further. It does inject a doubt into my mind about the desirability of lengthening progressively the duration of formal education for all, regardless of individual propensities.

In any case, at some point, it becomes absurd to think in terms of adding "more years" and we shall have to think of more fruitful years. This again is a problem for thoughtful educators, of which I am not one. I shall leave it for the moment.

Education for Production and Education for Leisure

It is time, indeed, that I should come to consider the purpose and nature of education. I have stressed that continued gains in productivity constitute the characteristic feature of our modern civilization: tellingly enough, it is the only one which nations formed by a different civilization than our own are eager to take over from us.

I have noted, as well, that economists champion more education because it serves to increase productivity. Productivity benefits the worker in two ways: (1) by an increase in the flow of goods he gets and (2) by a decrease in the amount of work he must do. When we think of less work or more free time, we are all too prone to consider it only in terms of a shorter work week. Considerations of increased holidays or increased longevity beyond the age of retirement are but different forms of one and the same phenomenon. It is the most telling index of our technological civilization that our life expectation has so increased: workers no longer work until they drop, because on the average they live longer than they used to and because individual or (increasingly) social provision can be made for old age.

If one reflects on the career of a hypothetical young man who goes to work at the early age of seventeen, he has a long career of work stretching before him. We may make some revealing calculations. He can look forward to fifty-three years of life, of which he can expect to spend ten after retirement. The very most he can expect to spend at work each year, assuming forty-three years of work, is approximately 1900 hours per year. Taking these figures, which surely do not err on the side of optimism, the most our young man can expect to spend at work is less than 18 percent of the time of life he has before him. If he assumes that during the coming forty-three years, the average time worked will be forty-eight weeks and thirty-five hours per week (1680 hours per year), then the share of the time at work during his lifetime falls to 15.7 percent. I think it is permissible to state that work-time will absorb one sixth of the time he has before him.

Assuming that sleep will absorb one-third of the remaining time, our young man has one-half of his prospective life unconsumed by work or sleep. In more striking terms, a man's waking hours (two-thirds of his whole mature life) will be divided one-quarter for work and three-quarters for free time. I find it surprising that people seldom make such simple arithmetical calculations—calculations, moreover, which are likely to shed light on pressing problems.

Let us by all means so educate our young man so that his hours of work will be more productive. Of course, if we delay his entry into work by one year, it will mean so many hours less (possibly as much as 1900 hours) available to him in his lifetime. At the same time it may well be that the loss of one year of work consumed by education might add to his economic capability in such a way that the life-product for the total hours remaining will be increased, not diminished—and, indeed, so increased that the shortening of the normal work year to come may ensue. All this is quite right.

But what seems very wrong is to educate our hypothetical young worker for one-quarter of his waking hours to come, and not for the other three-quarters! I am quite willing to recognize that not all of the three-quarters is, in fact, available time: much of it is taken up by travel to and from work—but even during this trip the fruits of education may appear. Using public means of conveyance, one may as well read Pascal as look at comic strips. In short, all the waking hours ahead of us—those hours not consumed by work—depend for their use upon the education we receive.

Let me put it another way—and for this purpose I shall provisionally adopt the vocabulary of aristocratic civilizations which contrast the laborer bent upon his task, and the gentleman of leisure who bears his head high, *os sublime*. In our day the man who is all the time a "gentleman of leisure" has utterly disappeared. But the laborer who was nothing but laborer, a mere "hand," has also disappeared. The man of our day is part laborer, part gentleman of leisure. If we want to call work "slavery," then the contemporary is a good deal less than "half-slave" and a good deal more than "half-free": look to the foregoing figures.

The case for developing the average man's skill as a laborer is unanswerable, since among the benefits procured, despite the loss of work time, is the progressive enlargement of that share of time during which he is a freeman, a "gentleman." But the greater the share thus liberated, the more pressing it becomes to educate man for the fruitful use of this free time. Sebastian de Grazia puts thing very nicely when he used the term "free time" negatively, to signify that part of time which is "saved from the job," while reserving the term "leisure" to signify something positive, "a state of being in which activity is performed for its own sake or as its own end." And he says: "To save time through machines is not easy. To transform free time into leisure is not to be easy either."[18]

While the contrast here drawn between "free time" and "leisure" may well be deemed excessive, it does point to a major problem of our times which is well expressed in the popular expression "How shall I spend my time?", or even better the childish question: "What shall I do with myself?" According to the way we spend our time, we improve or harm ourselves—and it is truly a question of *ourselves* and not of such externals as our job or status.

No term is clearer than that of "culture": it means something done to us for our improvement, and something we do to ourselves for improvement. There is a wealth of examples to show that a man who has not been cultivated can, later in life, cultivate himself. But it would be optimistic to believe that more than a small minority are capable of this—most of us depend for our cultivation upon the good start given us by our teachers.

In short, future generations, which can look forward to an increasingly lighter burden of work, and to an increasing share of free time, require a liberal education.

And those so aristocratically minded as to think that the delights of art and thought can be enjoyed but by the "happy few" play a fool's game. We live in majority societies where beautiful things will be wiped out unless the majority appreciates them. The selfish sage (were these terms not contradictory) who wants the harmony and silence of Nature only for himself will find the silence destroyed by noisy hordes and the landscape ruined by bulldozers unless he can convert the majority. "Convert or perish" must be the motto of the self-regarding man of taste. Surely it is better, as indeed it is more natural, to undertake such conversion for the good of one's fellow men and especially of coming generations.

A *Trivium*

Education then has a dual purpose: to make man's labor more productive, and his leisure more fruitful. And the greater the gains in one direction, the more necessary is progress in the other. But here a great difficulty arises. I have expressed doubts about the feasibility and advisability of successively lengthening the term of formal education. If it must be lengthened in order to accommodate increased productivity, how much more must we lengthen it in order to make room also for a liberal education? If that is the problem, we are, indeed, in trouble. But I think, or hope, that the formulation above is erroneous. It contains two assumptions, both of which I reject: the first is that education for efficiency and education for improvement are radically distinct, and that to give both is twice as much trouble and takes twice as much time; the other is that the time presently spent in education is well employed.

Would anyone doubt that the art of correct expression (literature) and the art of rigorous reasoning (mathematics) are basic both to business and to culture? I would contend that the acquisition of these two skills is far the most important part of education.

I would draw the sharpest contrast between mental skills (such as I have just mentioned) and factual knowledge. We are lazy, and most of us have to be driven very hard to progress in lucid exposition and correct inference. However, such progress as we do make becomes part of our personality. It is otherwise with factual knowledge: we receive it from outside, store it, and it wastes away in storage. Factual knowledge does not become a part of us—no more, be it noted, than what is in the "memory" of a computing machine is an integral part of it: you can change the content of its memory; it still is the same machine. Personal experience has made me most strongly aware that we forget factual knowledge.[19] Therefore I ask: How much of the history, geography, physics, chemistry, biology, or geology taught at school do we remember? And since these things are going to be forgotten anyhow, instead of wasting upon them efforts better applied to the gaining of durable skills, one may as well present them in the form of educational films which will at least associate vividly in a child's mind with a given historical event. I regard it as very important that a child should realize ecological relationship, the dependence of human life upon its natural environment, and while it can be expected that he will remember how the rains come and the simple circuit of water, it is idle to hope that he will memorize the pathways of biosynthesis and photosynthesis. Nor is it good to grade on the basis of how much is remembered:[20] proper grading should be on the degree of achievement in the use of mental skills. These are what truly survive the end of the formal educational process. To the two named already, I would add a third, as soon as gifted expositors[21] have found means of making it readily accessible to the young: this I would call the art of checking factual statements; of measuring whether the evidence in favor of a given statement is sufficient to carry conviction; of asking the right questions, the answer to which would clinch a case.[22]

This art, along with literature and mathematics, would constitute my *trivium*.

Of course the art of correct expression is considerably enhanced if a great deal of translating is required—and without hesitation, I would suggest Latin as the other language from which and into which translations should be made, for its prosaic neatness offers such a useful contrast with the colorful vagueness of English.[23]

But as I have no qualifications as an educator, it is most foolhardy to venture so far.

Disciplina Facit Mores

My excuse for venturing as far as I have arises from my insistence upon the acquisition of skills as revelatory of the nature of Education. "Getting education" is not like being given a car; it is more like becoming capable of swift and prolonged swimming. What one really learns is to use one's powers. Brain specialists now tell us that we intellectuals use but a small fraction of the resources of our brain. I feel sure that they are right, and our descendants should be stimulated to do better. This is, to a considerable degree, a moral problem. Lack of attention, the great original fault of the mind, is properly a lack of courage—"'tis good enough" is a lack of honesty. Everything which Xenophon says in his *Cyropedia* regarding the necessity of a hard training for the body is valid for the mind. It seems to me a shocking paradox that one praises the exacting trainer who forms athletes, and that the same hard-driving spirit is not demanded of or approved in trainers of the mind.

Factual knowledge we acquire throughout our life according to opportunity and need, and we lose it through disuse. But it seems clear that the capacity to use the mind is acquired in youth only: and it is therefore a betrayal of youth, and of mankind, not to challenge this capacity so as to give it the fullest development. It takes moral virtue to respond, and response develops moral virtue.

The Ancients used to say, *Disciplina facit mores*.[24] It is true, indeed, that the way of life depends upon education. It seems that this venerable truth is best understood in our day by the commercial community, whose advertisements are increasingly aimed at the receptive mind of the child, to educate him for conspicuous consumption. Strangely enough intellectuals seem to make little of this truth.

We are all anxiously asking ourselves what is the future of individual liberty. The answer lies in our hands. Our power to preserve or procure it cannot be efficiently exercised by the means which seemed decisive to late eighteenth-century and early nineteenth-century minds. Experience has made us fully aware that the establishment of institutional devices offers no durable and solid guarantee of freedom. We have seen the collapse of too many constitutions and the abuse of others. We realize that whatever the influence we expect from political institutions upon mores, mores have a far stronger influence upon institutions, which stand or fall, work well or ill, according to the mores of the people. But *disciplina facit mores*. The tone and style of society depend upon education. Of this the ancients were so convinced that Xenophon's *Republic of the Lacedaemonians* deals mainly with the educational system. The persistence and right use of the political institutions depend upon the will of the adult, whose character and judgment have been formed in the educational institutions.

But let us look closer. It is at least a twenty-five-hundred-year-old debate whether "right conduct" should be taught by the pedagogue, or by parents. In Rome there was no question but that such instruction fell to parents: the family was called the "seminar of the Republic." In the Middle Ages, when the teaching establishments were run by the clergy, it was only natural that they should impart religious principles. The day-school system, prevalent in France, naturally leaves moral education to parents; the boarding-school system prevalent in England seems to turn it over to teachers. Presently most of our contemporaries are convinced that right conduct is not efficiently taught by "laying down the law," by way of *diktat*, but by responding to the child's anxieties. As a Catholic, I must and do believe that man has a natural appetite for the good, which only needs to be encouraged and enlightened. So here again it is not a question of imprinting upon the mind a code coming from outside, but of fostering a faculty of the individual.

How school can contribute to this process is quite a problem. Only two positive ways occur to me. First, in literature, a choice of authors with strong ethical content, and these, indeed, seem to be preferred by children (the preference of French children for Corneille, as an example). Second and mainly, the ceaseless practice of virtue in study. *Laborare est orare*: learning to do an honest piece of work is apprenticeship in virtue. A slovenly performance is a spurning of God's gifts and should never be tolerated. And here again, direct familiarity with great authors, as championed by Robert M. Hutchins, is inspiring.

Incidentally, Americans can never cherish enough the independence of educational establishments which exists in their country, not in mine, and which makes it possible to develop experiments, such as the teaching from "great books" practiced at St. John's College in Annapolis.

Education and Equality

We must not only teach intellectual honesty, but also practice it. Liberal thinkers of the past held that progress in education would promote equality. This now seems, to say the least, very doubtful. What is in doubt is not that equal opportunity for education should be afforded to all children. What is in doubt is that, on the basis of equal opportunity, a society of equals will result. Of course we have been and are moving toward equality of opportunity in schooling,[25] an evolution wherein the European countries lag behind the United States.[26] We all favor this equalization of opportunity, but we no longer trust that this equal nurture of children will result in the equal development of adults. This was believed by some eighteenth-century liberals on philosophic grounds; men, born equal, and receiving equal treatment, should develop equally.

Modern educators, who do not rely upon metaphysical assumptions but speak from experience, tell us that children and youths are quite unequally receptive to education. The longer and more elaborate the curriculum, the more pronounced the disparity becomes. I have been told by American high school teachers that they felt an obligation to help along the stragglers, but, in so doing, failed to provoke and stimulate the gifted; contrariwise the French *lycée* professor addresses himself to the elite of the class.

It would be a crime against our descendants if education were slowed down to the pace of the least apt, and limited to their ingestive capacity. Education must perforce have for its maxim: "To each according to his capacity." From very different performances by students, there naturally arises a hierarchy within the generation reaching manhood. This hierarchic ordering sits well with an increasingly integrated society. I find it hard to understand how "progressives" can at the same time cherish centralization and champion equality. Integration means nothing other than bringing a great number of individuals into one organization, which naturally assumes a pyramidal shape, and has more grades and rungs the larger it is. A society of large organizations (never mind whether they are called public or private) is a society of many grades; this corresponds very well to the great hierarchy of grades which arises out of education. Michael Young has called the resulting social system "Meritocracy."[27]

This seems to be the modern pattern. Great anxiety has been expressed as to its implications for individual freedom; however, much depends upon what one means by freedom. If one thinks of freedom as enlarged in proportion to means and narrowed in proportion to constraints, one will find it hard to deny that the common man's freedom on balance has increased, and is continuing to increase. The model is not incompatible with freedom in private life but with equality.[28] It is a natural law of organizations—quite flagrant in organisms—that the more elaborate the organization, the more differentiated and hierarchically structured the roles. Increasingly, incompatibility will be found between the equality proclaimed and its practice. What allows us to believe that we are moving toward greater equality is that there is still a great deal of pre-technological inequality to be liquidated. It is an ironical thought that the more long-drawn-out the process of liquidating antiquated and now dysfunctional inequalities, the more it will help to mask the emergence of a new strongly inequalitarian system. While people are still discussing the abolition of Lords by birth, they are but faintly aware of the new lordships.

However the inequalitarian system we are moving into has much to offer the "inferiors." Not only will they have little to envy their "superiors" as to the material conveniences of life, but the "inferiors" will do less work and will be subject to far less strain than the "superiors." We are witnessing a great upward shift of responsibility and a great downward diffusion of leisure. The advantages of a lower position may, indeed, become such as to tempt even some of the highly qualified.

Aurea Mediocritas

The expression of *aurea mediocritas* may, indeed, become a true description of the common man's condition in a technological civilization. Freed from want and worry, leaving it to a responsible elite to dispose of his work and to insure his welfare, our man can spend a great deal of time according to his taste. He can paint or drink, raise flowers or make the air ugly with the sound of his outboard. The aspect of our civilization already depends and will increasingly depend upon his taste. In this sense (though not in its management) our society promises to be increasingly democratic. In every past culture, religious rites and public edifices have been taste-forming. During the Middle Ages and, indeed, up to recent times all the tunes of popular songs were drawn from Church music composed for the glory of God; Athenian citizens discussing on the Pnyx, faced the beauty of the Parthenon. In our day, a managerial elite, obsessed with the progress of efficiency, has little time or thought to spare for the formation of taste. That is a glaring deficiency which the teaching community must seek to repair.

Just as it is important to express oneself lucidly, so it is important to speak in a voice which does not grate upon the ear: and, for everyday life, the latter is the more important. It is a very good thing that modern transportation makes it easy to visit "beauty spots," but their beauty can easily be destroyed by the behavior of visitors. As men are closely packed, manners are more indispensable to their enduring each other's company. We are not merely, or even mainly, a thinking machine. We are a sensitive organism. The joys of the mind are experienced by only a few. Is that a good reason to regard them as superior? I think not. I think the more important experiences are those of our affective nature, and that its right cultivation will come to be recognized as the most important part of education. How is this to be achieved? This is beyond my ken.

But I would stress that our Christian faith, perpetually presenting to our minds the passion of Jesus, thereby stresses that the Incarnation was the assumption of our sensitive nature, and so dignifies it. This had been the basis of a policy directed toward the lessening of what human sensitivity has to endure; it can also justify a policy directed toward enriching this sensitivity. And the body of teachers, promised as they are a major influence in society, will therefore find itself stressing the development of our capacities in that direction.

Notes

1. Note that the rearing of Romulus and Remus by an isolated foster mother (called tellingly a she-wolf) is meant to excite wonder.
2. Because military capacity was so much in the minds of the Spartans and so colored their institutions, one should not jump to the conclusion that theirs was an aggressive city. Thucydides shows that its leaders tried to avoid or terminate war. It may be, however, that the small numbers of Spartans compared to the large number of their subjects was a motive for military vigilance.
3. See *Moeurs des Sauvages Amériquains comparées aux Moeurs des Premiers Temps*, par le Père Lafitau de la Compagnie de Jésus, 2 vols. (Paris: 1724).
4. See Friedrich Engels: *Anti-Dühring*, second part, chapter 4. "Without slavery, no Greek city, no Greek art or science; without slavery, no Roman Empire. And

without this basis of hellenism and Roman empire, no modern Europe. We should never forget that our whole development, economic, politic and intellectual had as its prior condition, a state of affairs in which slavery was quite as necessary as generally acknowledged. Thus we have reason to say: without ancient slavery, no modern socialism."

5. For a minority, does not mean for privileged classes alone. It is well known that the Church seeded medieval Europe with so many schools that, as an historian puts it: "Except in thinly populated districts, there were few parts of Western Europe in which a boy needed to go far from home to attend a regular grammar school, where in addition to instruction in reading, writing and religion, he could acquire Latin both as a spoken and as a written language, and perhaps even rhetoric and logic, which were still regarded as 'trivial' subjects, to be learnt at school." William Boyd, *The History of Western Education* (London: 1921 and 1947). It is equally known that promising subjects could hope to rise to the highest Church dignities, and indeed to the Holy See. The same seems to have been the case in China.

6. Seneca, *Epistle*, 90.

7. See Louis Bonald's *Observations sur l'ouvrage ayant pour titre Considération sur les principaux évènements de la revolution française* par Mme la barrone de Staël (Paris: 1818).

8. *A Voyage to Laputa*, chapter 4 (first published in 1724).

9. Lettre du Père de Premare, Missionaire de la Compagnie de Jésus, au Père Le Gobien, de la méme Compagnie, November 1, 1700, in *Lettres Edifiantes et Curieuses* (1781 ed.), vol. XVI, pp. 394 seq.

10. See in Joseph Needham's admirable *Science and Civilization in China* (Cambridge: 1956), pp. 154 ff. the table displaying the lags between China and the West in mechanical and technical inventions: the median lag of the West is ten centuries!

11. I find the data collected by Eva Mueller very impressive, if one remembers firstly that American opinion is averse to public spending, and most averse to the raising of taxes, and secondly that American usage offers alternative financing of education. No less than 60 percent of people consulted agreed that government should spend more on education, and as many as 41 percent persisted in this assertion even if such spending had to be financed by the raising of new taxes. No other item of public expenditure obtained so high a score when the condition of increasing taxes was included in the query. Eva Mueller, "Public Attitudes towards Fiscal Programs," *Quarterly Journal of Economics* (May, 1963).

12. Bureau of the Census. *Current Population Reports*, "Labor Force," November, 1957, Series P-50, No.78.

13. The most convenient presentation of the whole subject is offered in the October, 1962, supplement to *The Journal of Political Economy*, a supplement entitled *Investment in Human Beings*, and organized by Theodore W. Schultz. Therein can be found references to the many relevant papers published elsewhere.

14. For a crisp, clear statement of the findings, and a critical appraisal, see H.S. Houttaker, "Education and Income," *The Review of Economics & Statistics* (February, 1959).

15. See reports of the U.S. Commissioner for Labor Statistics, especially the results of the April, 1962 survey of persons unemployed five weeks or more in 1961.

16. I choose the dividing line of seventeen because, from the American statistics available to me, this seems the age beneath which the very great majority already attend school under present conditions.

17. Skeptics can be convinced by this rough calculation. Take 60 million fully employed as the equivalent of the occupied labor force, strike off 50 hours per year and per person: that is a loss of 3 billion hours of work. Assuming that 1.5 million youths are kept at school instead of doing 2,000 hours of work a year per head: that is also equivalent to 3 billion hours.
18. Sebastian de Grazia, *Of Time, Work and Leisure* (New York: The Twentieth Century Fund, 1962).
19. A quarter of a century ago I spent two years steeped in the French administrative correspondence of the Revolution and Empire relating to the "Continental blockade." As the author of a book on this subject, I was asked last spring to say a few words about it in a broadcast discussion. I found that I had to turn back to my book, which I studied almost as if it had been written by another man—the main difference being that some pages acutely brought back to me the excitement felt when I discovered this or that enlightening report.
20. No quiz is a measure of educational attainment.
21. I have in mind such admirable examples of pedagogic exposition as G. L. S. Shackle's *Mathematics by the Fireside* for younger children, or G. Polya's *Mathematics and Plausible Reasoning* for older students.
22. The development of decision theory and information theory should, in time, give rise to an elementary course in the art of evidence.
23. If not Latin, then French, but let it be pre-Romantic French.
24. *Disciplina facit mores* is, indeed, the appropriate theme of an essay contributed to honor my eminent friend, Robert M. Hutchins.
25. I say "equality of opportunity in schooling" rather than in education because that part of education which is received at home, of course, depends upon the knowledge and solicitude of parents. And you could not abolish this advantage for some without a general loss to society.
26. I understand that Japan is here also ahead of European countries.
27. Michael Young, *The Rise of Meritocracy 1870–2033* (London: 1958).
28. The French have a telling term for this: "la liberté du particulier."

6

A Better Life in an Affluent Society

I

Contemporary society is preoccupied with wealth. There is no need here to distinguish between capitalism and communism. It is a well-known fact that the great declared objective of Soviet economic planning is "to attain and to surpass the American standard of life."

Every country employs statisticians to compute the annual increase in its national wealth. If the increase is substantial, the government prides itself on it; if it is small, the opposition finds in it a grievance capable of rallying public opinion behind it. In democratic countries, the political organizations that are most firmly entrenched are the ones that seek to advance the pretensions of one group for a larger share of the national wealth, and those that seek to defend the present share of a group against such pretensions. Public affairs consist to a large extent of pleadings and pressures concerning the division of wealth, and to some extent of more technical discussions concerning its increase.

The United States, which is at present the wealthiest country, provides the ideal which all other countries seek to attain. It is therefore natural to arrange other countries on a scale according to the distance that separates the average wealth of their inhabitants from the average wealth of an American. The most forceful argument which is produced nowadays in favor of collectivism is that economic planning is the most rapid method for advancing on that scale.

II

All this is familiar enough—so much so that we must gain distance if we are to find it surprising and thus, make it a subject for philosophical

Reprinted from *Diogenes* 33 (Spring, 1961): 50–74. Translated by H. Kaal. Used by permission of the publisher.

reflection. This is easily done. Whether we look at the philosophers of ancient Greece, or at the prophets and priests of Israel, or at the authors of ancient Rome, we find that every one of them condemns the individual's passion for wealth and warns us of the corruption that results from a general state of prosperity. There are great differences in tone between them: Some would have man renounce worldly possessions altogether, and live in as great a state of poverty as is compatible with bare survival; but these constitute only a minority. The majority approve of modest comfort, but recommend that man confine his desires to that. Both these attitudes can be found in Christian morality: To the few it offers the vow of poverty; to the many it preaches the moderation of desires.

There is no better witness to the fact that the desire for wealth has always existed, and always been indulged in to some extent, than the fact that it has always been denounced. The desire for wealth is natural, and at times it has been indulged in by the very people who denounced it. Thus Seneca the Elder wrote his epistles condemning luxury in surroundings of great personal luxury.

What is new is not that men desire wealth, but that the satisfaction of their desire has become the major aim of government, and the dominant concern of intellectuals. For a long time, the role of government was thought to be to oppose the concentration of wealth and to preserve among the people an austere morality, while the proper concern of intellectuals was thought to be with goods other than temporal ones. What is new is that wealth has suddenly become respectable.

The attitude of governments has certainly changed from complacency about the prosperity of some to concern with the prosperity of all. This change should not be attributed to socialist ideas; for the principles of socialism did not aim at collective prosperity. What they aimed at was the creation of a society free from internal strife—of a true community. The current of thought and sentiment that may be called "socialism" was diverted by another powerful current: the idea that prosperity as such was a good thing. It is in this way that contemporary socialism, in the form it assumed in Soviet Russia, has become more "chrematistic" than "communal."

The word "chrematistic," which was used just now, was, I believe, coined by Sismondi. It designates the science of wealth, which has become, in some measure, the master science of contemporary society.

III

The appearance of Rousseau's *Discours sur les Sciences et les Arts* was a great event in the history of social thought. The scandal created by his thesis shows what the attitudes of his contemporaries were. In this great exercise in rhetoric, which was his first work, Rousseau may not have aimed his guns properly. But his contemporaries were never in doubt as to what the core of his thesis was, namely, that the gradual change of needs, away from their natural state, was an evil. Hence, in opposition to the mass of classical and Christian literature, public opinion in Rousseau's time was already unshakably convinced that such a change of needs was a good thing.

Rousseau's reply to his numerous opponents was in substance: "But I only repeated what all the classical authors said." And their replies to this may be summarized thus: "That may be so; but nowadays we believe the contrary."

The contrary had already been believed for a long time. Around 1620, there appeared a typical pamphlet entitled *La Chasse au viel grognart de l'Antiquité*. The unknown author[1] contrasts in vivid terms the standard of life of his contemporaries with that of his ancestors. His narrative contains details which make the pamphlet a valuable document for the historian of the period. But it is not as such a document that it is of interest here, but rather as an indication that advances in standards of living were, as early as 1620, a fascinating topic.

To examine how this theme gained gradually in respectability, would be a task for the historian of ideas. For our purposes, it is sufficient to note that the theme of rising standards of living has not always had the place it occupies now, and that the wealth of nations has not always been regarded as the principal concern of governments and of intellectuals.

IV

The rise of this theme to respectability had to await the discovery that a gain in wealth is not necessarily made at the expense of others. There is a motif which runs through all classical condemnations of wealth, and which is so invariable and insistent that it cannot be overlooked: Desire without moderation is bad because a man who always satisfies his needs becomes their slave. But there is another motif which underlies and reinforces the first: In becoming the slave of his desires, a man seeks more and more power to satisfy them, and he finds this power in the employment of other men in the service of his own desires. Thus, in being enslaved by his needs, he tries to enslave other men.

Here we have an idea which has played a long and effective part in history, and which for this reason alone deserves our attention. It should be remembered first, that all ancient civilizations, as well as our own up to a certain period, have rested either on slavery or on one of the several forms of serfdom. Under the system of slavery, the master has complete control over the labor of his slaves, and the right to divide the fruits of their labor very unevenly between the gratification of his own needs and their subsistence. Under either system, wealth is measured by the number of slaves one owns, or of serfs one controls. Under the system of serfdom, the feudal lord does not have complete control over the labor of his serfs; but they owe him part of the fruits of their labor, or part of their time, or both. And under either system, it is true that wealth is acquired at the expense of others, or by the exploitation of man by man. Paradoxically enough, this idea was given its most effective formulation at a time when society had reached a stage in the process of transformation where the idea ceased to apply.

For hundreds or even thousands of years, the only source of wealth had been the exploitation of other men's labor. It seemed obvious that, even under the most favorable material and moral conditions, a family that had to rely on itself could only achieve a modest degree of comfort. Happy, if it knew how to content itself with the "fruits" of its labor— which is the original meaning of "frugality." The number of its arms (taking into account a certain coefficient of strength) determined the maximum extent of the land it could cultivate. To go beyond that, it would have needed slaves. It could, of course, be reduced to much less than the extent it was capable of cultivating, by having its land seized by the rich; whereas the rich, who engaged in such seizure, could only put their vast holdings to use by means of a large population of slaves or serfs. There was, therefore, what might be called an "upper limit" to the wealth of a free family without slaves; and such a family was always in danger of falling much below this level because its land was always in danger of being seized by the rich. On the other hand, the rich saw no limit to their wealth, provided there were enough slaves or serfs to do for them the necessary manual labor. Wealth was therefore based on seizure and exploitation. And it is quite natural that the desire for wealth should have been condemned, since it could only be satisfied by such means.

The wealth of nations was no less predatory in character than the wealth of individuals. Athens at the height of its achievement was not only a slave-owner's state; it also exacted heavy tributes from the numerous cities that formed part of its alliance. How much larger in scale, and how much more deplorable, was the case of Rome! If Rome passed from its original simplicity to great luxury, this was due entirely to its armies, which brought back spoils and assured tributes from all the shores of the Mediterranean. St. Augustine was not exaggerating when he said that the history of Rome was that of a band of robbers; and it is very appropriate that Brutus should be remembered as one of its heroes; for he seized property and practiced usury with such ruthlessness that he aroused the indignation of Cicero who was, nevertheless, accustomed to the ways of the financiers of the period. Finally, it might be noted that the wealth of Rome vanished as soon as Constantine chose to spend the tributes from the Mediterranean world in Byzantium.

As long as there is a fairly constant limit to production *per capita*, one man can gain wealth only by making use of another man's labor, and, therefore, some men only can gain wealth at the others' expense. All ancient civilizations rested on the unformulated postulate of a constant productivity of labor.

I would, no doubt, be reproached if I were to omit all mention of commerce as it was practiced for thousands of years. But for the moralists this was only a minor issue. (Plato was exceptionally hostile to it.) It would take too long to explain fully why this was so; a brief sketch will therefore have to suffice. When, during the Middle Ages, Italian merchants dispatched vessels to the Levant, they received, in return for a cargo of European products, a cargo of exotic products whose sale brought them large profits over the cost of the original shipment. But the main result of this exchange of exported European goods for imported exotic ones was to bring variety into the consumption of the rich. Since the capacity of ships was small, it must have seemed to a moralist that the import of exotic goods could only *whet* the appetite for wealth in the importing country, while the only way to *satisfy* this appetite was to bring pressure to bear on others.[2]

The key to all this is that production *per capita* appeared to be a given constant. It is here, then, that the enormous change that has come over contemporary society is to be located. It would, of course, be wrong to say that technical progress made its appearance only recently; no doubt, each generation made some progress over the preceding ones, apart from certain disastrous setbacks. But it was only recently that men became aware of progress and of its acceleration, and that their awareness in turn increased the rate of acceleration.

V

The great new idea is that it is possible to enrich all the members of society, collectively and individually, by gradual progress in the organization of labor, its methods and its implements; that this enrichment provides the means for a greater development of the individual; and that this development can be rapid and unlimited.

This idea is an enormous innovation. It would have greatly surprised the ancient reformers, who were all intent on improving the material lot of the masses and the morals of society. Their views, put forward at different times and in different places, bear such a striking similarity to one another that one could paint a single portrait of them all. Such a Galtonian portrait would look like this:

First the land, whose cultivation occupied the great majority of the labor force, should be redistributed in such a way that each family owned the entire extent it was capable of cultivating. Then these rural laborers should be freed, entirely or in part, of the heavy burdens that rested on them to the profit of the privileged classes. The latter would, from then on, no longer be able to enjoy excessive luxury in the cities in which they had tended to gather; and especially, they could no longer maintain a flock of domestic servants, keeping them thus from productive labor in the fields. The artisans who had also gathered in the cities, attracted by a rich clientele, would either return to the country or work for a more prosperous peasantry, when they saw the sources of their present income dry up. Since peasant families would live in modest comfort, their heads could give more time and care to the common interests of the neighborhood, and assemblies of heads of families would form the base of a pyramidal political structure.

There is no need to emphasize how much this bucolic picture differs from the reality of contemporary society. A brief evocation of the picture is enough. But it is worth pointing out that if this model had been realized, we could not now flaunt the growth statistics we are now used to.

VI

We do not find these statistics surprising enough. The reason is no doubt, that they are only cited for short periods, and this leads one to say things of which one does not feel the weight. A few years ago, a president of the French Council put forward, as a goal that could be attained, the doubling of the French standard of life in ten years. He surely cannot have calculated that if this rate of growth were to keep up for one hundred years, at the end of this long period, wealth *per capita*[3] would have increased 867 times.

There is no need to appeal to imaginary objectives. The same point can be made by citing goals that were in fact attained. In France, production *per capita* increased, according to the most accurate figures, by 3.5 percent *per annum* in the years 1949 to 1959. This figure is not very impressive. But if this rate were to keep up for one hundred years, wealth *per capita* would have increased 31 times.

The rates that can be noted nowadays are a great novelty. The United States has become the wonder of the world by the progress in its standards of life. But according to a noted statistician,[4] production *per capita* increased no more than seven times in the 120 years between 1839 and 1959, at the mean annual rate of 1.64 percent—a rate with which no advanced country would be content today.

Yet this rate, which appears so small nowadays, was enough to turn America's gain in wealth[5] into something like the fairy tale of modern times. This shows that this rate, which appears small at present, was relatively great in the past.

It is very difficult to form an accurate picture of changes in standards of life before the nineteenth century. But if one considers this question, the impression one gains is that technical progress was slow enough for its beneficial effects to be completely offset by population increases. This is what seems to have happened in Europe in the sixteenth century;[6] and it is, no doubt, what happened in India and China during the last three centuries.[7]

However this may be, the facts until very recent times were never striking enough to support the view, which has now become dogma, that a gain in wealth is possible for each and all, continually and at a rapid rate. This rate has even taken on an explosive character. The term "explosive" is not too strong for it. If we try to imagine some of the successive results of a rate which is supposed to keep up (e.g. 3.5 percent *per annum*), we find that we can easily enough imagine our standard of life doubled in twenty years; but its multiplication by 31 in one hundred years exceeds the imagination, and its multiplication by 961 in two hundred years no longer brings anything whatsoever to mind. We shall return to this inconceivability and to what it implies. But at the moment we should be troubled by another thought: If it is true that we are gaining wealth at such a rate, then surely we must give priority to the question of how to employ this wealth. The art of making use of human labor and of natural resources so as to produce a rapidly increasing flow of wealth, has been greatly developed. This calls for another art, that of making use of this wealth.

VII

If one were to write a history of questions that have been debated, one would see how at different times different questions came alive or died. One would like to think that a question which, at a given time, is so much alive that it attracts all the thought of the moment, is the most important question for the society of the time; and that a question which is neglected is so because of its lack of real value. But it is difficult to believe this. Intellectuals resemble Rabelais's Panurge more than one would like to admit, and while many intellects combine to make a well-known problem with rapidly decreasing yields their quarry, another problem which is important for society remains unexplored. Thus the attention given to problems of productivity certainly exceeds the golden mean, while the problem of "the good life" suffers from neglect.

In speaking of productivity, we think, no doubt, of gain in wealth as its end. But gain in wealth has in turn its end, and this is the good life. There is no need here, I believe, to discuss the extreme view, that a gain in wealth is indifferent to the good life. This doctrine is respectable enough when taught by saints who live according to it; but it is scandalous when taught by men who enjoy most of the comforts of life. I here take it to be certain that a gain in wealth contributes to the good life. But should one, for all that, subscribe to the view which is at the opposite extreme, that a gain in wealth is identical with a better life, so that the only sense we could attach to the idea of a better life would be that of being richer? If this doctrine were true, two men who were equally wealthy would, by definition, live equally well. But suppose one of us were asked to observe two or more wealthy men with equal incomes, and to say afterwards which of them led the best life. None of us would reply that the question was devoid of sense, when thus asked, in practice, to pass a value judgment, and none of us would hesitate to make distinctions. Since we are naturally inclined to take into account a man's generosity to his fellows, I will restrict the question by supposing that the degree of generosity is the same for all the men we observe, and that we only have to take into account the use each man makes of his wealth to better the life of his family. Again, we would not hesitate to say that the use which one man made was superior to the use made by another, or that means which were equally large were used to create lives which were not equally good. This brief psychological experiment shows that the problem of "deriving the best possible life from a given increase in wealth" is by no means a false problem. It can even be said that this problem can be posed in the same terms as the problem of productivity. In the case of the latter, we can ask: "Given a certain increase in the factors available for production, how can this increase be made to yield the greatest possible increase in production?" In the case of our problem, we can ask: "Given a certain increase in the products available for human life, how can this increase be made to yield the greatest possible improvement in human life?" What is output for the problem of productivity, is input for the problem of the good life.

We are not dealing, as has been shown, with a false problem. But we are dealing with a problem of extreme difficulty, as will be seen.

VIII

At first sight, the problem appears to be quite simple. For we are tempted to treat the case of increasing wealth for all families in a progressive society, by assimilating it to the case of increasing wealth for a single family in a static society. Given a family A whose income is 100 at the present time, we tell them that their income (real purchasing power) will be 200 in twenty years, 300 in 32 years, 400 in 40 years, 500 in 47 years, and 600 in 52 years.[8] It is then quite natural to suppose that this family can, in 47 years, live in the way a family does at the present time whose income is five times as high. There are at present a great many different ways of life among families whose income is five times the income of family A. We can call the attention of family A to what seems to us to be the best way of life in "the fivefold class." But we can do more: The families in the fivefold class occupy social positions which are superior to that of family A, and they have duties attached, either by necessity or by vanity, to their superior position. Hence our hypothesis is that family A will increase its income five times without any corresponding rise in the social structure. There is, therefore, no good reason why this family should assume the duties which rest at present on the families in the fivefold class. Thus, family A may not only live as well as does at present the wisest of the families in the fivefold class; it may live much better, if it does not assume the duties of that class.

This way of looking at things is the one that naturally comes to mind when we start thinking about the problem of increasing wealth. But does this picture not mislead us? If is does not, then it must be said that the wealth acquired by an overall increase during the last two hundred years has been very badly used. Suppose we conjure up the spirits of the Marquis de Mirabeau, de Quesnay, and de Turgot, and we announce to this tribunal that the wealth *per* Frenchman has, in two centuries, increased sevenfold (an arbitrary figure). If they knew only this figure which, incidentally, would seem improbably high to them, they would suppose that life in 1960 had an ease, a sweetness and a charm about it which are neither noted by present-day observers nor felt by the interested parties. If we could press the spirits to add details to their supposition, their descriptions would make us feel ashamed of the use to which we have put our increased wealth. Hence, if I am correct in thinking that value judgments can be passed on the use of increased wealth (and this is the inspiration of this paper), it must be admitted that the problem cannot be treated as it has just been sketched. It cannot be supposed that wealth as we measured it had increased as we calculated it, if quite different choices determined its use. The progress in standards of life for families in general cannot be conceived, as we did just now, in a *vertical* fashion—as if each family came to have at a given moment the same resources as a family with greater wealth at a preceding moment. Rather, this progress must be conceived as *oblique*—so that an income of 500 in the year 47 is still five times an income of 100 in the year zero, but is nevertheless not the same thing as an income of 500 in the year zero. Finally and above all, the use of increased wealth cannot be discussed in abstraction from its conditions.

IX

The conditions of increased wealth have been, and are, draconic. First and foremost among these conditions must be placed the *mobility of labor*, in several senses of the phrase: A man must be ready to change his way of working, his occupation and his place of residence; he must be ready to do otherwise, to do other things and to live elsewhere.

He must be ready to do otherwise; for if he were always to proceed in the same way, he would always produce the same amount in the same time and thus fail to do his share to increase the flow of commodities. He must be ready to change his occupation; for an increase in the total flow of commodities is not, and cannot be, achieved by simply multiplying by a certain constant each of the specific currents of which the total flow is composed at a given moment. He must be ready to move elsewhere; for increased production demands continual changes in the way the labor force is divided.

Metal production obviously would not be what it is if it were still carried on by tiny work crews, around furnaces in which the minerals were melted over a charcoal fire, fanned by the wind of a pair of bellows: and metal work obviously would not be what it is if it were still in the hands of village smiths. There is no need to expand on what everybody knows. But it should be emphasized that a society, in the course of increasing its wealth, constantly calls the individual from the place where he happens to be to a place where he will contribute more to production. This is indeed an imperative of productivity, and it might even be called its essential imperative.

This imperative calls for a reversal of all social values: That a man should have roots in one part of the world; that he should be attached to it because this is where the tombs of his ancestors are, the memories of his childhood and youth, the ties of blood and friendship, and in short, his loves and his duties; this has always been judged to be good, at all times and by all men. But it has now become an evil because it conflicts with the demands of productivity. The man who was firmly rooted in his soil and tied by blood and friendship to his neighbors was always the paradigm of a good citizen. He has now become a recalcitrant producer.

Stability used to be so highly regarded that at one time the main argument in favor of emigration was that it helped to rid the country of unruly elements, and thus to preserve general stability.

Since the peasantry is stable *par excellence*, it was traditionally regarded as the very backbone of a nation. The Latin authors were unanimous in attributing the decay of morals to the decline of the free peasantry, and to the migration to the cities of country people who had given up agriculture, discouraged by robbery, debts and the import of foreign grain. Nowadays the migration of the peasantry to the cities is regarded as the very condition of economic progress. In England, this migration took place in the first half of the nineteenth century, and it is this migration which Soviet economic planners are seeking to speed up. The countries that have emerged in turn as the forerunners of the new society, namely, England and the United States, pride themselves on having only a very small and gradually decreasing part of their population engaged in farming. And French economists deplore the fact that our fields still retain a much too large proportion of our working population.

Whereas the free peasantry used to be regarded as the healthiest part of a nation, it is now looked upon as its backward element. As late as the eighteenth century, the prime concern of social reformers was to guarantee and to extend the possessions of the peasantry,[9] and to free the peasants of obligations that oppressed them.[10] Nowadays the main concern of reformers is to diminish the number of peasant families.

But peasants are not the only people who are attached to the place in which they live. In the British as well as in the French press, one reads from time to time of the outcries raised by miners or industrial workers against the management's decision to close their mine or plant. It may seem to be enough to guarantee these workers reemployment in a different location. But this is to count for nothing the attachment men feel for the place in which they live. This attachment is all the more striking when the place offers to the outside observer no visible attractions whatsoever.

If men become attached to the place in which they live, they also become attached to their occupation and to a certain way of practicing it. The attachment to methods was evident in the case of the artisan: His great pride was the method taught him by a master. But his traditional method had to give way to newer and more productive methods, which are, moreover, constantly changing. Even in the United States, in industries as far removed as possible from the practices of the artisan, the workers show great defiance when any changes in work rules are proposed that would alter the composition of their crews.[11]

The mobility of labor, the *sine qua non* of productivity, is to my mind a topic of immense importance. But I cannot develop it further here. Let me, therefore, just emphasize that the growth of roots, or the attachment to, and love of, a place, an occupation and a method, which were once taken for attitudes that were good for society, are nowadays taken for attitudes that are bad for the economy; and that the virtues of stability and faithfulness to the past are now considered vices. The individual in a productive society must be a docile nomad, ready to go wherever the goal of the greatest possible productivity directs him. One might note here a moral paradox: For what is demanded of the resident of the City of Productivity is, in short, a certain capacity for detachment from temporal bonds, which is also required of the mystic. However, the former is rewarded for his detachment, not by an abundance of spiritual goods, but by a profusion of temporal ones.

X

In a society of men who are essentially displaceable, the notion of "morals" has no longer the sense it had for the classical authors, and it could no longer have it. The ancients thought of good morals as consisting essentially of faithfulness to the best examples set by one's ancestors. If I want to picture to myself good morals as they were formerly conceived, I think of a certain artisan of my acquaintance who, in the same place, practices with love and minute care the art his family had practiced for several generations; he cannot be tempted by novel products, and his great passion is to collect beautiful specimens of his art. Under the old system, such a man would be a model to his neighbors; but in reality, he is considered by them something of a character and treated almost as a stranger. Far from being influential in his neighborhood by reason of his virtue, he is never listened to because of his different point of view; and when he speaks out against the broadening of the street in order to preserve its charm, it is said (and this is true) that he does not own a car.

In a productive society, the individual must not only, in his role as producer, learn to look for the employment in which he can make the greatest contribution to the total product; he must also, in his role as consumer, learn to buy the commodities that are offered to him at decreasing costs. It is misleading to measure an increase in wealth by first taking the typical or the average income of an individual or a family, by then noting how much this income has increased in terms of current monetary units, and by finally dividing this increase by a cost-of-living index in order to arrive, by such a division, at a so-called "real" increase. For this is hardly the effective increase, except for the rare or even non-existent individual whose expenditures have in fact remained distributed in the way in which the items in the index are distributed. Following Jean Fourastié, we can obtain a much more significant measure, by taking the typical or the average income, expressed in terms of current monetary units, as our point of reference, and by dividing the price of each item by this nominal income. Increase in wealth will then no longer appear as a single "real" increase in income, but in the form of a multitude of real reductions in price, each different from each. The divergence between these real reductions is enormous. Thus, in less than fifty years, the price of electricity for household purposes, expressed in terms of a worker's salary, has fallen to four percent of what it was, and the price of a bed with a metal frame to 25 percent, while the price of crystal glasses has, on the contrary, risen by 50 percent.[12] It is then clear that, of two families whose incomes have grown in the same way, the one that looked for its consumption to articles whose real prices were decreasing, derived from this a feeling of increased wealth which was much more pronounced than that of the other family, which looked for its consumption to articles whose real prices decreased but little, or remained the same, or even increased.

This brings us back to the point that increase in wealth is not vertical but oblique. If a workingman's family had, in 1760, conceived the ambition of living in the way a certain family, ten times richer, lived at the time, and if it had remained obsessed with this ambition, it could not realize it when the statistician told the family that its wealth had now multiplied by ten. It could not build the same house, and obviously could not have the same servants.[13] Our family cannot enjoy the luxury or even the comfort of yesterday; but it can enjoy the abundance of today: a profusion of light and a rapidity of locomotion which a comfortable or wealthy family could not obtain formerly. Our family will congratulate itself on the improvement of its lot to the exact extent that its tastes run to what has become easy to obtain; and it will deny this improvement to the extent that its tastes remain with what is *not* easier to obtain. In other words, that family improves its fortune most which is the most *opportunist* in its tastes. And if there was, in general, no opportunism of tastes in our society, there could be no progress; for the products which could be offered at rapidly decreasing real prices could not find a market that expanded rapidly enough. Without opportunism, tastes would change too slowly, and the demand would cling to products whose costs were constant or on the increase. To meditate on this is to understand one of the conditions of economic progress.

It appears, then, that economic progress rests, in general, on the *opportunism* of the individual. The individual must be an opportunist in production; that is, he must be willing to exchange one role in society for another which is more productive. And he must be an opportunist in consumption; that is, he must direct his desires to objects that can be produced at decreasing cost. The well-being of the individual will then be a function of this double opportunism. And hence, also, the phenomena of irritation, anxiety and disenchantment will appear precisely to the extent that an individual lacks this opportunism.

A man who lacks this double opportunism not only fails to further the general progress; he positively hinders it. By refusing to change his place for more productive employment, he lowers the average productivity. By refusing to buy new products that may decrease in cost, he restricts their market and impairs their chances of actually decreasing in cost. He does not, therefore, only stand apart from the movement of the economy; he attracts the hostility of other men. Hostility to a man who fails to keep up with his time is a vague sentiment, but as we have just seen, may have a rationale behind it. The more importance one attaches to the speed of economic progress, the stronger this sentiment tends to become. A man who lacks the required opportunism finds, then, that he is subject to the pressures, not only of the circumstances, but of public opinion as well, and this may lead him to behave *as if* he were endowed with this opportunism. And his behavior "as if" may in turn result in inner tensions. Psychoanalysts seek the origin of such tensions much too often in infantile experiences when they may quite simply lie in present pressures.[14]

XI

We have thus arrived at social questions, after taking the indirect route which leads through the domain of economics. In *Emile*, Rousseau contrasts two models of the good life. On one model, a citizen subordinates all his interests to those of the community, and loves only his country. But this, according to Rousseau, is only possible in a small rustic society with very stable morals. It has always struck me as odd that so many students of Rousseau, beginning with Robespierre, should have tried to create his community of citizens under social conditions which, as Rousseau had expressly said, were incompatible with it. Because Rousseau looked upon the society of his time as already too large, too complex and too advanced for such a community of citizens, he proposed, in *Emile*, a completely different model: that of a retired life, untouched by social currents. But a productive society could not exist if everyone followed the advice given to Emile. Such a society could not even tolerate it if a minority followed this advice. Besides, when Rousseau made an effort, in the second part of his life, to follow his own advice, he constantly complained that his retreat was not respected; and this was almost two centuries ago.

The individual in a productive society can in no way be detached. He finds himself engaged in numerous social relationships which undergo constant change and exercise constant pressure. All of the traits of a productive society are to be found in the United States, probably because that country was settled by men who had cut all their ties in order to come there, and who, therefore, offered the least resistance to the mobility and the opportunism that we have found to be essential to productive society. The new situation in which man finds himself has also been examined most carefully in the United States. It was recognized there that the well-being of the individual, in his social relationships, was a matter of "adjustment."

Since the process of increasing wealth demands that the individual change his place, his neighbors and his practice, it is important that he accommodate himself easily and quickly to his new condition. Since he is displaceable in these various ways, he must also, if he is not to suffer from his displacement, be psychologically displaceable. That is to say, he must feel no more than a passing regret for lost contacts, and he must take vivid pleasure in making new ones—but only because these contacts are new, and not because they are of a certain kind; for these contacts, too, are destined to be broken by a new displacement. And since the wages of displacement are a growing variety of goods offered to him, he must adapt his tastes to what is thus put within his reach.

These are not, as is sometimes said, the characteristics of the American way of life, but those of a productive society in general. Nothing appears to me more ridiculous than the criticisms addressed to the American way of life by leftist intellectuals who, at the same time, celebrate the gains of Soviet production. It is clear that these latter gains, which are incontestable and striking, have implied, and still do, the same process of displacement, the same duty of mobility and the same tendency to opportunism which we have noted. And all this takes place on a much larger scale because of the greater speed of the movement, and because this movement is, in Russia, directed by a strong central government.

XII

The only "leftists" who are in a position to find fault with the characteristics of the American way of life, are those who are steeped in the traditions of the peasant and the artisan. For a very long time now, there has been a "leftist" movement which is not "chrematistic," which is in revolt against all use of power, and which conceives of an ideal society in something like the following way: Men are not subjected to constraint; they are not spurred on by vanity or by the desire for more wealth; each relationship between them rests on common bonds, which assure that they are naturally drawn together. The soil, the tombs of the ancestors, faith, memories, intermarriage; all these combine to create a natural community which, in turn, inspires individual conduct. It follows from the very nature of the social setting that any tasks, required in the interest of the community, will be carried out voluntarily and in common; and that any decisions affecting the whole will be taken together. For a long time it was thought that this had been the state of nature, and that the power of one man over another, and the exploitation of man by man, were the result of artificial institutions; once these were destroyed, society would return to its former Arcadian state.

No one nowadays thinks of reestablishing the Arcadian state everywhere. Rousseau already pronounced this to be impossible. Nor does anyone think of making it flourish where the conditions for it may all be thought to be present—which is what Rousseau wanted to do on the island of Corsica. Take, for example, certain regions in Africa, which are free from the pressures of an exploding population and where social intercourse is still centered around each village community. No one would dream of suggesting that progress consisted in ridding these regions of everything that was opposed to an Arcadian state; rather, progress is taken to consist in developing these regions on the model of our productive society. Thus the Arcadian ideal is quite dead as far as its positive implications go; but its negative implications linger on. We want a productive society, and yet deplore the features it necessarily has. These appear especially black when compared with the Arcadian dream which continues to haunt us.

XIII

Here lies the conflict which we must try to resolve. Contemporary society is built with the end of greater efficiency of production in view, and on the principle of an ever-increasing flow of goods and services. This principle implies, on the one hand, that the individual as a producer must be mobile, ready to change his place for more productive employment elsewhere; and, on the other hand, that those appetites must be aroused that are the easiest to satisfy. In this society, the material and moral well-being of the individual is a function of his opportunism.

It should be noted that in such a society advertising is by no means the parasite it is thought to be. In view of the fact that there are facilities for producing certain things and not others, the guidance of the consumers' tastes to things that are easy to produce at decreasing costs, forms an integral part of the whole mechanism. Advertising of products, though not of brands, would survive even if the economy were to be socialized. It is in this form that advertising can be seen to emerge in Soviet Russia.

It certainly cannot be denied that the individual in such a society finds himself subject to the pull of the general current. And one may, if one likes, call this "alienation." It can, however, be said that the obligation "to keep up with one's time" under which the individual finds himself, does not differ radically from the obligation to remain in one's place under which he would be in a primitive society. It is difficult to see why conformity to change should be harder to bear than conformity to the *status quo*. Of course, to be uprooted time and again, hurts whatever there is of the habitual within us; but it is equally certain that, in a static society, to encounter great obstacles to change, must hurt whatever there is of the restless within us. The "good conscience" one has in a static society, after one has made one's contribution to the maintenance of good morals, has its analog in a dynamic society: in the satisfaction we feel after having done our share to gratify the needs of others.

XIV

Of course, all these needs are not of equal value. Here our task becomes more precise. An individual in a productive society receives from society a certain amount of credit; and the more efficient he is in helping others to obtain what they desire, the greater the amount he receives. As long as he is busy increasing his credit, the value of what others desire is indifferent to him. This indifference gives to the "motive of profit" its amoral character. It would be wrong to think that only a capitalist acted from this motive. The individual in a productive society who changes one job for another that is better paid, without caring about the quality of the desires he serves, also acts from this motive. In fact, this motive is the general law which governs the "placement" of men in any such society. Now the individual in such a society is not only indifferent to the value of what others desire; it is even in his interest to arouse and maintain those desires in others that can be satisfied with the least effort on his part.

It follows from this that, in a productive society, the individual has no incentive to guide the desires of others towards worthier objects, but instead a strong incentive to guide them toward objects that are easier to produce. He must therefore take an interest in the satisfaction (and in the excitation) of the desires of others, but show no interest in their quality. If these desires appear to him badly guided, his attitude in this respect may be described, in flattering terms, as tolerance, but could be described, in more accurate terms, as interested complacency. Nevertheless, since he must live with others, he is affected by the kind of life they come to lead, as a result of such gradual changes in their desires. If he has sold intoxicating beverages, he must put up with the inconvenience of living among intoxicated people.

We thus arrive at the following truth: Although an individual has an immediate interest in serving the desires of another, irrespective of their quality, he has, of necessity and in the long run, an interest in the quality of the kind of life his contemporaries lead.

We can imagine the producer being pushed by an "invisible hand" to the place where he can best serve the preferences shown by the consumer. But we do not feel that there is an "invisible hand" which arranges the products around the consumer, so as to bring them into harmony and to display a style of life which will bring out all of the consumer's potentialities as a human being. For a generation now, efforts have been made to improve on the workings of the "invisible hand" which were formerly left to themselves—efforts, that is, to bring to perfection the mechanism of production. This mechanism now issues a flow of commodities of ever-increasing abundance and variety. But what an average family selects from this flow is ill assorted, fails to serve its purpose, and looks like a collection of odds and ends. We feel uncomfortable in front of a shelf of books whose principle of selection was the award of a literary prize. The same lack of style characterizes our contemporary way of life.

XV

The Latin word *amoenitas* designates the pleasurable features or the charm of a perspective. Neither a wild place nor a functional building can be called "amene," only a place which is delightfully fit for human habitation. Since this is the proper meaning of the word, it seems to me well chosen to signify the quality which we would do well to bring into the midst of our lives. I am pleased to see that this word figures already in the English legal vocabulary, and that it should have entered into it precisely in connection with the "external costs" of industrialization. "The loss of amenities" means that industrial construction may have taken away some of the pleasant aspects of a place. Conversely, a systematic effort to render a place more agreeable is called, in the United States, "to create the amenities." The word means then, fortunately, what I have in mind, which is the harnessing of our productivity to amenity.

Advanced nations are nowadays very proud of their productive capacity. They will have better reason to be proud of it when this power will be used to make life more agreeable—that is, to develop amenity.

A good indication of our present state is the excessive importance we attach to vacations. We think of these not only as a pause in the current rhythm of our lives, but also as a change of place, away from where we usually are. It is hard not to conclude that the great value we attach to this pause and to this change implies a very unfavorable judgment on the nature of our daily rhythm and on the merits of our place of work or residence. A man whose life was more happily arranged would hardly have such a strong desire to escape.

Too much attention has been devoted to the progress of productivity, and is still devoted to it every day. It is time to devote some attention to the progress of amenity.

XVI

"My concern is to increase the amenity of life." Here we have a very imprecise statement. But lack of precision is not lack of sense. It is rather as if the statement contained too much sense. If I were to say "My intention is to increase my knowledge," no one would reply "I do not know what you have in mind." What someone might say to me is "I do not know what kind of knowledge you want to acquire," for it may be Greek philosophy, the theory of games, nuclear physics, abstract painting, or atonal music. And after I have made it clear what kind of knowledge I am after, my interlocutor may ask whether this kind deserves, more than any other, the expenditure of effort I propose to bestow on it. Similarly, my statement concerning amenity must be made more precise before it can be discussed. And this is what I will now try to do.

Man is a sensitive, working and social being. As a sensitive being he perceives forms, sounds, odors; and his sensitivity is the source of enjoyment and suffering. The lack of this sensitivity is an imperfection, its development a step towards perfection. External conditions that offend this sensitivity, or oppose its development, are an evil, while external conditions that cultivate or delight it are good. And this is part of amenity.

As a working being, man may be harnessed to his task, riveted to his function; he may feel that he is held to his work by an imperious external force or by a cold or malevolent destiny; he may struggle against this necessity which is imposed on him from without, or feel resentment towards it; he may dream of freeing himself from his enslavement to his task. And all that these feelings make him suffer is an evil. On the other hand, it is good, and one of the greatest goods we can enjoy, to be absorbed in, and delighted by, one's task; to look upon interruptions as necessary means for doing an even better job; to regard one's task as the best use one could make of one's life. And this, too, is part of amenity.

Finally, as a social animal, man lives necessarily with others. He may encounter indifference and even malice; he may feel that he annoys others, that he is deprived of esteem or affection. And this is a great evil. But he may also find himself in good company; he may encounter good will made more agreeable by pleasant manners. Good company will not only provide him with immediate pleasures; it will also cultivate him and carry him to the degree of social perfection of which he is capable. Happy, if he finds in his circle some who can arouse in him the feelings of love and admiration. And this is also part of amenity.

Thus, the nature of our physical surroundings, its relationship to our work, and to the nature of our social contacts; these are, it seems, the chapters into which a discussion of amenity would be divided.

Notes

1. This piece was published by Danjou and Cimber in their *Archives curieuses de l'histoire de France*, Second series, vol. 2, pp. 361–387.
2. This is borne out by a passage from Montesquieu concerning Poland: "A few lords own entire provinces; they force the laborers to let them have a greater amount of grain, so they can send it abroad and procure for themselves the goods which their life of luxury demands. If Poland did not trade with any country, her people would be happier. If the great had only their grain, they would give it to their peasants to live on. Too large an estate would be a burden to them, and they would give some of it to their peasants. Since everyone would own herds which yielded hides and wool, there would no longer be enormous sums to pay for clothing. The great would still love luxury; but since they could not find it in their country, would encourage the poor to work." *L'Esprit des lois*, book XX, ch. XXIII. Montesquieu, incidentally, is not opposed to international commerce under different conditions.
3. By "standard of life" is here meant "production per capita." The produce is, of course, calculated at fixed prices.
4. Raymond W. Goldsmith; the paper referred to was presented, on April 7, 1959, to the Joint Economic Committee of the United States Congress, and published in its *Hearings on Employment, Growth and Price Levels*. The figures used here occur on page 271.
5. It should be noted that the annual growth in production was much greater than here indicated, viz. 3.66 percent, but also that the annual growth in population was 1.97 percent. It is per capita that production increased by 1.64 percent; and it is increase per capita that constitutes a measure of progress in standards of life.
6. Cf. four articles by E. H. Phelps-Brown and Sheil Hopkins in *Economica*, August 1955, November 1956, November 1957 and February 1959.

7. According to Abbot Payson Usher, the population of China fluctuated, since the beginning of the Christian era, between a minimum of 54 and a maximum of 79 million; only in the seventeenth century did it begin the gradual growth that brought it up to 600 million. India around 1522 had perhaps up to 100 million inhabitants, which is far less than the nearly 500 million that now inhabit the peninsula. Cf. Usher, "The History of Population and Settlement in Eurasia," *Geographical Review* (January, 1930).

8. These calculations are based on the rate of progress of 3.5 percent per annum, which was mentioned above.

9. This goal was persistently pursued in France during the eighteenth century. It inspired the ordinance of Chancellor d'Aguesseau against the extension of the rights of mortmain. It also inspired the decrees of the Revolution that abolished these rights altogether—though by decreeing that a peasant's holdings were to be divided equally among his heirs, the revolutionaries violated all the principles of economics and did great damage to the progress of agriculture and the welfare of the population.

10. This is illustrated by the abolition of all feudal rights during the French Revolution.

11. This theme played a major part in the American steel dispute of 1959.

12. *Documents pour l'histoire des prix* , by Jean Fourastié and Claude Fontaine: the period covered is 1910–1955.

13. The question of servants shows better than any other that a general increase in wealth cannot place the poorer families in the position previously occupied by the wealthy families. In fact, the rich have always had servants; hence, it is obviously impossible for all to have servants. This question also shows that the position of the richest families cannot but suffer in the course of a general increase in wealth; for this raises the price of men, as compared with the price of objects.

14. One might also find in these pressures the origin of the remarkable role which the nightmare has played in contemporary literature.

7

Technology as a Means

We live in an Age of Opportunity. Our modern civilization is far superior to any other in terms of power, and thereby we enjoy undreamed of possibilities to foster the good life not for a tiny minority, as in earlier societies, but for the multitude. This is a wonderful privilege; nonsensical therefore is the attitude of those who regret not having lived at some former epoch: no matter that their personal circumstances might have been better, their means of improving the circumstances of their fellowmen would have been slighter. It is right to rejoice in the greatness of these means: it is proper to feel responsible for their personal and optional use.

We should be aware of two important features which qualify our Age of Opportunity. First the Opportunity—and to stress it I use the capital—is primarily a collective, a social Opportunity, and not primarily an individual opportunity in the sense of "Go West, young man." It is true enough that the powers of Man, in advanced countries, have been multiplied by a factor of a hundred; but the statement would be obviously untrue applied to the individual; we have not become, severally, so many Hercules. This new wealth of powers pertains to societies, it is managed by the managers of great organizations, we only get individually the benefits of these forces, benefits the nature of which depends upon the judgments of their managers. Thus the conditions and style of life of individuals depend upon the management of the social Opportunity.

The second qualification is more difficult to express but it is of capital importance. We can quite confidently expect that the increase of our collective powers shall continue and the probability of its acceleration

Reprinted from *Values and the Future: the Impact of Technological Change on American Values*, edited by K. Baier and N. Rescher. (New York: Macmillan, 1969):217–232. Used by permission of the author.

is great. However, we should not confuse the gross increase in powers with a net progress of Opportunity. In every realm there exists a relationship between past and future action, past action placing constraints upon future action. In so far as these constraints are of a psychological nature, we are apt to regard them as capable of being broken. But there is another aspect: the changes wrought by action in the environment. As long as human action was an insignificant scrabbling of rare and feeble insects, this did not mortgage future action. Indeed there is an essential difference between American history and that of Europe or the far longer history of Asian civilizations: the migrants who came to America from Europe, bearers of a relatively advanced technology, found unlimited natural resources unaffected by any previous uses. But as we grow capable of ever heavier actions which ever more profoundly modify the environment, such modifications become more important data for future actions. Therefore even though we can think of our powers as due to increase, it does not follow that we can think of the Opportunity afforded to each generation of our successors as allowing to each progressively greater latitudes of choice. Whether such latitude shall in fact increase or decrease we cannot say for certain. This we should think of as a function of increasing means and increasing constraints. What we may call "the balance of net Opportunity" is very favorable in our day; we must at least envisage the possibility of its being less favorable in terms of what might lead to our descendants judging that we have handicapped their moving toward a good life by our improvident use of an exceptionally favorable balance of Opportunity.

I take it that our concern is to place our descendants in circumstances conducive to the flowering of *la pianta uomo*, according to the expression of the poet Alfieri, which strongly suggests the dual aims of prosperity and quality, as indeed the Roman salute *vale* implied wishes both of good fortune and of worthiness. Strongly felt and unclearly conceived, this concern inspires to men of good will the advocacy or the performances of "moves" which are seldom rationally related to an overall view of the social system and an understanding of its many internal links, and which are often fertile in undesired after-effects and side effects. Unwanted effects wax in importance as the moves become heavier and as we are packed closer. Of this we have grown quite sharply aware: therefrom the many laudable efforts of our day to take a general view of society, to speculate upon the improvements which can be contrived within one generation, and to provide so to speak a general picture within which we can place the initiatives and innovations.

Of major importance is the placing in this picture of "scientific and artificial aids to man" to use the felicitous expression introduced by Robert Owen in 1820.[1] Alvin Weinberg rightly stresses that we can often employ "technological fixes" to deal with social problems rebellious to treatment by attention to alteration of human behavior; thus so to speak calling in the technologist to cut the Gordian knot we cannot untie.[2] This approach is to be welcomed because it represents techniques as means to achieve social ends, means to be consciously employed. And this is their true nature. Unfortunately they are currently seen or sensed quite otherwise.

Life in Western society is a new fatalism, a feeling that our future is determined for us by the autonomous course of a superhuman agency, whose godlike nature is acknowledged by the reverent use of the capital: Technology. It showers upon us benefits of its own choosing, it makes demands we may not deny. It blazes the trail of the future like a mythical Juggernaut's chariot, it drives us down if we stand in its way, and bears us from success to success if we cling to its side. Thus Technology is represented as an idol which richly rewards its servants who do not question its course.

This attitude displays our natural bent toward superstition, which seems in no way abated by our partaking of a scientific civilization. Indeed we prove more naive than the primitives; when they made idols of natural forces it was at least true that these were outside their control and generated in a manner they could not understand, which is of course not true of Technology.

It would be hard to find a phenomenon more dependent upon human decisions than the evolution of techniques. Indeed while the current decision as to its autonomy comes from the quickening of its pace, this acceleration itself manifests more conscious and deliberate decision making.

That the evolution of techniques depends upon human decisions, this is the pivot of my paper. If so, then how are these decision made, by whom, and on what grounds? What above all are the values which enter into such decision making and determine the choices? Recognizing that the system moves under the impact of a great variety of decisions made by a variety of groups, and that it can not be otherwise, the values which inspire discrete decisions assume a decisive importance. To what degree are the values taken into account here and there consistent with one another and with ultimate values regarding the condition of *la pianta uomo*? If the consistence is doubtful, how can it be improved? How can the ultimate values be injected to a greater degree into the discrete decisions? These are the questions I wish to raise. These are questions which are not meant to be answered, whose function is to become a demanding presence in our minds.

But first of all I must solidly establish the pivotal proposition.

At all times in every state of society the material existence of men rests upon the practice of reliable modes of operation. These reliable modes we called "arts" up to the 18th era or century: for instance I can find in my library "the art of the charcoal burner," "the art of the candle maker," "the art of the bricklayer" and so forth.[3] A new word crept in as a mere adjective: technical. Technical meant what pertains to the arts; then "technique" comes to displace "art," a displacement correlated with the increasing role played in the performance of operations by machinery and especially machinery moved by nonanimal energy.[4] Note that when Europe came into regular communication with China, and to a far greater degree with India, we found the arts (in the extensive and traditional sense) in most aspects more advanced in those parts of the world than in our own: our best informers, the Jesuit missionaries, marveled at the skill of Asian workers using instruments of amazing lightness and cheapness. The taste which Europeans, at least since the Germanic invasions, have shown for heavy instruments—in peace or war—was to us a handicap until the intervention of new motive powers[5] turned it into an asset. Enough thereupon: the point I am concerned to make is that techniques are properly ways of doing things which depend essentially upon resort to powered machinery.

This is a very important point: because it follows therefrom that the introduction of a new technique depends upon the provision of the adequate machinery, in other words upon an *investment*. Nobody would deny this but many will forget when discussing how society will be molded by technological progress, and such forgetfulness justifies my stressing the obvious.

In those activities which we still call "arts," and which require no significant capital expenditure[6] one may speak of a spontaneous course of change. Someone does a thing differently or does a different thing, and others imitate it. This is called progress by those who prefer the new style. Such changing in the arts (in the narrow sense) depends upon individual actions and reactions. At no time is there a massive input, subject to a decision made by wielders of collective resources (no matter whether it be a private or a public collectivity).

On the contrary such inputs are necessary, such decisions are called for in the case of a technical innovation which can be made operational only by setting up an important and costly apparatus, and which becomes of social importance only by multiplication of similar apparatus. The theme of the inventor unable to find the financier thanks to whom the idea shall be all fact has often been treated in the nineteenth century as a personal tragedy: thus Balzac draws a parallel between the unrecognized poet, Lucien, and the unrecognized inventor, David.[7] In our day the lack for financial support for the putting into operation of a proposed innovation is dealt with from another angle—not the loss to the balked inventor but the loss to society from the lack of this innovation or the lag in its introduction. Thus Charles Wilson writes: "The most striking contrast between Britain and France at this period (first half of the nineteenth century) is the higher rate at which, in Britain, inventions were adopted, developed, and passed into application. No nation in the world showed more vivid inventive genius than the French, but a high proportion of their inventive talent proved abortive or was put to profitable use elsewhere—notably in England and Scotland."[8] The important point here is that new techniques matter socially by "passing into application."

Wilson rightly calls attention to the "rate" of their passing into application, but there is another consideration of moment to us: the selection of those which do pass into application. It will prove a help to clarity if we broach these questions from the angle of an "underdeveloped economy." However loosely used, the term of "underdevelopment" has a concrete and precise meaning: a country is so called in proportion to the lack of application therein of techniques which are current elsewhere. Such was Japan before the Meiji era: it now ranks among the advanced economies, thanks to the great effort which was made to put into application techniques already available.[9] It implies no underestimation of the inventive genius of the Japanese—whereof there is abundant proof—to state that the exceptional pace of their economic progress has been due essentially to the vigorous putting into application of techniques proven elsewhere.

If we now turn to countries which were dubbed "underdeveloped" when Truman formulated (in 1949) his famous "Point Four," we find that they stood in relation to the complex of techniques current in the "advanced" countries in a relation differing by an order of magnitude from that which characterized the Japanese situation in the 1860s. The techniques prevailing in advanced countries and therefore potentially applicable in an "underdeveloped" economy, can be thought of as a backlog of available techniques. The will to put them into application is constrained by the volume of resources which can in total be allocated to that purpose: it follows that a selection must be made, no matter by what complex of decision-processes; and the larger the backlog the smaller the share thereof which can efficiently be transferred within a given period of time. Now insofar as the social pattern and the modes of life depend upon techniques, their evolution shall take a different course in the case of different selections.

I am not certain that the true variety of courses available to an underdeveloped economy is adequately recognized. The general idea which at first inspired development policies was that which had been formulated by Marx: i.e., that the most advanced country today offers to the less advanced the image of their future. If one resorts to the widely used (and very questionable) criterion of national product or income per capita, one is tempted to say that Japan has caught up with what Britain was when Marx wrote: but surely the Japan of today bears no resemblance to Victorian England. To press the point further, Spain has almost the same per capita income as Japan, but there is very little likeness.

Will you explain the enormous differences between Victorian England, present-day Japan, and present-day Spain wholly by differences in social values and attitudes? If so you entirely abandon the notion that "as Technology goes, so goes Society." For my part I do not jettison it: I seek to put it in its place. It is true that the course of technological change has an enormous impact upon society: but it is no less true that social values are reflected in the course of technological change. If Japan has more general education not only than Victorian England and modern Spain, but more, as I believe, than any Western European country today, this is not an outcome of superior wealth (it is not superior) generated by technology: it is an outcome of deeply imbedded values prior to espousal of industrial civilization, values presumably acquired from China many centuries ago. I cannot resist quoting from a textbook used in the primary schools of China long before the impact of the West.[10] It incites children to study not only by stating that "the man who has not studied is ignorant of justice and social duties," but by offering them picturesque examples: Tche-yin who so loved study that as his poverty forced him to work all day and did not allow him to use a lamp by night, he collected glow-worms to read by their light; Tchou mai-Tchin, who lived by collecting wood, and, as he carried it back from the forest, tied a manuscript to the longest perch so that he could read as he walked. Li-mi, who, while leading cattle, rode a buffalo and read from a book tied to the animal's horns!

To cut short what might become a digression, and to summarize: the techniques current in an advanced country constitute for an underdeveloped country a backlog of potential change from which a selection has to be made, which has social consequences and which is inspired by social values prevailing in the adopting country.

I have just stressed that, in the case of an underdeveloped economy, there must be a choosing, within a backlog of available techniques of those that shall be put into operation. I want to suggest that the same situation obtains, *mutatis mutandis*, in the case of the most advanced economy. In the case of the United States itself, there is a backlog of available techniques, out of which some have to be selected for their prior putting into operation. The difference lies in that for the underdeveloped country the backlog is made up of techniques which are in practice in more advanced countries while for the U.S., the backlog consists in techniques which are being worked out in its own laboratories.

At the present moment in the U.S. there are innovations which are operational only in a single or a very few pioneering instances: such an innovation shall not become a concrete factor in social life until it has become widespread; and this requires much operational investment. Other innovations have not yet been put into application anywhere but have reached such a stage of technical development that they need only an adequate allotment of investment to bring them into local and limited operational existence. Still other innovations are at earlier stages of development, the provision of more funds can precipitate their maturation. We may thus work up through the applied research stage up to the novelties which are clearly conceivable.

From the moment when a novelty is clearly conceived (I understand this to be called the Hahn-Strassmann point)[11] to the time of its being in such widespread practice that it can be said to be "socialized," its progress at various stages requires successive inputs of resources, which we may think of as successive "generations" of investments. It is our custom to draw a dividing line between the expenditures required to make the innovation operational (investments in the traditional sense of the word) and those required to bring the innovation to the point when it can be brought into operation (research and development expenditures, for short R&D). This custom is grounded in history: in the nineteenth century, investments to put into application were heavy and recorded expenditures (as they have remained), while expenditures to work out an idea to the point of feasibility were light and unrecorded expenditures (a momentous change has occurred here).

During the last twenty-five years a prodigious rise has occurred in R&D expenditures; as their estimates are highly subject to methods of classification, let us be content with the conservative estimate that the volume of such expenditures has multiplied at least twenty times. Therefrom of course an enormous operation of vistas and stimulus to our imagination. We find ourselves thereby incited to picture American society in the future as one where everything which is now conceivable shall have been socialized. The picture we can thus draw is surely erroneous: it must be erroneous in terms of a near future, because it is not feasible to make all this socially operational in a short time, in view of the amount of resources it would require. It is probably erroneous in terms of the distant future because other inventions shall have intervened and other interests shall have gained vigor. Therefore if we deduced the American society of the future from what seems feasible or likely in American laboratories today, we would be committing a mistake no less than that of deducing the Indian society of the future from the techniques used today in the United States.

But also, and this is far the more important point, this whole realm of the feasible must perforce play in American decision making the role of a backlog out of which the techniques assumed to be the more valuable are in fact selected. Further it seems to me that this backlog is increasing, and that, as a consequence, the selection has to be sharpened and that the future offers a greater variety of possibilities, as the range of the feasible from which choices have to be made gains in extension.

That the backlog is increasing is admittedly a hypothesis. It seems to me highly plausible. Let me say how it is based. As I said it is customary to divide investment expenditures from R&D expenditures. Great and legitimate attention has been paid to the multiplication of the latter. Very little—indeed none that I know of—has been paid to the changing ratio between the two. Investment expenditures have not kept pace with the growth of R&D expenditures, indeed they could not conceivably have done so as such pace-keeping would have implied their absorbing more than the whole national product! Therefrom a presumption that however much the capacity to implement has grown in absolute terms, it has dwindled relatively to the swelling of potential innovations. In other words, as much more becomes technically feasible, much less of the technically feasible can be *embodied* in socially operational plant and equipment. The likelihood of its being so (and I repeat it is not given as a fact) is not impaired by the reliable evidence which can be adduced showing that some innovations become operational in our day much faster than other innovations in the nineteenth century: that is entirely compatible with nonactivation of other potential innovations.

While changes in classification would no doubt affect the ratio between the variables R&D and investment, they surely would not do so to the extent of changing the general picture. To doubt then that there occurs a relative decline in the capacity to embody and an increasing backlog, one would have to give more weight than seems reasonable to two suppositions which are mere "intuitions." Possibly the communication of external benefits tends to cheapen the implementation of innovations; possibly the delivery of potential innovations by R&D does not keep pace with the input of resources therein. In these propositions figure terms too indefinite to allow any checking. Let us then say that there may be "something in them"; which would then tend to reduce the imbalance between what is offered as achievable by R&D and what can be undertaken through investments, and thus to slacken the increase of the backlog. The relations hypothesized are perhaps toned down but not substantially altered.

They can perhaps be represented by thinking of an "R&D country," whose population is engaged in digging, refining and fashioning goods which reach the "land of Society" only in so far as they have been picked up and transported by "ships." These ships stand for the operational investments. There being an imbalance between the output of the R&D population and the capacity of the fleet, there must be a selection of what shall be picked up. The decisions taken thereupon influence the character of change occurring in the land of society but also they exert an influence on the labors of the "R&D land" which shift from what is least picked up to what is most picked up.

As one perceives the determining importance of such decisions, therefore one is led to ask: by whom are these decisions made, and on what grounds?

The traditional answer would be: business executives make these decisions, on grounds of market expectations. Let us develop this answer. Never mind that these decisions are made by a few, senior executives of important firms, they are and have to be taking into consideration the value judgments of the great many on whose buying the fortunes of firms depend. The great merit of business lies in its being fundamentally a servant, while government is fundamentally a master. Government comes at the front door and makes demands, business comes at the tradesman's door and makes offers. These must be palatable. If the innovation takes the form of a new process cheapening a commodity or service already in wide use, businessmen know that such cheapening shall be welcomed. If the innovation takes the form of a new good or new service, business executives will try to make sure that consumers are ready to welcome it. In short the very idea of profit-making is to use resources (inputs) in the manner deemed apt to elicit maximal response, that is on the criterion of maximizing the expectation of response; and as the use of resources is ceaselessly reallocated through the feedback of actual responses, it can be claimed that the system tends to produce the best possible selection of techniques.

The validity of this answer is limited, firstly by the simple observation that the industries living from discrete sales to individuals are not by a long way the chief seats of innovations. It is well known that the bunching of innovations occurs in industries closely tied to government, government supported or having the government as their main customer. To this point I shall return later.

The second restriction called for is that the market allows only a limited, and, as it turns out, a biased expression of consumer preferences. The individual buyer by the very act of buying manifests his positive appreciation of the product sold to him; he has no symmetrical means of manifesting his negative appreciation of the nuisances attending the operational process or the use of the new product. By the power of his own purse he can acquire a "good," by the same power he can not dismiss a "bad." Thus the operations of the market do nothing to stem the flow of nuisances, which remains unrecorded in national accounting itself, based as this is solely on the sales and purchase transactions of a market economy. To stem the flow of nuisances, it may be necessary to substitute for technique A, a technique B which is not superior (and may be inferior) in terms of the individual goods it allows individual buyers to acquire, but whose merit lies in its being less productive of diffuse nuisances. Such a shift can not occur as a consequence of discrete actions by individual buyers, it requires government intervention either prohibiting technique A or putting upon it so heavy a money charge as to make it market-wise less advantageous than technique B.

The authorities will find it relatively easy to produce such a shift when the nuisances arise from the use of a process by large firms. By their very dimension these offer easy targets to public opinion and public action. And because of their ample means they are well able to achieve the shifts called for. Unfortunately the bulk of the nuisances attending modern society flow from consumer behavior rather than from that of large firms. This is not often said because the statement violates what a politician once told me some thirty years ago is "The First Law of Politics": In the case of any evil you wish to denounce, said he, put the blame on the smallest possible number of people in order to attract the largest possible number of votes.

Instinctive adherence to this "law" leads to underestimation of the part played by homemade nuisances in the global flow. As more goods enter the home, more refuse flows out, ranging from the dumping of cans to the dumping of motor cars. Homemade nuisances pose a major strategic problem: how far can they be remedied by changing the physiochemical nature of entries into the home (so that as they go out they dissolve more easily: paper containers instead of metal or glass containers etc.); how far must it be remedied by vast public endeavors of removal (a magnified sewage system embracing as well as liquids, solids, fumes, and if feasible, noises)?

Whether we are concerned to improve producer behavior or consumer behavior or to repair their side effects by public undertakings, we run up against the human propensity to act in view of discrete and immediate satisfactions with little regard for more general and distant states of affairs. There is no doubt that the large car powered by an internal combustion engine is a major nuisance in towns, which would become far better places if people moved about in small cars powered by electricity: but manufacturers are well aware that consumers enjoy the large car and the childish sense of power afforded by the internal combustion engine. The cluttering of the valleys of Kentucky by the massive fall-out produced by strip mining of the hillsides is a scene of vandalism: but what buyers require from mining corporations is the cheapest possible coal.

It is all too easy to place the blame upon producers: ultimately it lies in the vigor of our individual concern for immediate maximum getting, combined with the weakness of our collective concern for generating an optimal long-term state of affairs.

This is not, as some say, a trait of our industrial age, though our greater power has sharpened its nefarious effectiveness. Asia Minor formed a most prosperous part of the Roman Empire: in the intervening centuries improvident private and public use of its resources stripped it of woods, starved it of water, made it a land of poverty.

At no time in history have the public authorities exerted as powerful an influence as they do presently upon the daily lives of the subjects.[12] This influence is made possible by the operational development of the techniques of transport and communications. This influence can be exerted, and in part is exerted, to improve the setting of human lives. In so far as future changes in ways of living depend upon the progress of techniques, government exerts thereby a major influence. This influence is exerted by two chief channels: firstly investments which have an innovational character, which are made for the putting into application of new techniques, now occur with far greater density, in firms tied to the government than in firms working for a multitude of individual buyers. By firms tied to the government, I mean those establishments, whatever their legal character, whose services depend upon public decisions. Paradoxically enough state-owned firms whose services are addressed to the large public are often less tied to government decisions than are private firms who have the government as their main customer.[13] When the government passes orders which require innovational investments the cost of which is perforce taken into account in the costing of the product or service provided, it exercises upon the nature of innovational investments an influence no less powerful than by the alternative means of their direct subsidization.

But however important the part played by government in causing the implementation of feasible innovations,[14] it plays a far greater role at the earlier stages of innovation, that is in R&D. It is well known that the major part of R&D expenditures are financed by the government. This means that government is implicitly the selector of the kinds and lines of research to be encouraged.

We fail to grasp the importance of this because we are still haunted by the images of the scientist or artisan who pottering in a shed, come out respectively with major scientific findings or seminal investments. Pasteur used no great means nor did the Belgian waiter Lenoir who built the first motor car. Things are not done this way in our time; and indeed one wonders whether, if a breakthrough happened to be achieved in this artisan manner, it would command any attention. A century or more after the supersession of the artisan by the factory in the realm of production, the same phenomenon has occurred not only in the realm of development, which stands nearest to production, but also in the higher realms of applied research and even fundamental research.[15] Much hardware is called for, and however necessary to findings, its use also adds prestige to their announcement. Just as large establishments have come to dominate the field of industry, so it is in the field of research itself; the material quality of the plant and equipment, the talents of the associates, contribute to the intrinsic worth of the output, and the label to its reception.

This being the state of affairs, the allocation of funds becomes a determining influence. A promising scientist naturally wishes to work with the best instruments, in the best company; these are to be found in the sectors which are most favored by the allocators of funds. Therefrom a cumulative process whereby the lines of research which attract the most money in consequence are magnets to talents, which further justifies their being favored.

As the progress of research leads development, which leads the implementation of new techniques, and as the introduction of these in the social field influence the pattern of social arrangements and individual lives, the guidance exercised upon R&D in general and more especially upon research, by the power of the purse, is a determining influence of our social future. The process of allocation might be called the "Ministry of the Future."

Indeed this Ministry of the Future exerts not only a powerful concrete influence on what the future shall be but also it exercises even today a notable influence on our views of the future, which are of course shaped by what we hear of research in progress.

Let me take a concrete instance. Our civilization is characterized by increasing expenditure of power. We have acquired this energy from the burning of stores: ours is an incendiary civilization. I find it a most striking thought that if we relied upon the burning of wood for the present-day expenditure of energy, we would burn up all the forests of the world in three years.[16] This does not mean that we are in any danger of lacking materials for burning: while estimated reserves of oil, including that which can be retrieved from shells and bituminous sands would cover only some sixty years of consumption at the present level, coal represents no less than 600 years of present consumption, while beyond that we can, as it has been dramatically expressed "burn the rocks" to produce atomic energy.[17]

However, there exists an alternative to the burning of our dwelling place. As against the stores we can burn there are flows we can utilize. The yearly flow of solar energy into upper atmosphere is equivalent to fifty thousand times our yearly consumption of energy; considering only that part of solar energy which hits bare ground it alone represents a yearly supply equivalent to five hundred times our yearly consumption.

It is not necessary to worry about the false problem of the exhaustion of energy stores to appreciate the importance of shifting gradually our procurement of energy from burning to the utilization of continuing flows. This would be an enormous improvement of our collective manners which are those of drunken soldiers, using anything they can lay hands upon to make a fire. Such a shift would have great social and moral implications. I do not find them contemplated in pictures of the future: the reason lies in there being so little research in that direction.

A field which is not so neglected but which is very parsimoniously endowed is weather control: this obtains, I gather, seven million dollars per year.[18] And yet if we understood the movements which occur in the atmosphere, we might dispel hurricanes in the making. It appears from Lloyd's account that Hurricane Betsy cost this organization some twenty million pounds sterling and another ten to other insurers.[19] This should stir the imagination to consider the damage wrought by similar hurricanes in the poorer countries of the world which are not in a position to make good the losses suffered. Here we have a type of research of enormous importance to the underdeveloped countries.

And this instance raises a major moral question. The rich countries of the world alone have the human and material resources required for important research. While this great advantage has been at least fairly earned, it does not follow that it should be used for the exclusive advantage of the nations which have earned it. On the contrary, because research resources are concentrated in the advanced countries, therefrom follows a moral obligation to use them in the best interests of mankind generally. Impeding the formation of hurricanes would be a boon to the countries most affected, which are also the least able to repair the damages. The imagination may go beyond this and picture an improvement of the regime of rains in India: what a boon that would be.

Surely it is right that those who lead in research should address efforts to objects of moment to large parts of mankind. But it is hardly surprising that government support for R&D in advanced countries should give little weight to the welfare of other nations: it does not give very much to the welfare of our own people.

In the United States four-fifths or more of government-financed R&D expenditures are for purposes of international power politics and national prestige. The Department of Defense absorbed 62.3 percent, NASA, 17.2 percent, which add to nearly 80 percent; while the largest part of the 10.1 percent devoted to the Atomic Energy Commission was also destined to military ends. The author from whom I take these figures (referring to fiscal 1963) comments: "Of course products and processes which increase productivity or demand in other sectors of the economy may arise from military and prestige oriented programs. But these benefits—commonly referred to as 'spillover'—are strictly incident to the main purpose; there is also some reason to believe that the spillover from military and space programs has been quite modest in recent years."[20] I pretend to no expertise on this great subject. The fact of importance here is that most of this R&D is not meant at all to enhance the amenities of life for the multitude.

As it would be impolite to press my critique of what is done in the United States, I turn to the instance of the supersonic transatlantic plane. I have never felt happy about this: it is of course an achievement, nor can its usefulness be denied. But usefulness in the case of resource applications is comparative: is this the best that could be done for people with that amount of endowment?

This raises the question of speed. Many people find it extremely exciting that the speed of transatlantic travel should increase by ever greater leaps. The speed will be more than doubled when the supersonic plane goes into service, possibly in 1969, but the speed may be again multiplied perhaps five times by 1984, when the hypersonic plane could be in service, provided the required resources are applied to the stages of research, development and production. New York would then be within forty minutes flight from London.[21]

How wonderful! In the 1820s such a journey took twenty-five days. In 1838, the *Great Western* achieved the crossing from Liverpool in the breath-taking time of fifteen days. What gains have we not achieved in speed, and how much greater they become in successive periods! Yes, but there is another way of looking at the same phenomenon. The economy of travel time achieved by the *Great Western* was ten days, the economy expected of the supersonic plane is more than three hours, and the economy which might conceivably be obtained from the hypersonic plane would be less than three hours. If on a time graph from 1820 to 1984 you plot successive gains attained or hoped for, the shape of the curve shall be very different according to your choosing as ordinate either the speeds achieved, or the economies of travel time: in the first case the curve rises by ever larger leaps, in the second case by ever smaller fractions.

This exemplifies a general proposition dear to my friend Ely Devons, i.e., that graphic representation of phenomena depends upon basic value judgments. If the value which inspires me is pride in human achievements, I shall naturally use the speed curve and no other view of the phenomenon shall be of interest to me; if on the other hand the value which inspires me is the improvement in human lives, then I shall use the second curve. This shall then lead me to estimate the benefits accruing from the successively faster planes in terms of savings of travel time for increasing numbers of travelers. However important the figures obtained for such savings of time per year, if we place them in a balance, with on the other side the man hours of travel time which can be saved on the "journey to work" by equal expenditures, then the gain from greater transatlantic speed must seem very much the lighter one.

By this comparison I find that the social benefits of speeding up transatlantic flight are well below the opportunity cost: that is the social benefits which might be conferred by an alternative use of equivalent resources. Of course my presentation is very rough. It is meant merely to illustrate an attitude, i.e., that public support for technical innovation is justified by the relevance of the innovation to the improvement in the ways and quality of life, and that its contribution in that respect is to be weighed against the contributions of alternative uses of resources.

I doubt whether anyone would dispute the principle; but it does tend to be forgotten in the climate of understandable excitement generated by a fast succession of "feats." A feat in any sector of technical endeavor rightly attracts praise and moral credit, and this moral credit lends force to demands for further and larger support. Thus public funds get channeled toward what is most exciting and impressive rather than toward the more serviceable in terms of people's daily lives. As more talent gets involved in that direction, more political weight is acquired in the elite circles where the process of distribution takes place.

The enormous contribution which the laboratories made to the war effort stands at the source of their great leap forward in material and social status: the association of a great deal of research and development with power requirements has persisted or has been renewed. It is then perhaps not surprising that the model of the war machine should however unconsciously color the thinking of many researchers, and that many advances, however unrelated to military purposes, should work toward imparting to society some characters of the war machine.

It may well be a dual play of unconscious associations which generates in so many of our contemporaries an anxiety about "the Society which Technology fosters." There is, to my mind, some absurdity in the exhortations we hear to adjust to a technological society. Why should we? Is it not more reasonable to harness the processes of innovation to procure a life rich in amenities and conducive to the flowering of human personalities? No generation has been more free to lay the foundations of the good life. But we shall not be free if we do not become aware of our freedom.

Notes

1. Robert Owen: *Report to the County of Lanark*, Part 1 (Glasgow, 1821).
2. Alvin Weinberg, Acceptance speech for the University of Chicago Alumni Award, June 2, 1966. Published in French in *Analyse et Prévision*, October 1966.
3. I refer to the *Description des Arts et Metiers* published from 1761 to 1769 in Paris, Duhamel du Monceau et al.
4. Cf. my article of *Preuves*, April 1965.
5. "Meaningful" is the title of Denis Papin's treatise on steam power (1690): "A New Method to Elicit Very Powerful Forces at a Low Cost."
6. Note that architecture forms an exception of great moment, being far the most important of arts, and requiring vast investments, but I must bypass this great subject.
7. This is in the series *Les Illusions Perdues*, where "les souffrances du Poète" and "les souffrances de l'inventeur" are discrete parts.
8. Holmyard, Singer, and Hall: *A History of Technology* (Oxford, 1958), vol. V, ch. 33, p. 800.
9. Japan should be ranked much higher in terms of techniques than it is according to the criterion of per capita income, the critique of which is outside of my present subject.
10. The work referred to is the San-tseu king with the commentary of Wang-Tcin-Ching, as translated and edited by G. Pauthier under the title *Le Livre Classique des Trois Caractéres* (Paris, 1873).
11. I am indebted for this expression to an as yet unpublished essay by Robert W. Prehoda on *The Future and Technological Forecasting*.
12. The use of the term "subjects" is entirely proper relatively to what is being discussed. As Rousseau put it "in a legitimate form of government, the associated are collectively called the people, and are severally called citizens as participants to the sovereign authority, and subjects as subject to the laws of the State" (*Social Contract*, bk. I, ch. 6).
13. See Murrey L. Wiedenbaum "Les entreprises privées à destination publique," in *Analyse et Prévision*, vol. 2 (1966), pp. 493–498. An earlier if shorter English version has appeared in *Challenge*.
14. In order to quantify the role of government in the innovational investments one would need to separate such investments from that large part of the investments currently made in society which have no innovational character. I made no such distinction in my earlier confrontation of R & D expenditures with investments in general, deeming it unnecessary to what is but a suggestive approach.
15. Cf. Norman Kaplan, ed., *Science and Society* (Chicago, Rand McNally, 1965).
16. All figures quoted from a study made for OECD by E. Jantsch.
17. W. R. Derrick Sewell: "Humanity and the Weather," *Scientific American* (Spring, 1966). The author is editor of *Human Dimensions of Weather Control* (Chicago: University of Chicago Press, 1966).

18. Their figures were given in the *Financial Times*.
19. If I stress this point, however obvious, it is because of the utterly silly statements one often encounters, about a minority of the world's population "enjoying" the major part of "world income," as if world income were a given fact available for distribution, instead of being a mere fanciful aggregation of the very different products of very different activities in different countries.
20. Frederic M. Scherer, "Government Research and Development Programs", in Robert Dorfman, ed.: *Measuring Benefits of Government Investments* (Washington, D.C.: The Brookings Institution, 1965).
21. My authority here is C. L. Boltz, scientific editor of the *Financial Times*, in the August 3, 1966 issue.

8

The Treatment of Capitalism
by Continental Intellectuals

We view with grave concern the attitude of the Western intelligentsia to its society. Man possesses mental images, representations of the universe on progressive scales, of the things and agents therein, of himself and his relation to them. These images can be roughly likened to ancient maps adorned with small figures. Rational action, in a sense, means to go by the maps available to the ego, however inaccurate. The breadth, richness, and precision of these representations or maps are due entirely to intercommunication. Education consists in conveying a stock of such images and fostering the natural faculty of producing them. In any group, chosen at random, it can be observed that members are unequally active in communicating such representations; in all organized societies known to us a fraction of the members is specialized in dealing with representations. Their importance to society is very great; "rational" individual or collective action must be taken on the basis of what is "known," of the images of reality which have been given currency. These images can be misleading. "Rational" action based on bad "maps" is absurd in the light of better knowledge and can be harmful; the study of primitive societies yields a quantity of illustrations.

It is rational, subjectively, to tilt at windmills if we firmly believe them to be wicked, dangerous giants holding fair princesses in bondage. It is, however, a sounder view to regard them as a not very efficient device to capture an irregular energy for the purpose of grinding grain. We may happen to dislike the miller, who may be a bad man, but it is, at best, poetic fancy to regard him as blighting the countryside by the spread of his evil wings. The Western intelligentsia is not exempt

From *Capitalism and the Historians*, edited by F. A. Hayek (Chicago: University of Chicago Press, 1954): 91–121. Used by permission of the publisher.

from such nightmares, resulting from a grafting of strong feeling onto a weak stem of positive knowledge.

Positive knowledge is an understanding of our surroundings which allows us to move toward our goal by the best route. Indeed, some understanding of the forces at work in these surroundings has made it possible to put them to work for our purposes. It is a fact of experience that we can alter the arrangement of men (society) as well as the arrangement of things (nature). As in the former case, this calls for knowledge. To the ignorant, social devices will always appear needlessly complicated; so does a machine. Indeed, any organic structure, as we know, is far more complex then an inorganic one. Men, however, are less willing to admit ignorance in the realm of society than in that of nature: *de re mea agitur.* In this social realm, moreover, the criterion of judgment is a dual one.

Men pass judgments of value, some of which are ethical and relate to *bonum honestum*; these latter are never applied to agents or agencies known to be witless. Taken to see a steel furnace, a small child or a savage may be terrified by its roaring and call it "wicked." This view, however, will be dropped as soon as it is understood that the furnace has no spirit. No informed person will think of the furnace as evil because it is fiercely red, lets out occasional streams of burning lava, and feeds on gritty scrap iron and coal that is black. It is merely a device, instrumentally good, since it leads to the production of tools and machines, serving men's purposes. Nor will any reasonable person blame the furnace for the badness of some human purposes served by the machines (such as aggressive war). It is understood that the device is a good servant and that men alone are accountable for evil uses. A schoolboy obdurate in the animist view of the furnace would be shown by his schoolmaster that this is superstition. The same teacher, however, may regard "capitalism" in the same light as the ignorant and superstitious schoolboy regards the furnace. He will see in it an evil monster, author of hurts and wrongs, not a device as useful as the furnace in the production of tools.

It is quite true that moral considerations have their place in the assessing of social devices, while they do not seem germane to the assessing of engineering devices. For in social devices moral agents are involved. Therefore, social devices are subject to a double criterion: efficiency and morality. A discussion of the harmony of these criteria in general involves metaphysics. We shall attempt to remain on a humbler plane. As the notation of good and bad (morally) applies only to consciences, a device can be bad only indirectly. There is a clear case against a device which makes men worse; such is the criterion on which Plato relied to call the politics of Pericles bad. It has been held by some of the greatest minds of mankind that we grow worse through the development of our wants and better by cutting them down. The Stoics pointed out that we become slaves to our desires, and the Cynics stressed that each desire given up is a degree of freedom gained. The early Church Fathers taught that by attention to worldly goods we place ourselves under the sway of the "Prince of this World." More recently Rousseau took up this theme with enthralling eloquence. If this view is adopted, then devices which tend ever to enlarge the scope of our wants by successively satisfying them and by inducing hopes of meeting ever new wants are bad indeed. The social device of capitalism is bad, but so are, by the same token, the engineering devices of industry. This view, however, is not avowed by contemporaries; on the contrary, they are anxious that men's wants should ever increasingly be satisfied. Therefore declamations against "money" do not seem to make sense. If men desire "goods," of course they desire money, which is the common denominator of these "goods," the door opening to them; and the "power of money" is nothing but the *reification* of the power of these goods over men's desires.

It is the proper function of the spiritual and moral teacher to show men the worthlessness of some of the things they do desire. Impeding the acquisition of these things by temporal authority tends to cause lawbreaking and to create a complex of criminal interests. These are among the clearest examples of the deteriorating effect of social devices on human character. The civilized world has marveled at the existence of a powerfully organized criminal society beneath the surface of American life; this mushroom growth was occasioned by the driving underground of drinking and has been given a new lease on life by the driving underground of gambling. These phenomena warn us that a result contrary to the intention may be obtained when social devices are used to raise the moral level of human behavior. It is, moreover, well known that any attempt to change man's actions by means other than a change in his spirit is usually futile and anyhow not a moral improvement.

To the intellectual the social device of capitalism offers a displeasing picture. Why? In his own terms, here are self-seeking men in quest of personal aggrandizement. How? By providing consumers with things they want or can be induced to want. The same intellectual, puzzlingly, is not shocked by the workings of hedonist democracy; here also self-seeking men accomplish their aggrandizement by promising to other men things they want or are induced to demand. The difference seems to lie mainly in that the capitalist delivers the goods. And all through the West the fulfilling of political promises seems to be a function of capitalist achievement. Another aspect of the capitalist device which makes it unpleasant to the intellectual is the "degradation of workers to the condition of mere instruments." In Kant's words, it is always immoral to treat other men as means and not as ends. Experience teaches us that this is not an uncommon behavior, nor is it peculiar to capitalism. It is Rousseau's view that such treatment is inherent in civilized society, which multiplies random contacts based on utility rather than on affection, and that it becomes more and more widespread as contacts increase and interests overlap. Marx's view is less philosophical, more dependent on history. The nascent capitalist, he says, found already at hand a population which had been treated as tools by previous exploiters before being seized by the enterprising bourgeois, and the existence of a proletariat which could be treated in such a way originated in the expropriation of the farmers. This is what obliged the workers, bereft of their own means of production, to work for others who disposed of such means. If this theory (obviously inspired by the enclosures) were true, capitalism would have found it most difficult to obtain "wage slaves" in the countries where land was most readily available (i.e., in the United States).

It is not impossible that the mental picture of capitalism has suffered from a dichotomy which classical economists found necessary for logical purposes—the dichotomy of the consumer and the worker. The entrepreneur was represented as serving the consumer and using the worker. Such a dichotomy can be introduced even in the case of Robinson Crusoe, whose physical resources (considered as "the worker") can be represented as exploited in the service of his needs (considered as "the consumer"). This reification of two aspects of the public was intellectually tenable at the outset of what is known as the capitalist era. Heretofore, indeed, the buying public of manufacturers had been sharply distinguished from the working public of artisans, engaged chiefly in producing luxuries consumed by the rich, who lived on unearned takings from the produce of the land. But precisely in the capitalist era the wage-earning producer of industrial consumer goods and the market buyer of such goods have become increasingly identified. It would be a striking illustration of social evolution to find out what fraction of manufactured consumer goods has gone to the wage-earners employed in manufacturing. This fraction has constantly increased under capitalism, so that the dichotomy has become ever a more theoretical concept. It is almost unnecessary to point out that the dichotomy is intellectually useful in any economy where division of labor obtains; in the same manner the Soviet worker is used in the service of the Soviet consumer. The difference lies in the fact that he is used more mercilessly as a worker and gets less as a consumer.

A large part of the Western intelligentsia of today forms and conveys a warped picture of our economic institutions. This is dangerous, since it tends to divert a salutary urge to reform from feasible constructive tasks to the unfeasible and the destructive. The historian's contribution to the distortion of the picture has been under discussion, especially his interpretation of the "Industrial Revolution." I have little to add. Historians have done their obvious duty in describing the miserable social conditions of which they found ample evidence. They have, however, proved exceptionally incautious in their interpretation of the facts. First, they seem to have taken for granted that a sharp increase in the extent of social awareness of and indignation about misery is a true index of increased misery; they seem to have given little thought to the possibility that such an increase might also be a function of new facilities of expression (due partly to a concentration of workers, partly to greater freedom of speech), of a growing philanthropic sensitivity (as evidenced by the fight for penal reforms), and of a new sense of the human power to change things, mooted by the Industrial Revolution itself. Second, they do not seem to have distinguished sufficiently between the sufferings attendant upon any great migration (and there was a migration to the towns) and those inflicted by the factory system. Third, they do not seem to have attached enough importance to the Demographic Revolution. Had they used the comparative method, they might have found that a massive influx into the towns, with the resultant squalor and pauperism, occurred as well in countries untouched by the Industrial Revolution, where they produced waves of beggars instead of underpaid workers. Given population pressure, would conditions have been better without capitalist development? The condition of underdeveloped and overcrowded countries may provide an answer.[1] Methodological oversights of this type, however, dwindle into insignificance in comparison with conceptual errors.

The vast improvement achieved in workers' conditions over the last hundred years is widely attributed to union pressure and good laws correcting an evil system. One may ask, on the other hand, whether this improvement would have occurred but for the achievements of this evil system, and whether political action has not merely shaken from the tree the fruit it had borne. The search for the true cause is not an irrelevant pursuit, since an erroneous attribution of merit may lead to the belief that fruit is produced by shaking trees. Lastly, one may ask whether the "hard times" so bitterly evoked, and for which capitalism is arraigned, were a specific feature of capitalist development or are an aspect of a rapid industrial development (without outside help) to be found as well under another social system. Does the Magnitogorsk of the 1930s compare so favorably with the Manchester of the 1830s?

It is remarkable that the historian should fail to "forgive" the horrors of a process which has played an obvious part in what he calls "progress," precisely in an age addicted to "historicism," where excuses are currently found for horrors going on today on the plea that they will lead to some good, an assertion as yet incapable of proof. Surely indignation is best expended on what is happening today, events which we may hope to influence, rather than on what is beyond recall. Nonetheless, instances readily come to mind of authors who have stressed the hardships of the British working classes in the nineteenth century while finding nothing to say about the violent impressing of Russian peasants into kolkhozes. Here bias is blatant.

Can we find specific reasons for the historian's bias? I think not. The attitude of the historian would present a special problem only if it could be shown that it was he who originally brought to light the evils of capitalism previously unnoticed by the remainder of the intelligentsia, thereby altering the point of view of his fellow-intellectuals. But this is not in accordance with the facts. Unfavorable views of capitalism, whole systems of thought directed against it, were prevalent in large sectors of the intelligentsia before historians exposed the past wrongs of capitalism or indeed before they paid any attention at all to social history. It is probably the main achievement of Marx to have fathered this pursuit, which originated and developed in an anti-capitalist climate. The historian is no aimless fact-finder. His attention is drawn to certain problems under the influence of his own or other current preoccupations related to the present day. These induce him to seek certain data, which may have been rejected as negligible by former generations of historians; these he reads, using patterns of thought and value judgments which he shares with at least some contemporary thinkers. The study of the past thus always bears the imprint of present views. History, the science, moves with the times and is subject to the historical process. Furthermore, there is no philosophy of history but by the application of philosophy to history. To sum up, the historian's attitude reflects an attitude obtaining in the intelligentsia. If he manifests a bias, it is one pertaining to the intelligentsia in general. Therefore it is the intellectual's attitude which must claim our attention.

Sociology and social history are disciplines much favored nowadays. We would turn to them for help. Unfortunately, their scholars have given little or no attention to the problems centering on the intellectual. What is and what has been his place in society? To what tensions does it give rise? What are the specific traits of the intellectual's activity, and what complexes does it tend to create? How have the attitudes of the intellectual to society evolved, and what are the factors in this evolution? All these problems, and many more, should be tempting to social scientists. Their importance has been indicated by major thinkers (such as Pareto, Sorel, Michels, Schumpeter, and, first and foremost, Jean Jacques Rousseau). The infantry of science, so to speak, has not followed; it has left this vast and rewarding field of study uncharted. We must therefore make shift with the scanty data in our possession, and we may perhaps be excused for the clumsiness and blundering of an ill-equipped attempt.

The history of the Western intelligentsia during the last ten centuries falls easily into three parts. During the first period the intelligentsia is levitic; there are no intellectuals but those called and ordained to the service of God. They are the custodians and interpreters of the Word of God. In the second period we witness the rise of a secular intelligentsia, kings' lawyers being the first to appear; the development of the legal profession is for a long time the main source of secular intellectuals; amusers of noblemen, progressively raising their sights, provide another, very minor, source. This secular intelligentsia grows slowly in numbers but rapidly in influence and conducts a great fight against the clerical intelligentsia, which it gradually supersedes in the main functions of the intelligentsia. Then, in a third period coinciding with the Industrial Revolution, we find a fantastic proliferation of the secular intellectual, favored by the generalization of secular education and the rise of publishing (and eventually broadcasting) to the status of a major industry (an effect of the Industrial Revolution). This secular intelligentsia is by now far and away the most influential, and it is the subject of our study.

An enormous majority of Western intellectuals display and affirm hostility to the economic and social institutions of their society, institutions to which they give the blanket name of capitalism. Questioned as to the grounds of their hostility, they will give *affective* reasons: concern for "the worker" and antipathy for "the capitalist"; and *ethical* reasons: "the ruthlessness and injustice of the system." This attitude offers a remarkable superficial resemblance to that of the clerical intelligentsia of the Middle Ages (and a striking contrast, as we shall see, to that of the secular intelligentsia up to the eighteenth century). The medieval church centered its attention and its work on the unfortunate. It was the protector of the poor, and it performed all the functions which have now devolved on the welfare state: feeding the destitute, healing the sick, educating the people. All these services were free, provided out of the wealth shunted to them by church taxes and huge gifts, vigorously pressed for. While the church was forever thrusting the condition of the poor before the eyes of the rich, it was forever scolding the latter. Nor is its attitude to be viewed merely in the light of a mellowing of the heart of the wealthy for their own moral improvement and the material advantage of the poor. The rich were not only urged to give but also urged to desist from their search after wealth. This followed most logically from the ideal of the Imitation of Christ. The seeking of worldly goods beyond bare necessity was positively bad: "Having food and raiment, let us therewith be content. But they that will be rich fall into temptation and a snare and into many foolish and hurtful lusts which drown men in destruction and perdition. For the love of money is the root of all evil" (I Tim. 6: 7–10). Obviously a faith which warned men against worldly goods ("Love not the world, nor the things that are in the world" [I John 2:15]) could not but regard the most eager and successful seekers after such goods as a vanguard leading the followers to spiritual destruction. The moderns, on the other hand, take a far more favorable view of worldly goods. The increase of wealth seems to them a most excellent thing, and the same logic should therefore lead them to regard the same men as a vanguard leading the followers to material increase.

This latter view would have been most unrealistic in the material conditions of the Middle Ages. In so far as wealth was drawn from land which received no improvements, and in so far as the well-endowed did not make productive investments, there was nothing but disadvantage to the many in the existence of the wealthy (though this existence did give rise to the artisan industries from which there long after evolved the industries serving the people; further, it was instrumental in the development of culture). It is perhaps a fact worthy of notice that the modern use of profit, expansion from retained earnings, arose and was systematized in the monasteries; the saintly men who ran them saw nothing wrong in extending their holdings and putting new lands under cultivation, in erecting better buildings, and in employing an ever increasing number of people. They are the true original of the non-consuming, ascetic type of capitalist. And Berdyaev has truly observed that Christian asceticism played a capital part in the development of capitalism; it is a condition of reinvestment. It is tempting to mention that modern intellectuals look favorably on the accumulation of wealth by bodies bearing a public seal (nationalized enterprises), which are not without some similarity to monasterial businesses. They do not, however, recognize the same phenomenon when the seal is missing.

The intellectual thinks of himself as the natural ally of the worker. The partnership is conceived, in Europe at least, as a fighting one. The image is imprinted in the intellectual's mind of the long-haired and the blue-bloused standing side by side on the barricades. It appears that this image originated in the French Revolution of 1830 and became generally popular during the Revolution of 1848. The picture was then projected backward into history. A permanent alliance between the thinking few and the toiling many was assumed, a view to which romantic poetry gave expression and currency. The historian, however, can find no evidence of such an alliance in the case of the secular intelligentsia. No doubt the clergy was committed to the solace and care of the poor and unfortunate, and indeed its ranks were continuously replenished from the lowest orders of the people; the clerical intelligentsia was thus the channel whereby the talented poor rose to command princes and kings. But the lay intelligentsia, growing away from its clerical root, seemed to turn its back on the preoccupations of the church. Evidence of its interest in what came in the nineteenth century to be called the "social question" is up to that time remarkably scant. There is, however, abundant evidence of a sustained fight by the lay intellectuals against the welfare institutions of their day, administered by the church. During the Middle Ages the church had amassed immense wealth from pious gifts and foundations for charitable purposes. From the Renaissance to the eighteenth century these accumulations were returned to private possession through far-reaching confiscation. In this process the intellectuals played a major role. Servants of the temporal power, they started from the simple fact that the wealth of the church was least amenable to tax; they moved by degrees to the idea that property was more productive in private hands and hence that private enterprise was the best servant of the prince's treasure. Finally, it became a truism that the prince lost his due and the subject his chance by the piling-up of wealth in undying hands (cf. D'Aguesseau's report on perpetual foundations).[2] The lay intellectuals took little account of the social needs fulfilled by the institutions which they sought to destroy. Beggars should be rounded up and led to forced labor; this was the great remedy, in sharp contrast to the medieval attitude. It is not an undue comparison to liken the attitude of the secular intelligentsia to that of the most rabid opponents of the social services in our day, except that they went so much further, taking an attitude which we may find recurring in our times a few generations hence, if the social services should happen to claim a large part of the national wealth in a poor economy.

In direct contradiction to the friars who were to live in poverty with the poor, the secular intellectuals started out as companions and servants of the mighty. They can be called friends of the common man in the sense that they fought against distinctions between the high- and the lowborn and that they favored the rising plebeian—in point of fact, the merchant.[3] There was a natural bond of sympathy between the merchant and the civil servant, both waxing important but both still treated as social inferiors. There was a natural resemblance in that both were calculators, weighers, "rational" beings. There was, finally, a natural alliance between the interests of the princes and those of the merchants. The strength of the prince bound up with the wealth of the nation and the wealth of the nation bound up with individual enterprise; these relationships were perceived and expressed as early as the beginning of the fourteenth century by the secular councilors of Philip the Fair of France. The legal servants of the princes tended to free property from its medieval shackles in order to encourage an expansive economy benefiting the public treasury. (All the terms here are anachronistic, but they do not misrepresent the policies of those times.)

Hostility to the money-maker—*l'homme d'argent*—is a recent attitude of the secular intelligentsia. Any history of European literature must cite the names of the numerous money-makers who patronized intellectuals and apparently earned the affection and respect of their protégés; thus the courage shown by the men of letters who defended Fouquet (after the imprisonment of this financier and finance minister by Louis XIV) testifies to the depth of the feelings which he had inspired. The homes of Helvetius and D'Holbach must of necessity figure in any history of the ideas before the French Revolution. These two *hommes d'argent* were much admired by their circle, while the person most popular with French intellectuals at the time of the Revolution was the banker Necker. Again, in the Revolution of 1830, a banker— Laffitte—occupies the front of the stage. But this is the parting of the ways. Later, intellectuals cease to admit the friendship of capitalists, who, in turn, cease to be possible figureheads, as Necker had been.[4]

Strangely enough, the fall from favor of the money-maker coincides with an increase in his social usefulness. The moneyed men whom the French intellectual of the seventeenth and eighteenth centuries had liked so well had been chiefly tax farmers (publicans). The economics of tax farming are simple. The farming companies rented the privilege of collecting a given tax by paying a certain sum to the exchequer. They saw to it that much more than the official levy flowed in to their coffers; the margin constituted their gross income. When the costs of collection had been subtracted, the remainder was clear profit. This procedure is certainly more deserving of the name "exploitation" than any modern form of profit-making. Moreover, these profits were only rarely used for investments enriching the country. The tax farmers were renowned for their ostentatious consumption. As their privilege was valuable, they conciliated influential people at court by "helping them out" very freely. Thus the tax farmer combined all the features commonly attributed to the "bad capitalist" without any of the latter's redeeming features. He produced nothing, he profited in proportion to the harshness of his agents, and he retained his privilege by corruption. What a paradox it is that this type of money-maker should have been popular with the intellectual of his day and that unpopularity should have become the lot of the money-maker at the time when his chief form of money-making became the manufacture of goods for popular use!

Until the late eighteenth century the secular intelligentsia was not numerous; its average intellectual level was therefore high. Moreover, its members were educated in ecclesiastical schools, where they received a strong training in logic, which the "scientific education" of our day seems unable to replace. Therefore these minds were prone to consistency; it is remarkable how common a quality consistent reasoning was in their works, as compared to those of our contemporaries. For minds thus equipped, as soon and in so far as they insulated earthly concerns from spiritual truths, the criterion of earthly good was bound to be what we call efficiency. If, with Descartes, we insulate what occurs in space and comes directly to our notice, we can validly state that one movement is greater or less than another and validly call the "force" which causes it greater or less. If social events are regarded as movements, some of which are considered desirable, then it is "good" that these should be produced, the forces which tend to produce them are "good," and devices tending to call them forth and apply them to the object are better or worse in proportion to their efficiency. It is a naïve belief of many European intellectuals that "efficiency" is an American idol, recently installed. But it is not so. In anything which is regarded *instrumentaliter*, as an agent for the production of another thing, the greater or lesser capacity of the agent is to be taken into account, and Descartes repeatedly spoke in this sense of the greater or lesser *virtus* of the agent. It seems clear that, the more one tends to a monist conception of the universe which sets up the wealth of society as the result to be attained, the more one must be inclined to equate efficiency in the service of wants and desires with social good. Strangely enough, however, such an evolution of intellectual judgment did not occur in the last hundred and fifty years coincidentally with the evolution toward materialist monism. Ethical judgments disastrously detached from their metaphysical basis sprang up in disorderly growth to plague temporal action.

It seems at least plausible to seek some relation between this change of attitude and the wave of romanticism which swept over the Western intelligentsia. Factory builders trampled over the beauties of nature precisely when these were being discovered; the exodus from the country coincided with a new-found admiration for country life. A sharp change of surroundings divorced men from ancient ways precisely when folkways were coming into fashion. Finally, town life became life with strangers precisely at the moment when civil society was proclaimed insufficient for man's comfort, and the necessity of communal feeling and affection was stressed. All these themes are to be found in Rousseau. This major philosopher was well aware that the values which he cherished were in opposition to the progress of Western society; therefore, he wanted none of this progress: no successive quickening of new wants, no monstrous bellying of towns, no vulgarization of knowledge, etc. He was consistent. Western intellectuals, however, were not to be diverted from their enthusiasm for progress. Therefore, at one and the same time, they thought of industrial development as a great spreading of man's wings and of all its features which were in sharp contrast with the "shepherd" values as deplorable blemishes. Avidity was responsible for these blemishes, no doubt—and also for the whole process! There is a natural homogeneity of the attitudes relative to a certain general process.

The intellectual is really of two minds about the general economic process. On the one side, he takes pride in the achievement of technique and rejoices that men get more of the things which they want. On the other hand, he feels that the conquering army of industry destroys values and that the discipline reigning there is a harsh one. These two views are conveniently reconciled by attributing to the "force" of "progress" everything one likes about the process and to the "force" of "capitalism" everything one dislikes.

It is perhaps worthy of note that precisely the same errors are made in respect to economic creation as are made on the metaphysical level in respect to Creation, since the human mind has but limited capacities and lacks variety even in its mistakes. The attribution to essentially different forces of what is considered good and what is considered bad in the tightly knit process of economic growth of course recalls Manichaeism. Error of this type is not dispelled but tends to be aggravated by retorts taking Pope's line that all is well and that every unpleasant feature is the condition of some good.

It is not surprising that the discussion of the problem of evil in society should tend to follow the pattern of the more ancient and far-reaching discussion of the problem of evil in the universe, a matter upon which far more intellectual concentration has been brought to bear than upon the more limited modern version. We find the secular intelligentsia passing judgment on temporal organization, not from the point of view of adequacy to the end pursued, but from the point of view of ethics (though the ethical principles invoked are never clearly stated or perhaps even conceived). One hears Western students stating that the welfare of the workers must be the aim of economic leaders; that, although this aim is achieved in the United States and not achieved in the USSR, it does inspire the Soviet leaders and not the Western leaders (or so the students say); and that therefore the former are to be admired and the latter condemned. Here one finds one's self very clearly in a case of jurisdiction *in temporalia, ratione peccati*. The secular intellectual in this instance does not judge social devices as devices (and the device which achieves the workers' good out of the leaders' indifference *ex hypothesi* is surely an excellent device as compared to that which produces no workers' good out of the leaders' solicitude!), but he steps into the shoes of a spiritual guide, with perhaps insufficient preparation.

Taking a sweeping view of the attitudes successively adopted by the lay intelligentsia of the West, we shall say that it started out in reaction to the spiritual jurisdiction of the clerical intelligentsia, in the services of the temporal powers, and concerned itself with bringing rationality into the organization of earthly pursuits, taken as given. Over the centuries it battered down the power of the church and the authority of revelation; thereby it gave free rein to the temporal powers. Temporal power takes the two basic forms of the sword and the purse. The intelligentsia favored the purse. After liquidating the social power of the church, it turned upon the sword-bearing classes, especially upon the greatest sword-bearer, the political sovereign. The weakening of the ecclesiastical power and of the military power obviously gave full freedom to the moneyed power. But then the intelligentsia turns again, proclaiming a spiritual crusade against the economic leaders of modern society. Is this because the intelligentsia must be at odds with any ruling group? Or are there special causes of antagonism toward business executives?

The intellectual wields authority of a kind, called persuasion. And this seems to him the only good form of authority. It is the only one admitted by intellectuals in their utopias, where the incentives and deterrents of material reward and of punishment are dispensed with. In real societies, however, persuasion alone is inadequate to bring about the orderly cooperation of many agents. It is too much to hope that every participant in an extensive process will play his part because he shares exactly the vision of the promoter or organizer. This is the hypothesis of the "General Will" applied to every part and parcel of the economic body; it goes to the extremes of unlikeliness. It is necessary that some power less fluctuating than that gained from persuasion should lie in the hands of social leaders; the intellectual, however, dislikes these cruder forms of authority and those who wield them. He sniffs at the mild form of authority given by the massing of capital in the hands of "business czars" and recoils from the rough sort of authority given by the massing of police powers in the hands of totalitarian rulers. Those in command of such means seem to him coarsened by their use, and he suspects them of regarding men as wholly amenable to their use. The intellectual's effort to whittle down the use of alternatives to persuasion is obviously a factor of progress, while it may also, carried too far, lead society into the alternatives of anarchy and tyranny. Indeed, the intellectual has been known to call upon tyranny for the propping-up of his schemes.

The intellectual's hostility to the businessman presents no mystery, as the two have, by function, wholly different standards, so that the businessman's normal conduct appears blameworthy if judged by the criteria valid for the intellectual's conduct. Such judgment might be avoided in a partitioned society, avowedly divided in classes playing different parts and bound to different forms of honor. This, however, is not the case of our society, of which current ideas and the law postulate that it forms a single homogeneous field. Upon this field the businessman and the intellectual move side by side. The businessman offers to the public "goods" defined as anything the public will buy; the intellectual seeks to teach what is "good," and to him some of the goods offered are things of no value which the public should be discouraged from wanting. The world of business is to the intellectual one in which the values are wrong, the motivations low, the rewards misaddressed. A convenient gateway into the intellectual's inner courtyard where his judgments are rendered is afforded by his deficit preference. It has been observed that his sympathy goes to institutions which run at a loss, nationalized industries supported by the treasury, colleges dependent on grants and subsidies, newspapers which never get out of the red. Why is this? Because he knows from personal experience that, whenever he acts as he feels he should, there is unbalance between his effort and its reception: to put it in economic jargon, the market value of the intellectual's output is far below factor input. That is because a really good thing in the intellectual realm is a thing which can be recognized as good by only a few. As the intellectual's role is to make people know for true and good what they did not previously recognize as such, he encounters a formidable sales resistance, and he works at a loss. When his success is easy and instantaneous, he knows it for an almost certain criterion that he has not truly performed his function. Reasoning from his experience, the intellectual suspects whatever yields a margin of profit of having been done, not from belief in and devotion to the thing, but because enough people could be found to desire it to make the venture profitable. You may plead with the intellectual and convince him that most things must be done this way. Still he will feel that those ways are not his. His profit-and-loss philosophy can be summed up in these terms: to him a loss is the natural outcome of devotion to a thing-to-be-done, while a profit, on the other hand, is the natural outcome of deferring to the public.

The fundamental difference of attitude between the businessman and the intellectual can be pinned down by resort to a hackneyed formula. The businessman must say: "The customer is always right." The intellectual cannot entertain this notion. A bad writer is made by the very maxim which makes him a good businessman: "Give the public what it wants." The businessman operates within a framework of tastes, of value judgments, which the intellectual must ever seek to alter. The supreme activity of the intellectual is that of the missionary offering the Gospel to heathen nations. Selling spirits to them is a less dangerous and more profitable activity. Here the contrast is stark between offering "consumers" what they should have but do not want and offering them what they avidly accept but should not have. The trader who fails to turn to the more salable product is adjudged a fool, but the missionary who would so turn would be adjudged a knave.

Because we intellectuals are functionally teachers of truth, we are prone to take toward the businessman the very same attitude of moral superiority which was that of the Pharisee toward the Publican, and which Jesus condemned. It should be a lesson to us that the poor man lying by the wayside was raised by a merchant (the Samaritan) and not by the intellectual (the Levite). Dare we deny that the immense improvement which has occurred in the condition of the toiling many is chiefly the work of the businessmen?

We may rejoice that we minister to the highest wants of mankind; but let us be honestly fearful of this responsibility. Of the "goods" offered for profit, how many can we call positively harmful? Is it not the case of many more of the ideas we expound? Are there not ideas nefarious to the workings of the mechanisms and institutions which insure the progress and happiness of commonwealths? It is telling that all intellectuals agree to there being such ideas, though not all agree as to which are obnoxious. Far worse, are there not ideas which raise anger in the bosoms of men? Our responsibility is heightened by the fact that the diffusion of possibly mischievous ideas cannot and should not be stopped by the exertion of the temporal authority, while the merchandising of harmful goods can be so stopped.

It is something of a mystery—and a promising field of investigation for historians and sociologists—that the intellectual community has waxed harsher in its judgments of the business community precisely while the business community was strikingly bettering the condition of the masses, improving its own working ethics, and growing in civic consciousness. Judged by its social fruits, by its mores, by its spirit, capitalism of today is immeasurably more praiseworthy than in previous days when it was far less bitterly denounced. If the change in the attitude of the intelligentsia is not be to explained by a turn for the worse in what they assess, is it not then to be explained by a change which has occurred in the intelligentsia itself?

This question opens a great realm of inquiry. It has for long been assumed that the great problem of the twentieth century is that of the industrial wage-earner's place in society; insufficient notice has been taken of the rise of a vast intellectual class, whose place in society may prove the greater problem. The intellectuals have been the major agents in the destruction of the ancient structure of Western society, which provides three distinct sets of institutions for the intellectuals, the warriors, and the producers. They have striven to render the social field homogeneous and uniform; the winds of subjective desires blow over it more freely; subjective appreciations are the criterion of all efforts. Quite naturally, this constitution of society puts a premium upon the "goods" which are most desired and brings to the forefront of society those who lead in the production of "goods." The intelligentsia has then lost to this "executive" class the primacy which it enjoyed when it stood as "the First Estate." Its present attitude may be to some degree explained by the inferiority complex it has acquired. Not only has the intelligentsia as a whole fallen to a less exalted status, but, moreover, individual recognition tends to be determined by criteria of subjective appreciation by the public, which the intelligentsia rejects on principle; hence the countervailing tendency to exalt those intellectuals who are for intellectuals only.

We do not presume to explain, and the foregoing remarks are the merest suggestions. Our ambition is merely to stress that there is something to be explained and that it seems timely to undertake a study of the tensions arising between the intelligentsia and society.

Notes

1. Do we not see such countries in dire need of capital for the employment of surplus labor crowded off the land? Be it noted that such labor can be employed on terms which seem to us humane only on condition that its produce serves foreign and richer markets. But, in so far as it destines its wares for the home market, hours have to be long and pay short to make the merchandise salable to a poor population. Indeed, the initial factories seeking to serve an ample fraction of the local population cannot fail to employ their workers on terms much lower than those which were previously commanded by artisans serving only a narrow market of wealthy landowners. Therefore the Industrial Revolution is logically accompanied at the outset by a fall in real wages, if one compares, somewhat unduly, the previous reward of the artisan with the present reward of the factory worker.
2. This report, which prefaced the French Royal Edict of August, 1749, lays down the principle that the accumulation of land in collective hands which never release their holdings impedes the availability of capital to the individual, who should find it possible to obtain and control a "fund of wealth" to which he may apply his energy. Readers of this and other state papers will perhaps subscribe to

the equation: "The ideas of the French Revolution, I mean those which inspired the ministers of Louis XV."

3. The merchant, of course, was also an industrial promoter, since he ordered from artisans the goods which he offered for sale.

4. One of the later instances being, of course, that of Engels.

Part Two:

Problems of Postwar Reconstruction

"A country which seeks to preserve both stable exchange rates and the freedom of its citizens to acquire foreign currencies, must be ruled in its policies, not by internal considerations but by the necessity of keeping in step with the other countries: it must act as a part of the whole, as a member of a system. When this is grasped, it seems obvious...that this discipline will prove more or less acceptable, according to whether [it] is more or less harsh."

—"Money in the Market," 1955

9

France: No Vacancies

A Dollar a Month

A dollar a month will pay a wage earner's rent in Paris [in 1948–Eds.]. Our authority for this assertion is the Communist-dominated Federation of Labor Unions, the CGT. In setting forth its demands for a minimum wage to ensure a decent living, it produced a worker's budget in which the expenditure on rent was put at 316 francs. (In this analysis, all figures will be stated in dollars at the rough valuation of 300 francs to the dollar).

Against this figure one may set the estimate of the conservative Union of Family Associations. Thinking in terms of families, this source sets the expenditure on rent, providing adequate space, at a dollar and a half for a man and wife with a child and a baby; for a family of six the expenditure on rent should go up to a little less than two dollars.

Artificially Low Rents

Such cheapness is amazing. In the CGT budget, rent is reckoned as equal in cost to transport to and from work. To put it another way, a month's rent for an individual worker costs little more than six packets of the cheapest cigarettes. For a large family of six it costs as much as eleven packets of cigarettes (cigarettes, now unrationed in France, cost 15 cents a packet).

Even in a worker's very modest budget such an expenditure absorbs but a small part of his income, 2.7 percent of the minimum income demanded by the CGT; as little as 1.2 percent of the income of a six member family as calculated by the Union of Family Associations.

Reprinted from *Verdict on Rent Control*, ed. F. A. Hayek; IEA Readings, no. 7 (London: Institute of Economic Affairs, 1972). Used by permission of the publisher and the Foundation for Economic Education, Irvington-on-Hudson, New York.

Against such estimated blueprint budgets we can resort to actual declarations of wage-earners canvassed by the French statistical services. It appears from their budgets that, on average, rent makes up 1.4 percent of wage earners' expenditures; for white collar workers rent goes up to 1.7 percent of total expenditures.

In practice there are many rents lower than a dollar a month; rents of half-a-dollar are not uncommon. Nor should it be assumed that the lodgings are necessarily worse, for price and comfort, as we shall see, are unrelated.

Such low rents are not a privilege confined to wage-earners. Middle-class apartments of three or four main rooms will frequently cost from $1.50 to $2.50 per month. Rents paid by important officials or executives range from $3.50 to $8 or $10 a month. There is no close correlation between income and rent. Rent seldom rises above 4 percent of any income; frequently it is less than 1 percent.

It is not then surprising that Parisians spend on entertainment every month far more than they pay for three months' rent.

Here Lies an Apartment

This may seem a very desirable state of affairs. It has, of course, its drawbacks.

While, on the one hand, you pay no more than these quite ridiculous prices if you are lucky enough to be in possession of a flat, on the other if you are searching for lodgings you cannot find them at any price. There are no vacant lodgings, nor is anyone going to vacate lodgings which cost so little, nor can the owners expel anyone. Deaths are the only opportunity.

Young couples must live with in-laws, and the wife's major activity consists in watching out for deaths. Tottering old people out to sun themselves in public gardens will be shadowed back to their flat by an eager young wife who will strike a bargain with the janitor, the *concierge*, so as to be first warned when the demise occurs and to be first in at the death. Other apartment-chasers have an understanding with undertakers.

"Bootleg Housing"

There are two ways of obtaining an apartment which death has made available. Legally, if you fulfill certain conditions which give you a priority, you may obtain from a public authority a requisition order;

you will usually find that the same order for the same apartment has been given to possibly two or three other candidates. The illegal method is the surest. It is to deal with the heir, and with his complicity immediately to carry in some pieces of your furniture. As soon as you are in, you are king of the castle.

Buying one's way into an apartment will cost anything from $500 to $1,500 per room. At such prices you may also share flats which the tenants will agree to divide. As for wage-earners, they may as well give up hope of setting up house; they will have to stay with their families or live in very miserable hotels by the month.

In short, rents are very low but there are no lodgings available. Nor are any being built. And practically none have been built for the last twelve years.

There are some 84,000 buildings for habitation in Paris: 27.2 percent of them were built before 1850, 56.9 percent before 1880. Almost 90 percent of the total were built before the First World War. Most of the additional new building was carried out immediately after that war; then it slackened, and by 1936 had practically stopped.

Parisian Plight

Even a very lenient officialdom estimates that there are about 16,000 buildings which are in such a state of disrepair that there is nothing that can be done but to pull them down. Nor are the remainder altogether satisfactory. To go into sordid details, 82 percent of Parisians have no bath or shower, more than half must go out of their lodgings to find a lavatory, and a fifth do not even have running water in the lodgings. Little more than one in six of existing buildings is pronounced satisfactory and in good condition by the public inspectors. Lack of repair is ruining even these.

Owners can hardly be blamed. They are not in a financial position to keep up their buildings, let alone improve them. The condition of the owners can hardly be believed. To take an example of a very common situation, here is a lady who owns three buildings containing thirty-four apartments, all inhabited by middle-class families. Her net loss from the apartments, after taxes and repairs, is $80 a year. Not only must her son put her up and take care of her, but he must also pay out the $80. She cannot sell; there are no buyers.

When the owner tries to milk a little net income from his property by cutting down the repairs, he runs great risks. Another person postponed repairs on his roofs; rain filtering into an apartment spoiled a couple of armchairs. He was sued for damages and condemned to pay a sum amounting to three years of the tenant's paltry rent.

The miserable condition of owners is easily explained. While rents since 1914 have at the outside multiplied 6.8 times, taxes have grown 13.2 times and the cost of repairs has increased from 120 to 150 times the 1914 price!

Rent Control Takes Root

The position is, of course, as absurd as it is disastrous. An outsider might be tempted to think that only an incredible amount of folly could have led us to this. But it is not so. We got there by easy, almost unnoticed stages, slipping down on the gentle slope of rent control. And this was not the work of the Reds but of successive parliaments and governments, most of which were considered to be rather conservative.

Legacy of First World War

The story starts with the First World War. It then seemed both humane and reasonable to preserve the interests of the families while the boys were in the army or working for victory. So existing situations were frozen. It was also reasonable to avoid disturbances at the end of the war. The veterans' homecoming should not be spoiled by evictions and rent increases. Thus prewar situations were hardened into rights. The owner lost—"temporarily," of course—the disposition of his property, and the stipulations of law superseded agreement between the parties. This was only for a time.

But by the time the situation was reviewed in 1922, retail prices had trebled with rents still at their prewar level. It was then plain that a return to a free market would imply huge increases, an index to them being provided by rents in the smallish free sector, which hovered around 2 1/2 times the 1914 rents. The legislators shrank from this crisis. Wages were by then three and a half times what they had been in 1914, and the expenditure on rent in the worker's budget had shrunk from something like 16 percent before the war to around 5 percent. In our times habits become quickly ingrained. Instead of regarding rent as constituting normally one-sixth of one's expenditures, one took it now as being normally one-twentieth. Also, a "right" had developed, the "right" to dig in. Always very sedentary, the French now had struck roots in their rented lodgings.

The legislators decided to deal with this matter in a prudent, states-manlike manner. So the tenant's right to retain possession was confirmed but the rent was raised slightly. Successive increases were granted in further laws, all hotly debated. A new owner-tenant relationship thus took shape. The owner was powerless either to evict the tenant or debate the price of rent with him, because the state took care of that. The price rose but slowly, while in the meantime the field of regulation was progressively enlarged to bring in such flats as had not been previously regulated. New buildings put up since 1915 were alone left unregulated to stimulate construction. This exception was not to endure for long.

The Fear of Liberty

No systematic view inspired this policy. It just grew from the fear of a sudden return to liberty which seemed ever more dangerous as prices rose. And, of course, if one had to control the price of rent, one could not allow the owner to dispossess tenants, because in that case he might so easily have made an agreement secretly with the new tenant; so rent control implied necessarily the denial of the owner's right to evict.

What then happened to rents under this regime? In 1929, with retail prices more than six times what they had been in 1914, rents had not even doubled; real rents, that is, rents in terms of buying power, were less than a third of what they had been before the war.

Law-making on rent control continued, indeed no single subject has taken up so much of the time and energy of Parliament. But the improvement in the condition of the owners, when it came, was not the work of the legislators. It was brought about by the economic crisis which lowered retail prices. Thus, by 1935, rents then being almost three times their prewar level, retail prices were down and owners obtained almost two-thirds of their prewar real income. Or rather they would have obtained it had not the Laval government then decided on a cut of 10 percent in rents as one of the measures designed to bring down the cost of living and implement a policy of deflation.

When the Popular Front came to power in 1936, the process of devaluations started again, retail prices soared, and real income from buildings crumbled from year to year.

Then came the Second World War. The return to liberty which had been devised for 1943 was, of course, shelved, and all rents were frozen, including this time those of recent buildings which had till then escaped.

The Busy Law-Makers

Since the Liberation, an order in council of 1945 and two laws in 1947 have intervened, bringing up to 119 the number of laws or quasi-laws on the subject since 1918. The new laws have provided for increases jacking up rents. Apartments built before 1914 can now be rented at prices 70 percent above the 1939 price. But while rents increased 1.7 times, retail prices rose more than fourteen times. In other words, the buying power of rents was set at 12 percent of its 1939 level, already greatly depressed as we have seen. The buildings put up since 1914 were more severely treated on the assumption that the ruling rents in 1939 had been more adequate. The permissible increase over 1939 levels was set at 30 percent, thus keeping the buying power of these rents at 9 percent of what it was before the Second World War. It was further specified, for buildings dating back to 1914 or earlier, which comprise as we have noted nine out of ten of the total stock, that their rents should in no case be more than 6.8 times the 1914 rent. This in spite of the fact that retail prices were then 99.8 times as high as in 1914.

In short, owners of new buildings have been allowed to get in terms of real income less than a tenth of what they got before the Second World War.

Owners of old buildings, that is, nine-tenths of all buildings, have been allowed to get in terms of real income either 12 percent of what they got in 1939 or a little less than 7 percent of what they got in 1914–whichever is the lesser, the law took care to specify!

The Price Predicament

If on the other hand a builder were now to put up flats similar to those in existence, these new apartments would have to be let for prices representing from ten to thirteen times present rent ceilings, in order to reward the costs of construction and the capital invested. According to an official source, a report of the Economic Council, a wage-earner's apartment of three small rooms and a kitchen now renting for $13 to $16 a year (!) would have to be rented for $166 to $200 a year; and a luxury apartment of 1,600 square feet floor space would have to be rented for $55 to $70 a month, compared with the current price of $14 to $17 a month. Obviously, as long as the rents of existing buildings are held down artificially far below costs, it will be psychologically impossible to find customers at prices ten or twelve times higher, and hence construction will not be undertaken.

Such is the differential between the *legal* and the *economic* price of lodgings that even the most fervent advocates of freedom are scared at the prospect of a return to it; they shudder at the thought of a brutal return to reality. They feel that if the right to dismiss tenants were restored, and the right to bargain and contract with them, evictions could not be executed, the whole nation of tenants sitting down to nullify the decision. The thing, they say, has now gone too far, the price of rent is too far removed from the cost.

Hence the strange plans which are now being considered by the French Parliament. It is proposed to maintain a right of occupation, a right to retain one's lodgings, and it is proposed to arrive at a "fair price-fixing." That is, the true service value of every flat would be fixed according to floor space, the value per square meter being multiplied by a coefficient according to the amenities, situation and so forth. Thus the "fair rent" would be ascertained. But it would not be wholly paid by the tenant. He would benefit by a special subsidy, an inflationary measure of course, as are all subsidies. Nor would the larger part of this fair rent be paid to the owner. It would be divided in slices. A slice to correspond with the cost of upkeep would be paid to the owner, not directly but to a blocked account to make sure it was spent on repairs. A much bigger slice for the reconstitution of the capital investment would not go to the owner at all, but to a National Fund for Building. Thus the dispossession of the owners would be finally sanctioned. They would be legally turned into the janitors of their own buildings, while on the basis of their dispossession a new state ownership of future buildings would rear its proud head.

Road to Ruin

Possibly the French example may prove of some interest and use to our friends across the sea. It goes to show that rent control is self-perpetuating and culminates in both the physical ruin of housing and the legal dispossession of the owners. It is enough to visit the houses in Paris to reach conclusions. The havoc wrought here is not the work of the enemy but of our own measures.

10

The Political Consequences
of the Rise of Science

What political consequences can we see, and to some degree fore-see, as flowing from the rise of science? We can expect such conse-quences to be considerable. There can be no civilization unless society affords ample credit to men of thought. As their character changes, so does society. In the history of European civilization it is easy to ob-serve, first, a long era during which the men of thought were all men of God, clerics; then a gradual emergence of the men of law, who finally became the most favored and dominant type of intellectual. As we can tie great changes in political ideas and institutions to this displacement, we therefore have good reason to predict great changes from the super-session of the jurist by the scientist as the most favored and dominant type of intellectual.

The cathedrals of Europe are standing witnesses to the faith of the Middle Ages. The clergy formed the First Estate, whose duty it was to exhort and guide all members of society, above all, the rulers, who were thought of as "bound in conscience." But the interests of princes, the rifts within the Church, the growing complexity of society, all con-tributed to the promotion of the legal profession. This is not the place to describe the long, and partly unconscious struggle whereby the legal profession superseded the clergy as the dominant intellectual corpora-tion. Even in Catholic France, the long history of the Parliament of Paris shows us how this assembly of judges, under the *ancien régime*, intervened with increasing boldness in church affairs up to the point where the dominance of jurists was highly proclaimed, where the law-

Reprinted from *The Bulletin of the Atomic Scientists* (December, 1963): 2–8. Re-printed by permission of *The Bulletin of the Atomic Scientists*, © 1963 by the Educa-tional Foundation for Nuclear Science, 6042 South Kimbark Avenue, Chicago, Illinois 60637, USA.

yer-packed Assemblée Constituante dared to prescribe the organization and rules of the French church.

The age of lawyer predominance might be called the age of human scripture as against the age of Holy Scripture. Argument is no novelty, the Middle Ages were rife with it, but it turns no longer upon evidence of God's will but upon evidence of human will: the contract. If the contract can not be shown, it has to be presumed: society itself is a contract. I have shown elsewhere that the term "society," borrowed from jurists, has of necessity carried over its juristic meaning: in Roman law, society *is* a contract. Better, however, to put it in writing: this is the age of written constitutions. Parliaments are full of lawyers; "reading law" is the indispensable education of a gentleman.

Our formal political institutions are not only worked out and interpreted by jurists but also, what is far more important, they have been cast under the influence of the juristic mind, from which they borrow their character. Now I wonder how the predominance of the scientist will affect, first, the operation of these institutions and, in time, their nature.

Precedents Versus Technology

Unwittingly and indirectly, the scientist undermines the juristic order. Technology, that by-product of science which society at large regards as its end product, permits, nay commands, an accelerating pace of social change. Our expectation of and enthusiasm for progress are in contradiction with fidelity to "the ways of our fathers." But the "ways of our fathers," so dear to ancient moralists, have always served as a significant basis for jurists.

Precedent is the most ancient basis of law, and the safest. Pascal observed: "Custom alone maketh equity, and for no other reason than that it is accepted.... The art of subverting and upsetting commonwealths is to rattle established customs by delving to their source in order to display their lack of justice.... This is a game whereby all must surely be lost. Weighed in that balance, nothing will be found just" (*Pensées* III, 8). While we need not accept so extreme a view, we must observe that the countries where the individual is best guaranteed from arbitrariness are those English-speaking countries that have a great tradition of common law. Law legislated according to the dictates of reason has proved a weaker bulwark. Now the rapid course of change does strain the recourse to precedent, while it also belies the eighteenth-century confidence that a stable system of laws could be found, corresponding to a natural and necessary order of society, sure to persist once understood and established. We tend to think of society far less as an order, far more as an organization: while the rules of an order arise from considerations of equity, the rules of an organization shift according to its purpose of efficiency. The issue of "work rules" in the American steel strike of 1959 displayed the contrast between looking back to what is customary and looking forward to what is efficient.

Time was, when in the case of anything to be done there was a "right way" of doing it, a "true and loyal" practice, which could be checked by reference to the "good and respected masters." Now the judgment has been reversed: those who operate traditionally are a drag upon progress, since, by applying the same process, they take as much time to do the thing as was the case before, and thus impede the general social goal of doing far more in a decreasing amount of time. Thus the old idea of "due process" is hounded out of the productive realm. Judicial procedure is the sole remnant of the old idea of "the right way," and therefore an islet of stable procedure in a sea of shifting processes. Just how long can such an islet subsist, when it no longer corresponds to current attitudes? The French referendum of October 1962 testified that the utter disregard of procedures required in the constitution failed to shock the majority of voters.

As early as the seventeenth century, Malebranche expounded the doctrine that God works with the utmost economy of means, and implied that man's action is the less imperfect the greater the economy of means applied for a given result or, conversely, the greater the results from a given allotment of means. Still in this guise, this is the maxim of productivity which holds sway in our day. Efficiency is, without question, the characteristic virtue of the modern West, indeed the only one which the underdeveloped nations envy us and are willing to borrow from us. But who could deny that there is a conflict between efficiency and formality? And again, who would deny that forms are the guarantees of rights, formality the indispensable character of a juristic order?

Indirectly, science is a contributory influence to the dissolution of a juristic order. In the political realm, it is blatantly clear now that "the executive" is nothing like what Locke imagined: he saw it as a power subordinate to the legislative, and as "seeing to" the execution of the laws (*Second Treatise on Government*, chapter 12). This implied that a decision of the executive should look *back* to the laws in force, whereas we are well aware that such decisions in fact look *forward* to the results to be hoped for from them. Indeed the executive elaborates policies, which the legislative is required to implement by the voting of ad hoc laws. The initiative and the superiority lie with the executive and it cannot be otherwise in a society of rising expectations.

In our day, a commonwealth is nothing like a club, the rules of which are stable; it is more like an enterprise conducted for a sort of "collective profit," i.e., the year-to-year rise in the gross national product. Such a purpose of course calls for a continual adjustment of structures to the achievement of the purpose, and this takes precedence over the claims based upon custom and shatters the dream of an "ideal form" fitting an a priori idea. Social organization becomes a matter for systems engineering, and specific decisions become problems of operations research. Whether, and to what extent, one applauds or deplores such development, they have to be taken into account; they tend to downgrade the jurist and upgrade the expert, who, however, being a specialist, cannot play in society the same role as the jurist previously performed.

Scientist Politician

I have started with an indirect influence of science. Quite a few people, some of them eminent, feel that scientists will become the rulers of states—there could be no more direct influence. The scientist as statesman, as politician? This seems to me most improbable. The scientist signally lacks the qualities required in politics: they are antithetic to the qualities that make him a scientist.

The very first trait of a scientist is a disposition to give himself up altogether to the working out of one problem. Without distinction of working and leisure hours, and even in sleep, he tirelessly hunts his elusive prey. The whole of his attention is invested therein. He is therefore impatient of interruption, inattentive to extraneous matters, and but faintly aware of the questions asked of him and of the persons asking them.

A statesman, on the contrary, does not have one object of interest but a great many, and he does not choose them: they are forced upon him. In the course of his day, several different matters are brought to him, and he must be able to switch from one to another, expelling the preceding from his mind to be wholly available for the next. This is, in any case, a difficult feat, and quite impossible for a man whose disposition is to worry out one problem. Moreover, a good politician must be sharply aware of people. Wherever he goes, everybody looks at him—if not, he is not a successful politician—and he must give the impression that he notices every person: he antagonizes if he seems absent-minded. The political animal is available and alert, the scientist is absorbed: these are sharply contrasting propensities.

Nor does the contrast stop here: the scientist is scrupulous in his assertions, and the politician unscrupulous. This must be so, because the activities are so different. Let the scientist and the politician both "feel" that "if A, then B." The scientist would be unworthy of his calling if he did not spend the utmost care upon checking this hypothesis. But the statesman is in quite another position: a decision must be taken in time, and the more value the politician sets on B, the greater his anxiety to get done what procures B. He "feels" that this is A, and therefore is eager to procure A's acceptance. But he would fail therein if he said: "As B is of great value, and A has some likelihood of bringing it about, therefore let us do A." He is driven to assert that A shall yield B, thus transforming a value judgment on B into a certainty judgment on the A-B relationship. This we could not tolerate in a scientist. We accept it in a politician, pleased enough if he does not cheat us into accepting the A he wants for its own sake, by an empty promise that it is the way to the B we want.

Politics and science are quite different activities. In France, since 1789, we have seen a number of eminent scientists in politics: they have not been conspicuously successful, nor have they carried into their new field any distinctive behavior, other than a constructive interest in education.

It may be objected that in our day we witness a novel phenomenon, the rise of great research institutes, wherein a large number of scientists are associated with a considerable plant and supported by substantial financial resources. The head of such an institute, who is himself a scientist, has to show executive ability in running this enterprise and persuasive qualities in obtaining more funds. It is therefore quite conceivable that such executive functions should be a step toward politics. The scientist chosen as head must have been selected on the basis of his political disposition, and had the opportunity of developing it while filling this office. It is not at all improbable that we shall find some such people moving into political personnel. What is very doubtful is whether they will impart to this personnel the traits of the scientific community. More probably, on their way toward political office, they will have shed the character of scientist, and assumed that of politician. An analogy springs to mind: France had in succession two great prime ministers taken from the Church, Richelieu and Mazarin, but their administration bore little trace of their religious origin.

City of Science

That some scientists should individually become politicians seems to me of slight importance. What matters is the general influence exercised by the City of Science upon the larger City. I have already noted a form of influence, which is both very great and quite indirect: as scientific advances are translated into new processes, society undergoes structural changes, which are distant outcomes of scientific research though they were not its goals. Such changes create new problems for the treatment of which we are prone to consult experts, thought of as a variety of the genus scientist; we do this not so much on the basis of *similia similibus curantur*, but in view of a general belief in Science.

"We believe in science"—that is a conveniently loose mode of expression, which embraces a variety of attitudes. Thus Primus will say: "The progress of understanding is a great and glorious adventure in which I am eager to engage, and I most willingly submit to its rigorous discipline." While Secundus will think: "Science is not my business, but I confidently look to it for benefits that will accrue to me and my fellows." Primus feels called to the practice of science, Secundus looks to its yields; Primus will be a working scientist, Secundus a recipient of social dividends from progress.

The attitude of Secundus must perforce be uncritical: what "they" do in the City of Science is a mystery, the outcome is "magic." I find it hard to believe that the individual's loss of confidence in his personal judgment can be without political consequences. Indeed, my ignorance forces me to suspend judgment on such a threat to mankind as atomic radiation. If I leave it to scientists to assess the danger and to cope with it, why then should I meddle in political decisions minor by comparison? I shall do so only when my interests are directly involved, or my emotions immediately aroused.

Now let us turn to Primus: after having served a long apprenticeship, he has qualified as an active citizen in the Republic of Science. While a pioneer in one field, he must take on trust the findings of fellow scientists in other fields. Michael Polanyi has described the way in which standards are maintained by a few watchers over each field, so that confidence is warranted. But here again Primus himself abstains from personal judgment in matters that are not of his special competence.

What a contrast with the ubiquity of personal judgment that was assumed in the "Age of Reason"! Who would deny that the "Age of Reason" and the "Age of Science" have a common *fons et origo* in the self-assertion of man? But the subject, the "self" in which this confidence is placed, has shifted: it was "I" and now it is "we" (meaning in fact "they"). Hearing of a ticklish problem, a distinguished contemporary of ours will probably say: "This deserves the attention of a strong team, endowed with adequate resources." By adequate resources he understands the means of collecting the adequate data, and of checking by proper experiments the suppositions formulated. A *philosophe*, however, would have displayed a different reaction: "This intrigues me; I shall think it out." He would not have doubted his capacity to master the problem without equipment or personnel, but by the mere powers of the mind. These words of Hobbes, "*per rectam ratio cinatem acquisita cognitio*," could serve as the motto of the Age of Reason. There is a facile parallel between this contrast and that between industrial and artisan production. But such a parallel fails to catch a more fundamental difference. While a specific "bundle of scientific inputs" is good for a specific output of findings, the *philosophe* thought of his mind as good for any output, omnicompetent; his was an expression of supreme confidence in personal judgment. There was no subject on which he deemed it necessary to defer to the judgment of others, as a scientist of our day does when the matter falls outside his own field.

This attitude made for a regime of public opinion. Whatever problem came up, it was not thought of as a problem for experts, specialists: any thinking man could confidently advance his own view. "Thinking men" they saw as actually a tiny minority, but potentially all men were such: the natural light of reason, given to everyone, could come to be exercised by each in time. Thus, government by opinion, exercised first by men of letters, could progressively involve increasing portions of the population. But all this falls to the ground if opinion reached by mere ratiocination ceases to be trusted, as we come to think that valid findings require painstaking research.

Changing Nature of Discussion

As I happen to have been involved in the discussion of economic policy for nearly forty years, this affords me a field of observation. The character of such discussions has undergone a complete alteration. At the outset of the period, anyone boldly advanced views derived from ambiguous premises. There was almost no reference to factual data, then scarce in my country, there was no common terminology of well-defined concepts; indeed there was no effort to surmise how the recommendations made on grounds of principle would work out in fact. Today, the standards of discussion are very high in the French consultative bodies that associate representatives of the employers, the unions, and the farmers with civil servants and professors. And these standards rise every year: but in the meantime such discussion becomes increasingly incomprehensible, not only to the "man in the street," but also to the average lawmaker. While the improvement of the discussion is certainly helpful to national welfare, on the other hand its attendant esoterism runs counter to the democratic ideal of the informed and participating citizen.

"Technocracy" is a term of abuse, applied to such expert bodies. It carries an implication that their members have a common doctrine and interest; it is not so: what they have in common is a language, thanks to which they can agree on certain findings, and can spell out clearly their disagreements. As this language is their tool, they must successively refine it, and in so doing, they make it increasingly incomprehensible to the public, which therefore lends no ear to their discussion. This lack of audience involves a great risk. Confidence in governmental providence is increased by its consultation of experts, which indeed contributes to the prudence of its measures; but such consultative bodies afford no guarantee at all if the government turns imprudent or illiberal. The bodies have no powers of their own, their members are not accustomed to catching the public ear; and if they feel in duty bound to appeal to the nation against the government, their voices will not be heard.

I will venture to describe these bodies as having their eyes turned to the nation in order to assess requirements, and their mouth turned to the government for the utterance of advice. And that is good, but no substitute for bodies that have their eyes on the government to watch its doings, and their mouth turned toward the public to denounce the government's sins of omission or commission.

We must recognize that public opinion, in our modern democracies, falls very far short of what was imagined. The average citizen is involved in public affairs far more as a claimant than as a judge. He has expectations, he utters complaints, he formulates demands, and joins in pressures to advance his requests. But how these are to be met and conciliated with other data of the situation is a problem for "the management." If the problem is not satisfactorily solved, then the public is open to a "take-over bid": there is a change of management. Such self-centered political activity falls far short of the ideal of our ancestors, but it would be folly to belittle its value. Indeed, the most tangible difference between democracies and totalitarian regimes lies precisely in the freedom to press private claims, and in the sensitivity of public agencies. We should regard with the utmost suspicion all attempts to limit such freedom "in the public interest"; and we should be attentive to remedy those great inequalities in the ability to exert such pressure which arise in our day, no longer from differences in wealth, but from differences in the numbers of those having in common a special interest; we should see to it that each individual gets a hearing, which is not now the case.

Let us never listen to these haughty idealists who spurn a Babel of special demands and complaints, failing to recognize therein the voice of the people in its everyday reality. But of course such a Babel is problem-setting, not problem-solving, and throws the onus of problem-solving upon "the management." Now it is right that "the management" should have this task, but it is highly desirable that there should be a continuing general discussion of its performance, critical of what it is, suggestive of what it should be. And here lies the present weakness of political discourse. Democracies do have public pressing of special claims, and that is good; they have increasingly expert discussion of specific problems, and that is good. But general discussion seems inadequate.

Outcome-Aimed Versus Principle-Derived

Such inadequacy is hardly surprising. Not all matters lend themselves readily to general discussion; and matters of public interest are often not in the form best suited to the exercise of public attention.

Men have always joined with passion in discussions of right and wrong, wherein not one of us deems himself incompetent. Recently every French home was moved by the trial in Belgium of the thalidomide baby mercy-killers, and the problem was spontaneously posed in general terms: is a mother (any mother) justified in suppressing a child doomed to life-long monstrosity? The rule-making disposition was manifested by every opiner, who posited principles and argued from them. In keeping with this human disposition, the public discussions of the past have dealt essentially with principles—be it the conflict of principle with custom (as in the desegregation issue), or the conflict of

principle with principle (as in the "right to work" issue), or the derivation of specific rules from general principles. In short, public discussion is "law-minded" in wide terms, and indeed it is the business of
law-making which the theoreticians of democracy have attributed to
the people, either directly or mediated through their representatives.
Now as I noted earlier, while laws are turned out by the hundreds in
modern democracies, they are not so important nowadays as policies.

However far the nineteenth century carried Locke's idea that the
executive should be but the executor of the legislative power's pre-
scriptions, the twentieth century has been marked by a most striking
reversal. The executive is supreme; the legislative has not only lost its
supremacy, it has lost its independence in all countries but the U.S.
This seems an unavoidable feature of the Active State and, so much so,
that the more one calls for it, the more one belittles the legislative, as
shown by the American liberals who are in favor of a disciplined Congress. Now with the rise of the Active State goes a change in the character of the important political decisions; they are policies, not laws;
they are strategies aimed at maximizing some goods, or minimizing
some evils, or more generally at satisfying a complex of requirements.

Looking forward is essential: a proposal is advanced on the grounds
that it has a strong likelihood of bringing about a desirable state of
affairs; its justification lies in a future outcome, not in a previously
accepted principle. It would be absurd to say that taking decisions on
grounds of their expected future yield is a "new" thing. That is the
habitual mode of human decision. But while the early nineteenth century held this to be the proper mode in the realm of private business, it
held that in the realm of public affairs the proper mode was derivation
from antecedent principle. The entrepreneur should ask himself what
strategy would lead to the best outcome, and this was for each a problem involving the best possible knowledge of present facts, the best
possible understanding of the workings of a dynamic system of relations, and the best possible selection of the action inputs with a view to
the outcome. But, on the other hand, in public affairs, the question was
imagined to be: what is the standing rule relevant to this instance, what
is the known principle from which a rule should be derived, etc. Now a
great change has occurred: the forward-looking decision has invaded
the public realm—which means that the discussion of public affairs is
no longer a matter of ratiocination and rhetoric from *ex ante* premises,
but is an estimation of the most fruitful actions, a speculation on *ex
post* states of affairs.

Where the public financier of the nineteenth century would have affirmed that the budget must be balanced and that the note circulation must enjoy a given proportion of specie coverage, his counterpart in our day will seek a strategy achieving full employment (no more than a given percentage of unemployed) together with economic growth (no less than a certain rate of increase in the gross national product) and with price stability (no more than a certain rate of increase in one or more given price indexes). No recommendations of that nature can be made or criticized without hard work. Surely views of that nature are nothing but "opinions"; but they are not opinions cheaply come by: they are formed at the cost of a considerable expenditure of time and attention. Participation in discussions of that character requires an initial investment so considerable as to restrict entry to a few.

Nor should we see this with any surprise. We do not expect to find ourselves competent for the discussion of the management of, say, General Electric. The modern state being increasingly that sort of thing, only far more complicated, we feel equally nonplused. The major change that has occurred in the nature of the state tends to relieve its operations from general discussion. In fact, the modern state tends to operate under much the same conditions as a big business firm, subject to pressures and to a satisfactory "pay-off." Therefore, once more we must set great value upon the ability to exercise pressures and the opportunity to change the management; but we must also set great value upon there being, at every actual decision center of this great machinery, some qualified discussants.

I have noted here a great shift to outcome-aimed decisions from principle-derived decisions, and stressed that this shift narrows down the number of possible discussants, since it is only on matters of principle that participation requires no qualification. I should further note that the influence of science tends to shake confidence in principles. The experimental frame of mind becomes more common, and principles therefore become subject to verification of their validity by means of the outcomes which their application brings about. For instance, in education, the principle that teaching should be so paced as not to leave behind the least receptive will be jettisoned if it is found that it keeps the more gifted from starting creative production when they should (for example, mathematicians, who, it is well known, are at their most creative in still tender years). Similarly, the principle of minimum spread in the remuneration of teachers will be jettisoned if it is found to produce the emigration of elites, and so forth.

Our general ideas about society are of the same degree of simplicity as those which we had in the Middles Ages about the structure of the universe. Science has successfully moved us away from such pristine simplicity in the case of the universe. A similar phenomenon is due to occur in our conceptions of society. While this holds promise, there can be no question that it implies great danger. Simple common beliefs, robustly held, are the walls of a city: these are cracking.

No status is higher in our present society than that of the scientist: and justifiably so, since he is the artisan of all change. On this status he can safely rely to obtain ever increasing support from society to enlarge and enrich the City of Science; and indeed he can rightly claim that payments to the City of Science are a very unequal return for its "exports" to society: the City of Science could lay claim to most of the productivity gains achieved in the economy. This being so, the City of Science is the creditor, not the debtor of society in terms of commutative justice. However, being aware that their findings are causing the most fundamental revolution that ever occurred in society, scientists can hardly be indifferent to society's course, and say that the problems arising are not their concern. They do feel a responsibility; its manifestation by emotional interventions in politics is revealing, but inadequate. Will they find some more systematic and competent way of discharging the responsibility? It is not yet clear how this can be done: but we shall certainly see a great rise in the bargaining power of the scientific community which it can put to good purpose.

Support or Challenge

I have recently seen in the *Bulletin* a quotation from Gerard Piel, stating: "Wherever they have taken root, the two movements of science and democracy have mutually sustained each other...." Trusting to the automatism of such mutual support smacks of nineteenth-century optimism. That science can develop without a democratic form of government has been proved in Russia, and does not concern me here; my worry is that science, far from providing automatic support to democracy, constitutes a challenge to it, which we must find ways of meeting. Democratic government, as distinct from a democratic society, implies confidence in Everyman's common sense, in his sufficiency for passing judgments on matters of general interest, and it requires the invigoration of Everyman's self-confidence in this respect. Now the progress of science shakes my confidence in my own judgment: this table upon which I am writing I regard as solid, science tells me I am wrong, that it is mostly void; this I now believe, on the authority of science.

How can highly reputable writers speak of our age as one where the mind does not submit to intellectual authority! How do I know that there can be no speed greater than that of light, or that the proton has a mass 1,836 times that of the electron, or indeed that such things have any existence? Science says so, and I accept these beliefs on its authority, with no more thought of checking them than if I were a medieval peasant.

If I compare my attitude to what it would have been two or three centuries ago, I find that I trust far less to the evidence of my senses, rely far more upon scientific authority, and am far more aware of my ignorance. The formidable expansion of human knowledge shows up the poverty of my own: indeed this great age of science is, by way of corollary, an age of personal ignorance.

The more the standards of research rise, the greater rigor I feel impelled to bring into my statements, the narrower the range within which I feel justified in formulating conclusions. This psychological impact of science seems to me to work against sustaining this general confidence in one's judgment, which is basic to the conception of democracy. And because science saps such individual confidence, we have a problem, which I feel we can meet but which it would be imprudent to deny.

11

Money in the Market

All day long, we obtain from others goods or services, for which we pay out money: money serves as a general key to the variety of obtainable goods. It is so in every country: but each several country has its own national currency, which commands the goods available in its own realm, and those only. Consequently a problem arises when I desire goods or services present in another realm, which has a different key of its own. The foreign seller does not wish for my currency but for his own: means must be found of turning the one into the other; this will prove easiest when both keys are made of the same stuff; mine can then be recast into his own. If it is not so, then my buying depends upon my finding someone in my country who has obtained foreign currency which he wants to turn into our own, or upon the seller's knowing of someone in his country who desires a key to my national store of good; in either case, a transfer of keys occurs, known as Exchange. Let us illustrate it.

The Parable of the Innkeeper

In 1912, an English family spent its summer holiday in an out-of-the-way French village. A bill was presented, invoiced in francs: the English father had nothing but English gold sovereigns, then circulating in Britain. This did not embarrass the innkeeper: true, he had never seen coins stamped with the British Monarch's profile, but he was thoroughly familiar with the gold coins then circulating in France. Placing a twenty-franc gold piece by the side of the sovereign, he found the latter heavier (123.27 grains to 99.56), and it seemed to him that two sovereigns made up about the same weight as a fifty-franc gold piece

Reprinted from *Money and Trade*, ed. by Sir Wilfrid Eady (London: Batchwoth Press, 1955): 31-55. Used by permission of the author.

(50 francs = 248.9 grains; 2 sovereigns = 246.54). Therefore, without consulting anybody, he made up his mind to accept two sovereigns as equivalent to fifty francs. In this he was justified, because the French Mint bought the sovereigns from him on the basis of their fine gold content (113 grains to the sovereign), and recoined them into French gold pieces (224 grains to the fifty-franc piece). Thus English money could be physically converted into French money by melting and re-stamping. An assessment of relative values could be made by mere comparison of the coins, which, to be accurate, had to take into account, not only brute weights but the degree of fineness.

In 1932, the same English family returned to the same spot, again the head of the family had no other means of payment than those current in Britain at the time, i.e., pound banknotes. The aged innkeeper took these notes, laid them side by side with French notes, and this time learned nothing from the comparison. Obviously a physical conversion of the English notes into French was out of the question: the French Mint did not offer a high price for paper to be re-engraved with French designs. The English currency could not be turned directly into French currency, only into British goods; therefore its worth in francs hung upon the eagerness of other Frenchmen to obtain British keys. The 'weighing' of pounds had ceased to be a physical process, it was now a market process, a day-to-day confrontation of the French demand for pounds with the British demand for francs.

In the former case the rate of the exchange depended upon the unchanging balance of physical weights in fine gold between the national coins: it was therefore inherently stable; in the second case it depended upon the changing balance of claims between the two countries (the balance of claims with third countries entering into the picture): it was therefore inherently unstable; we shall in time attend to the means of stabilizing exchange rates under such conditions.

Coming now to our own days [1955–Eds.], a third journey of the same family presents a wholly different picture. The English travelers are not allowed to take pounds out of Britain: on the other hand the national authorities do grant them, at fixed exchange rates, a quantity of foreign currency units corresponding to a given, limited, amount of pounds. The innkeeper shall be paid in francs, but the sojourn will be short.

Inconvertibility

Our times have given the lie in many respects to the dictum that there is nothing new under the sun. Inconvertibility is one of our true novelties. 'Inconvertible currencies' is an expression familiar to students of history. But this historical inconvertibility was something quite different from the new inconvertibility, and the similarity of name is confusing: therefore we shall call the old inconvertibility 'irredeemability.'

If you will look at a pound note, you may read upon it: 'Bank of England: I promise to pay the bearer on demand the sum of one pound." This sounds meaningless to us: a pound is not the promise of a pound, it is a pound. The phrase, however, testifies to the ancient notion that a paper pound note was a promise to pay a gold pound, if the bearer of the note should so demand. Up to 1914, all currency notes were gold certificates (or gold and silver, or silver certificates, according to times and countries). The public or private establishments putting these notes into circulation were under obligation to redeem these notes on demand in coins of the realm (and this had come to mean gold coins in an ever increasing number of countries).

Monetary history is rife with occasions when the expansion of notes and/or the draining of metal reserves led to proclamations that the obligation to redeem the notes in coins was temporarily suspended. During this suspension, the paper currency was said to be inconvertible, that is payment in coins could not be exacted. This however did not preclude the bearers of such paper from acquiring foreign currency; they only found that their currency would not be taken abroad as equivalent to their national coins, since the national coin could not be obtained by taking the paper to the bank; hence the buying of foreign currencies would occur at fluctuating rates of exchange, depending upon the balance of international claims and not upon the respective weights of national coins. A currency inconvertible in this sense (i.e., irredeemable) would habitually depreciate in terms of foreign, redeemable currencies.

Convertibility in that older sense (redeemability) is not a quality which *some* currencies lack today; it is a quality which *all* currencies have lost. There is not, at present, a single currency redeemable in gold coins: not even the proud dollar. All currencies are inconvertible in the historic sense, that is are irredeemable: it is no novelty that currencies should find themselves in this position. It is a novelty that *all* currencies should find themselves in this position. The position in which the currencies *now* termed inconvertible do find themselves is on the other hand a wholly novel phenomenon, consisting in the prohibition of buying foreign currencies with one's own.* As we have seen, the faculty of buying foreign currencies at constant (or fairly constant) rates of exchange has often been lost: but the freedom of buying them had never been abridged before our day. One would have to delve far back into the centuries to find a faint simile in prohibitions to take specie out of the country.

It is the present practice, in the great majority of countries, that citizens wishing to travel, buy or invest abroad, have to seek permission from their national authorities. This is an unquestionable abridgment of freedom, and a striking innovation of our times. It must be stressed, not to condemn, but for purposes of clarity.

If the citizen's application is successful, the required amounts of foreign currency are granted to him by the authorities, i.e., sold to the applicant at a fixed rate of exchange. If the application is unsuccessful, the applicant may not seek to buy foreign currency at any price or by any means: that is a penal offense. This state of affairs constitutes "inconvertibility" in the present sense: a term both misleading and unwieldy, but still more convenient than would be an adequate designation of the situation: "convertibility of national currency into other currencies conditional upon administrative approval, and then assured at fixed rates of exchange."

Convertibility

Having defined inconvertibility, we should have no trouble in defining convertibility. But it is not so. Three different concepts of convertibility can be adduced, and none of them covers what experts mean by the much discussed "return to convertibility."

At present, national authorities control both the quantities of foreign currencies used by nationals and the prices, in national money, at which these currencies are acquired. A return to freedom is always possible, i.e., the dropping of both controls, as when rationing and price control are dropped for any merchandise; thus nationals would be free to ac-

---

*The private exchange of national for foreign currency was the subject of various exchange controls imposed by European countries, beginning with Germany in the 1930s. These controls persisted in Western Europe, in various forms, until the late 1950s, being relaxed for the first time in 1958. Exchange controls were not completely abolished in Great Britain until 1979; in the Soviet Bloc they lasted until the collapse of the USSR in 1991 [Eds.].

quire foreign currencies and the rates of exchange would be those resulting from the balance of demands; this we shall call simple convertibility. Human nature, however, is such that, faced with a situation
containing both unpleasant aspects (the limitation of our buying of foreign currencies) and pleasant aspects (a fixed rate of exchange), we
demand the reversal of the unpleasant aspect and assume the retention
of the pleasant aspect. What is generally thought of under the name of
convertibility is the *freedom to buy foreign currencies combined with
the guarantee of a fixed rate*. This is not an impossible state of affairs,
but it is not an easy one to secure. Redeemability, a third conception,
would carry with it both the freedom to buy foreign currencies and the
assurance of a fixed rate.

The three concepts all involve at least the citizen's freedom to buy
foreign currencies with his own. This freedom, however, is not contemplated in the current expert discussions over the so-called "convert-
ibly issue": what is at issue is whether the Bank of England should
make itself responsible for providing dollars against pounds, to foreigners currently earning sterling currency, and who prefer dollars.

As it is generally desired to go back to a state of affairs where individuals may freely acquire foreign currencies at fixed rates of exchange,
it seems the right procedure to seek how and why this state of affairs
has disappeared.

The Age of Redeemability

Consider a country with a purely metallic currency: domestic and
foreign payments are made in the same coin. Consequently an excess
of foreign payments over foreign income will produce a net export of
currency: there will be no difficulty in settling foreign claims, but internal difficulties will arise. The drain of specie will be experienced at
home as a constriction of currency available for domestic payments.
This is "good" for the re-establishment of external equilibrium and "bad"
for domestic prosperity.

It was Ricardo's contention that a decline in the volume of currency
available at home caused no other effects than a corresponding decline
in the price level at home, a general cheapening of home goods which
stimulated their exports, while conversely the swelling of currency at
home, which occurs in the country receiving specie by virtue of an
excess of foreign income over foreign payments, caused no other effects than a rise in the price level, making domestic goods more expen-

sive to the foreigner. These two effects would rapidly combine to re-store the balance of trade between two countries, without ill or favor-able effects upon the domestic activity of either. Experience belies the postulate that domestic activity is not effected. In fact a decline in the volume of domestic currency will produce a combination of irregular declines in home prices and declines in home activity; and conversely an increase in the volume of domestic currency will cause a combina-tion of irregular price increases and increases of domestic activity.

It is true that the decline in domestic activity affecting the country which loses currency will help as well as the decline in prices, towards the restoration of international balance: because of the decline in activ-ity, less foreign raw materials will be called for, because of the decline in real incomes (consequent upon the decline in activity), less foreign (as well as home) consumer goods will be bought. Conversely the coun-try gaining currency will import more, because its increasing activity and its increased real incomes will call for more raw materials and consumer goods drawn from abroad as well as from home. Thus it is quite true that the transfer of metallic currency from one country to another, consequent upon a disequilibrium of international transactions, will tend to correct this disequilibrium; but it is not true that it will achieve this without passing injury to the domestic activity of the country in foreign deficit.

The events follow exactly the same course when the countries have not a purely metallic currency but also a redeemable paper currency. In that case the money in circulation at home will be made up of coins plus notes, the latter backed by specie in the banks. As net foreign pay-ments are made in specie alone, an excess of payments abroad will impinge upon circulation, either by draining coins out of circulation or by draining specie out of the banks, causing them to call in notes. In-deed, as a banking system evolves over time towards the granting of credits which are a multiple of the gold backing, a given drain of gold must then cause a destruction of credits greater than the loss of gold.

Capital Movements

Such a shrinkage of the means of payment is hurtful to national ac-tivity: therefore it is vital to the proper functioning of the system that external deficits should be rapidly remedied. In the heyday of the sys-tem , one did not wait passively till the drain of the system produced an automatic righting of the balance, as outlined above: the central bank of the deficit country brought about a rapid righting of the balance by raising the price paid for money ("money rates"), a course which never failed to cause an immediate influx of foreign funds and/or retention of national funds previously exported. One might perhaps think of this process as avoiding a loss of money at the cost of paying more for its use. Thus the economy was spared the period of attrition inherent in the correction via loss of gold. This swift method of adaptation was made possible by the willingness of holders of liquid assets to move them across the globe in immediate response to the slightest difference in the rewards offered: a disposition induced by the certainty, bred of long experience, that the funds could be moved back at will. It may be unwise to underestimate the part played in this fluidity of funds by the existence of an acknowledged distributing center, the City of London.

From this description, it appears that the working of a world system of redeemable currencies rested upon the condition that the external deficits of individual countries would not be long lasting; if this happened, due to internal or external causes, the countries suffering successive losses of currency would experience increasing economic distress, a situation which any responsible government must want to relieve by restoring an adequate stock of currency, even at the sacrifice of redeemability.

The Lapse from Redeemability

A major war diverts national activity from sales abroad while it calls for enlarged supplies from abroad: therefore it causes a drain of specie. But it demands a domestic activity as great as possible and thus an ample supply of home currency: and it would be so even if the government balanced its expenditure, which it does not, therefore inflating the currency. This contradiction between more currency and less specie has repeatedly led to the suspension of redeemability, as in the case of the U.S. during their Civil War. It cannot astonish us that the phenomenon occurred in the European states, due to World War I.

But we may well ask why, contrary to previous experience, redeemability was never restored in its pristine perfection. Successively the various governments did place a stable gold value on their currencies, in some cases the same as before (Britain), in others much lower (in France one fifth), but gold coins did not go back into circulation: gold was paid out by the central banks against notes at the stated rates, but only in bulk and served only to settle foreign claims; gold moved from commercial banks across frontiers, it did not again move across the counter and from individual purse to individual purse. Strangely enough, in the country which had not lost but gained gold during the hostilities, in the United States themselves, coins were taken out of circulation (January, 1934).

What reason can be given for this disappearance of gold coins? A few figures may provide the answer. In 1890, the world stock of gold and silver money was estimated at about 8 billion dollars (the word billion is used in the American sense for thousand millions). Of this slightly more than half was silver. As the gold value of the dollar was, in 1935, brought down to 0.59 percent of its previous value, it appears that the 1890 metallic stock was equivalent to 13.5 billion dollars of today. Since that time, industrial production has risen, in the free world alone, 7.43 times. Assume that the needs for currency have moved in the same manner: the metallic stock should then be around 100 billions; the gold stock of the free world is, however, equivalent only to 35 billions, while the silver has been demonetized. This latter development had by itself shrunk the metallic supply relatively to economic activity well before 1914. Shortfalls in gold production, mainly due to refusals to raise its price appropriately, have since then accelerated the reduction of the metallic stock in proportion to economic activity. Hence the need to economize gold: it was taken out of circulation and served to cover, in ever smaller proportions, enlarged note circulations and banking accounts. This system is known, in jargon, as the Gold Exchange Standard.

But under such a system, external deficits dealt hammer blows to the national economy. Consider a country which uses a money supply amounting to 40 percent of its national income; let us assume that this money supply (i.e., notes and demand deposits) is backed by 20 percent of gold reserve: these then amount to 8 percent of national income. Now let us say that this country pays abroad yearly for goods, services, etc., 28 percent of its national income, and suppose that in a given year its income from abroad is only 24 percent of its national income; the external deficit is then only one-seventh of the volume of external relations: but it calls for settlement in gold amounting to 4 percent of national income; as the gold stock is 8 percent of national income, this stock will be halved. If this gold stock serves to back the money supply, that also will have to be halved! This would obviously be disastrous. Therefore the relationship between gold reserves and money supply was quite severed, and gold henceforth was devoted solely to external settlements. Symbolical of this change is the alteration of the Bank of England return on the outbreak of World War II: the 233 million pounds of gold which stood in the list of assets as backing for the note circulation were taken out and turned over to the Exchange Equalization Account: it was all needed for payments abroad.

Can Redeemability be Restored?

The restoration of a mandatory relationship between gold reserves and money supply does not seem feasible. The money supply of all sterling area countries amounted in 1952 to the equivalent of 25.7 billion dollars (according to the International Monetary Fund study). The monetary authorities of the area then held some 2.1 billion dollars' worth of gold plus 0.6 billion dollars capable of being turned into gold, a little over one tenth of their money supplies. Assume that a reserve requirement of one to ten were then established: twice in recent years, the sterling area has run an external deficit of well over a billion dollars (in 1949, 1.51; in 1951, 1.16); a similar episode, following the establishment of a statutory reserve requirement would cause a deflation of the money supply by well over one third! Nor would the problem be substantially altered if the requirement applied solely to the British money supply, then equivalent to 15 billion dollars. Nor is the difficulty specific to sterling countries: the aggregate of free-world non-dollar countries held in 1952 about 8.4 billions of gold plus 3.5 billions of dollar assets, amounting in all to one fifth of their total imports (60 billion dollars) and therefore capable of being affected by fluctuations in external balances to a degree disabling them from serving as a basis for about 80 billion dollars' worth of money supply.

On the other hand, if no relationship obtains between the money supply and reserves, an external deficit, draining away the latter, causes no effect upon the internal economy, capable of correcting the external deficit. Thus the deficit may proceed to far greater lengths than otherwise, indeed until external means of payment are utterly exhausted: an obvious way to stop this is to grant means of external payments only to the tune of gains achieved in external relations, and to apportion these means to the most useful purpose. This is the principle of exchange control. We thus understand how we have come to the present situation, and we realize that if we wish to rid ourselves of exchange control, some other method must be devised to check external deficits.

Substitutes for Exchange Control

We have a choice of two systems other than exchange control: the first course is to relinquish government control over the rate of exchange, the second is to increase central bank control over the internal economy. Either course will allow nationals to buy more freely abroad but neither will allow the nation to buy more from abroad. Much confusion arises over the notion that inconvertibility is an obstacle to trade. The amount of goods and services which residents of the sterling area may obtain from the dollar area is determined by sterling area's earnings of dollars for the goods and services it sells, plus the influx of dollars credits, and eventually grants. Whatever system obtains in the sterling area, the available amount of dollars constitutes the limit of dollar buying, stretched from time to time by losses of gold which must in time be recovered. This amount of dollars may be apportioned by the authorities according to their ideas of the most suitable employment, or it may be apportioned by a process of auction between sterling residents wanting dollars: the structure of imports will be different under the two systems, but the total volume of import trade will not be greater under the system of freedom: it may indeed be less.

If the demand for dollars is very active, it will push up the price of the dollar in pounds: such depreciation of the pound must cheapen sterling goods for the dollar buyers, more sterling goods will be sold and one generally assumes that therefore more dollar goods will be obtainable: this is far from certain. Assume that at one moment Britain is selling 100 million pounds' worth of goods and services to the dollar area, thus netting 280 million dollars: after a 20 percent devaluation these same things, selling at the same sterling prices, will bring 20 percent less in dollars (224 million) and to recover the same amount of dollar earnings, the volume of British exports must rise by one quarter: it will have to rise by as much as one half to net 20 percent more dollars than previously. The rise in dollar earnings through price depreciation, i.e., the possibility of obtaining more imports, is very uncertain. The more certain effect of exchange depreciation is to make foreign goods more expensive in our home currency and the consequent discouragement of import trade is the chief means whereby exchange depreciation procures equilibrium.

An unstable equilibrium attained by giving more domestic goods than before in return for less foreign goods than one previously obtained is not obviously a good thing, though many factors here have to be weighed: in fact there are few more intricate studies than that of the various effects of an alteration in the exchange rate.

Let us now consider the second course open to us. We want to do away with the apportioning of dollars by the authorities, but at the same time we are anxious that the exchange rate should not fall: this implies that the demand for dollars must somehow be calmed in order not to exceed the supply. This can be achieved by abating the domestic thirst for goods in general, by decreasing activity, which calls for imported raw materials, and decreasing real incomes, which call for imported food. Deflationary policies will dull the appetite of this nation. Is this a good thing?

If we wish to have freedom to buy foreign currencies while preserving reasonably stable rates of exchange, the internal economy must at all times be ruled by the overriding objective of keeping the demand for foreign currencies in equilibrium with the supply: therefore domestic policies cannot be determined by any other major objective, such as full employment, regular expansion and so forth.

As governments are now held responsible for welfare, it is to be asked whether a government acting in such a manner would not evoke serious, and justified, discontent. This is the heart of the convertibility problem. A country which seeks to preserve both stable exchange rates and the freedom of its citizens to acquire foreign currencies, must be ruled in its policies, not by internal considerations but by the necessity of keeping in step with the other countries: it must act as a part of the whole, as a member of a system. When this is grasped, it seems obvious, firstly, that it is more difficult to return to such membership after one has long departed from it than to remain within it, and secondly, that this discipline will prove more or less acceptable, according to whether the necessary discipline is more or less harsh.

The Pre-1914 Discipline

Whatever moralists, jurists and parliaments may advocate, formulate or decree, inequality is inherent in any system of relations. The City of London was the pivot of the pre-1914 system of commercial relations. Britain had lost its position as the chief industrial center of the world in the early 1880s but was the chief trading country and the hub of international finance. In the twenty years preceding World War I, Britain was the great market for international exports, and essentially for foodstuffs and raw materials, which constituted over four-fifths of her imports. This outlet was quite regularly enlarged at the rate of something like 2 3/4 percent per annum. This increased buying, necessary to the rise in British activity and living standards, afforded pounds to the sellers, who thus could also increase their imports.

Was this a world of extreme canniness in which other countries strictly avoided temporary deficits, and above all did not allow themselves chronic deficits? It was not. A system of international economic relations may be likened to a game which should be increasingly lively: it is therefore necessary that no player should ever be cleaned out, obliged to cut down his imports by one means or another and therefore the outlet afforded to the exports of others. The game leader, the City of London, was forever redistributing the counters: this gave time to make economic adjustments in an elastic manner; moreover, the provision of foreign credits helped deficit countries to improve their productivity: indeed some countries found it possible to play regularly beyond their means, thanks to a continuing influx of long-term capital.

No congestion of gold ever occurred in the world's then greatest creditor country, Britain: in twenty pre-1914 years England's accumulated intake of specie absorbed less than one-sixteenth of the amount of gold mined during the period; average net import of specie was equivalent to only 41 million dollars of today, and the largest intake in an exceptional year was only slightly above 120 million dollars of today. The intake of specie could be kept so small only through continual lending and investing abroad.

Britain was thus the moving spirit of the world economy. It is important to realize that she did not have to cut down her outgoing of pounds for merchandise or in credits, according to her foreign earnings: it was the other way around. She spent and invested abroad as fitted her, assured that the pounds thus sent out would return to her if not in payment for her goods then as balances in London. Any amount of pounds meted out to foreigners would find eager takers and holders. This situation does not obtain any more. England has ceased to provide an ever growing outlet for foreign goods: indeed the volume of her foreign buying is now less than in 1938.[1] Nor can England provide capital abroad in such quantities as she used to. Perhaps the main cause of this change lies in the unwillingness of foreign providers to use pounds in Britain, or the sterling area, and to their reluctance to keep pound balances in London. Britain must be cautious as to the amount of pounds she launches forth abroad because the recipients wish to turn them into dollars. There is, however, a remnant of the ancient city-ruled world economy, known as the sterling area. What in fact is the sterling area? It is the company of countries which are willing to hold pounds.

The Return to a System of World Convertibility

A world of convertible currencies must now center upon the United States. That country however does not have the same need for imports as Britain: its imports grow very irregularly and are cut back brutally when domestic fluctuations occur, which is understandable: if a country imports its whole supply of a certain material, a 10 percent cutback in consumption means a 10 percent cutback in imports; if, on the other hand, a country imports only 15 percent of its supply of this material, a 10 percent cutback in consumption may mean a two-thirds cut-back in imports. Nor do American banks provide finance for trade even between third countries as the City used to do: which again is understandable, as the U.S. are not a great sea-carrier interested in anything implying transport. Finally there is only a minute export of capital, comparatively speaking, concentrated on dollar countries. Indeed it seems that (excluding American governmental aid) American export of capital, at the height of her prosperity is less than the provision of capital by Britain and France to their monetary areas.

The great question mark then seems to be whether an ever-increasing outflow of dollars, for goods and services or in investments, will provide to the world of today the regular stimulus which was provided in the past by an ever-increasing outflow of pounds. If this occurs, a country like Britain can achieve convertibility with domestic comfort: if not, Britain can still achieve convertibility but only at the price of domestic discomfort.

The Position of Britain

Notwithstanding a 68 percent increase in the volume of her exports as against 1938, Britain, due to a fall of almost two-thirds in her previously important investment income, and due also to the far greater expensiveness of the primary products (which she buys) in terms of the manufactures (which she sells), can afford somewhat less than the volume of imports which she acquired in 1938. Her increased activity calls for a heightened quantity of raw materials, petrol and machinery: room has been made for these needs by a considerable decline in food imports and so-called nonessentials.[2] Clearly, if her activity is to increase, she will have to buy more raw materials: her exports must increase for that purpose. But if sterling residents are to be allowed to draw on foreign earnings for purposes of their own choice, which may well be so-called nonessentials, then these wants will compete for the available amounts of foreign currencies: therefore under this freedom, a greater increase of exports will be necessary to allow the acquisition of the increased raw materials supplies. If such an increase is not achieved, the choice made by the buyers of foreign currencies may restrict the means of expansion.

The increase in exports adequate to allow both for freedom and for greater supplies of raw materials hangs upon two conditions: there must be an increasing volume of world trade in manufactures, and Britain must win and maintain an adequate share of this trade. The first condition, under a world system of convertible currencies, depends chiefly on American policy. As to the second condition, if Britain, in the lines of goods which she offers for export, comes up against a growing competition from others whose productivity in those fields grows faster than her own, she may be able to achieve the desired objectives only by cuts in real wages. Or if she cannot achieve these objectives, her expansion will be hampered by her incapacity to pay the means to be imported from abroad.

External Convertibility

If we concentrate upon the notion that the true external problem is that of paying for the supply of goods regarded as necessary to the life and for the increasing welfare of the country, we can understand firstly the anxiety prevailing in official circles about the possible impact of true convertibility: given a limited supply of foreign currencies, how would the provision of vital supplies be affected by the freedom to use the nation's foreign earnings for other purposes? No one really knows beforehand. We can also understand how the problem of external convertibility has arisen.

Obviously a country can never have any difficulty in procuring the foreign goods and services desired if foreigners are willing to be paid in the buyer's currency. That was the happy position of Britain in the past. There was no question of finding pesos to pay imports from Argentine; the exporter's bank in Argentine was only too happy to pay him in pesos while acquiring a bill on London, which was desirable international currency, as good as gold for payments anywhere in the world. One may think of the pre-1914 world system as one in which City houses were putting into circulation international currency in the form of bills on London, currency which the banks of the whole world were using and glad to hold. One may also think of the developments since as a continuing "run" upon the City, foreign holders of bills on London proving increasingly eager to cash the bills on London in gold or dollars. At the outbreak of World War I, the *Economist* published a prophetic article underlining the importance to the world of the "bill on London" system of international currency and stressing that it would collapse if England intervened in the war. The process began with the refusal of American banks to hold bills on London: it was up to the British banks to find dollars for payments in the U.S. (and now the dollar area). The issue of external convertibility is raised because the banks of other countries also wish to encash bills on London in dollars.

When World War II broke out, Britain came to buy much more, while she sold less to other countries. Buying in the U.S. was conducted in dollars, as a consequence of which all the British gold migrated over the Atlantic up to the Lend-Lease agreement. Other countries, used to payment in pounds, continued to be so paid, but these pounds had ceased to command goods anywhere in the world, were good only as local money, and could not even be turned into British goods for want of the latter. Hence accumulated credits, known as the sterling balances. These were held in abeyance: at the end of the war the U.S. advocated their drastic reduction on the score that they were war debts incurred in the defense of the common interest; Britain however forbore to ask for any reduction. A problem was indeed set by Britain's current needs. Britain had to buy and those she wished to buy from were less eager for pounds than of yore: it was clear that Britain could only give her own goods. Therefore arose the so-called bilateral agreements. Britain would buy so much from Belgium and the Belgian National Bank would take up the pounds and sell them to its nationals wishing to buy sterling goods. Under the bilateral agreements, the pounds accruing to Belgian accounts were not to be turned to non-Belgians. This provision tended to oblige each country from which England bought to buy as much in return.

Since then, Britain has moved increasingly away from the principle of bilateral balance. Pounds earned by foreigners have been made transferable between certain countries, and finally the decision of March 19th, 1954, has made pounds transferable from any foreign country to another, outside the dollar area. This means that a foreign commercial bank in possession of pounds need not wait till one of its nationals needs them but may cede them to a foreigner–a practice which was current long before it was authorized.

Something more, and indeed something quite different, is widely demanded–to wit, that the Bank of England should, at the request of a foreign bank holding pounds, pay out dollars in exchange for them. This is a very different business. No matter in what foreign hands pounds paid out for British imports may end up, the commitment can be met out of sterling goods addressed to whoever wishes so to utilize the pounds. The logical worst which may then happen is a run on British goods, which is not such a bad thing. But if the Bank of England is bound to pay out dollars for pounds, this may lead to a run on its gold and dollar stock, which is very limited; and that precisely is what happened in 1947, when the Bank of England did assume such an obligation, which had to be promptly renounced.

It is felt that the pound would gain in stature if that obligation could now be assumed again and discharged with success. But the dangers are considerable. Firstly there is a danger that the British manufacturers may lose customers: at present British imports give rise to claims which may be encashed in British manufactures, not in American manufactures: if the pound is made convertible in dollars, some customers may shift their buying: as against this it is held that British industry is quite competitive. Secondly there is a danger arising from the fact that there is imperfect competition between the sterling area and the dollar area: even if sterling prices are competitive, still there are things to be found in the dollar area which foreign buyers would rather have than the things to be found in the sterling area.

The preparation of such a move as the convertibility of pounds in dollars calls for inconvenient measures. Because there may be important calls on Britain's reserves, British and sterling area buying from the dollar area has to be compressed in order to make way for buying in the dollar area via the pound by the foreigners. In order that they should not have excessive means to do so, the pound has to be made scarce abroad, and this is inconvenient to British exporters and for international trade in general.

Therefore there is a school of thought which advocates the preservation of pound inconvertibility in dollars and feels that the City of London might be again the center of a non-dollar trading area within which the pound would resume its ancient function of international currency: that is the inspiration of the so-called Strasbourg Plan. Others point to the fact that convertibility will be manageable only if the demand for dollars is diminished, and plead for a collective Western European tariff discrimination against dollar goods. The East-West trade issue grafts itself upon these preoccupations, as it is felt that the need for dollars would be less if some of the things currently obtained from the dollar area were obtained from the ruble area: it is however to be noted that Soviet rulers have grossly neglected precisely those productions which we would like to buy from them.

Conclusion

Two views may be taken of the problem: to some, Inconvertibility is "the wages of sin," the consequence of an improper conduct of internal affairs. There is something to be said for this view, but far less than is said. To others, Inconvertibility arises out of the formidable change which has occurred in human geography, over the last generation.[3] Leadership has passed from a group of Western European countries characterized by relatively scanty natural resources, having great, vital, and ever-increasing import needs, and interested in developing natural resources abroad for their own use, with their own capital, to a country abounding in natural resources, having little use for imports and little cause to invest abroad; a country moreover from which the former obtain a large fraction of their primary imports while it has little use for their manufactures. The world economy must adapt itself and this is not an easy process. Mutual comprehension, careful analysis, and a succession of unspectacular moves have already improved the situation almost out of recognition. Further progress will be made, quite possibly by complicated devices rather than through short cuts.

The following works are recommended:

Milton Friedman, *The Case for Flexible Exchange Rates* in *Essays in Positive Economics* (Chicago: University of Chicago Press, 1953).

J. R. Hicks, *An Inaugural Lecture,* in *Oxford Economic Papers* new series vol. 5, number 2.

Austin Robinson, *The Future of British Imports* and *The Problem of Living Within Our Foreign Earnings* (The Three Banks Review, March 1953 and March 1954).

J. E. Meade, *The Convertibility of Sterling* (The Three Banks Review, September 1953).

A. R. Conan, *The Sterling Area* (New York: Macmillan, 1952).

Sir Dennis H. Robertson, *Britain in the World Economy* (New York: Allen and Unwin, 1954).

A. C. L. Day, *The Future of Sterling* (Cambridge, U.K.: The Clarendon Press, 1954).

Roy Harrod, *The Dollar* (New York: Macmillan, 1953).

For British monetary regulations see the periodic surveys in the *Midland Bank Review* starting with the study in the issues of November 1947 and February 1948. For International Monetary Fund, *International Financial Statistics* and *Staff Papers*. For appreciations see the yearly report of the Basic Bank of International Settlements.

The pre-1914 situation may be grasped through:

A. K. Cairncross, *Home and Foreign Investment 1870–1913* (Cambridge: Cambridge University Press, 1953).

Werner Scholte, *British International Gold Movements and Banking Policy 1881–1913* (Cambridge, Mass.: Harvard University Press).

Benjamin Higgins, *Lombard Street in War and Reconstruction* (New York: National Bureau of Economic Research, 1949).

Notes

1. Cf. Austin Robinson, *The Future of British Imports* and *The Problem of Living within our Foreign Earnings* (the *Three Banks Review*, March 1953 and March 1954).
2. Cf. Austin Robinson, op. cit.
3. Cf. Roy Harrod, *The Dollar* (New York: Macmillan, 1953) and A. C. L. Day, *The Future of Sterling* (The Clarendon Press, 1954).

12

Reflections on Colonialism

I

The history of modern Europe is the history of an expansion occurring in two great waves: that of Western Christendom which began with the voyages of the Portuguese, and the expansion of Eastern Christendom across the Russian and Siberian plain. "Expansion," however, is too simple a term for various phenomena which to be properly analyzed must be subsumed under three great headings: conversion, commerce, settlement.

Under the first heading the European projection outward was spiritual. Missionaries at the cost of their lives sought to show the heathen the way to eternal life. And in a sense the various economic aid programs represent but a materialized version of the missionary spirit. To be sure, since our scale of values has altered, since we set less store on the Word of God than on technical know-how, we talk more about technical assistance than about salvation. But the basic attitude remains the same: let us teach the heathen–those without our knowledge–the way to a better life here and now.

Under the second heading, that of commerce, a different type of European went forth to seek goods for sale on the European market. Economists speak loosely of commerce having grown up *between* the various peoples of the world, as if indigenous Asian or African exporters shared equally in the development of world trade. Such was not the case, however. The conception of a world-wide market is a European conception, carried out by European "factors" installed abroad. World commerce was started to serve the needs of Europe and was conducted

Reprinted from *Confluence* 4 (October, 1955): 249–65. Reprinted by permission of the Summer School of Arts & Science and of Education, Harvard University.

between emigrant Europeans and stay-at-home Europeans. Time and again the local authorities sought to submit the European factors on their soil to local law or caprice; these attempts were punished by the exercise of European force. World commerce, in short, was run on lines laid down by ourselves.

The third type of European expansion involved settlement by Europeans, who took over large tracts of land by outright conquest or by the negotiation of contracts badly understood and soon repented by the sellers. If one compares the present map of the world with one of the fifteenth century, one can see at a glance that this peopling of outlying lands is quite the major phenomenon of modern history. In the fifteenth century the Europeans, including the Russians, were confined to the fringes of Eurasia. Today populations of European origin have overrun the American continent, Oceania, and Northern Asia, and are planted on the northernmost and southernmost parts of Africa. Contrary to general belief, "Europeans" are the people of the earth which have the most increased in numbers, because they have acquired enormous space.

Only a very insensitive mind could dwell with pride upon the European achievement. In balancing the good and evil which we have brought to other peoples, the work of our missionaries is incapable of outweighing our destruction of pre-existing communities: some peoples we have almost extinguished, others we have enslaved; there exists almost no non-European society which we have not hurt in some way, at the very least destroying its way of life, its values, its mores, its chances of autonomous development. We must be clearheaded, however; we can admit that it was all morally wrong, but we must recognize that at least one-third, and more probably one-half, of us would not be alive today had we not enormously enlarged our basis of life. None of the new nations of the European continent would exist; there would be no United States. That the most important Western nation has arisen out of colonialism is the foremost colonial triumph of European history.

We are eager to change our ways, of course. A cynic might observe that we can well afford to, considering how much of the planet has been permanently appropriated by "Europeans" (all through this paper, the term is used in its wider, historical sense). But we must be clear that our unqualified commitment to the principle of self-determination implies not only that the new nations are fully entitled to restrict international trade, or to deny access to their natural resources if they see fit, but also that they have complete freedom to select any form of government they desire. To be sure, nations recently promoted to independence have adopted political institutions drawn from one or the other of the Western nations; there is no certainty, however, that these institutions will work according to our customs, or indeed are suitable for all nations.

For the prerequisite of our political life is the alternation of political teams in office; and indeed what we think of as "democracy" is intimately bound up with this system of alternation, since our main liberties coincide with those which are necessary in order that the "outs" may rally the support whereby they can oust the "ins." Those who have been the spearhead of an independence movement, on the other hand, must naturally seek to encourage a consensus. Their success has been due to the active and organized support of their people; it is not natural that they should think of promoting an opposition. A one-party system which communicates the impulse downwards will tend to seem more suitable to the leaders of a new country than our system. In most western countries, moreover, with the U.S. a notable exception, there is no limit to what may be enacted into law, the limitations being provided by psychological *taboos*. In a new community these taboos may not be present, or may be very different from ours. We must be prepared then to find the politics of non-European peoples different from ours, and perhaps increasingly different. They naturally start with imitation, under the guidance of men who have had a Western training; but when the political interest of the unwesternized masses is awakened, characteristic features will appear. It is not implied that non-European standards of fairness will be lower than ours; historically it has rather been the reverse, but we must expect standards to shift until they settle down. These problems, while important, are not as immediate or critical as those which arise in territories where a substantial European population coexists with a more important non-European population, as is the case both in South Africa and in French North Africa.

II

The Pluricommunal State and the Democratic Principle. It has often been observed that the majority is by nature stronger than a king, and its sovereignty more absolute. A king is preserved in authority by the idea the people have of his right, an idea not different in nature from the ideas they have of other rights. The king must therefore regard every right existing in society as related to his own, and cannot undermine rights without undermining his crown. On the other hand, the majority has the power–as it is believed the people have the right–to alter, abolish or create rights. Indeed, it is because the kingly power was too weak to change rights in a manner suitable to the pace of social change that it gave way to a stronger authority. It has been stressed that the sovereignty of the people, by nature unlimited, is exceedingly dangerous to minorities.

To be sure, it has not turned out so in Western democratic states. This is because Western democracy developed in homogeneous communities, where people might find themselves in very different positions but not in inherently incompatible relationships; that is, they shared the same beliefs, the same customs. In such a community there does not exist *a* definite minority exposed to oppression. True, I may find myself overruled on a decision which matters to me, but it is highly improbable that I shall be overruled day after day with the same group of associates. I shall find myself in a decision-making majority on a second issue, in a minority again on a third issue, but a minority different from the former minority. It is convenient for the purposes of constitutional government to have two coherent *teams,* but this should not lead us to the supposition that within the nation there exist coherent *groups*, one of which will find itself in a permanent minority. Speaking of "two nations within one" is a figure of speech, and woe to the nation where it becomes a truth.

These remarks are trite, but they illustrate the dilemma posed when "two nations" really exist, two communities, distinct in origin, in language, in faith, in customs. In that case, the two communities can be made to live together in amity only under neutral law, under a government which obeys neither but serves both. If representative government is introduced, however, such a government will be representative of one or the other community, not of both. Palestine was for many years a headache to British statesmanship: this territory housed two distinct populations, Arabs and Hebrews; each "nation" had a "national will" but there was none common to both. In such a situation, the community weakest in numbers cannot accept, as the Hebrews would not, the institution of popular sovereignty; for the Arabs, who bitterly resented the settling of the land by the Hebrews, even though this was enriching the country and redounding to the benefit of all, would have exerted their communal will, made sovereign by their predominance in numbers, against the achievements and the very existence of the less numerous community. The problem was capable of no rational solution.

The same difficulty arises on North Africa, where France is caught between the conflicting demands of the settlers and of the "Arab" nationalists.[1] A century and a quarter after the landing of the French at Algiers, the European population in North Africa (to which the Italians and Spaniards have greatly contributed) is about equivalent to the population of North America a century and a quarter after the founding of New York. These people think of North Africa as a lesser New World; they would like to step up the influx of labor and enterprise from all the countries of Western Europe. Quite contrary to this wish, the nationalist leaders of the "Arab" populations, which have multiplied since the advent of the French, aim to set up independent national States, to which the settlers would be subject as non-voting aliens. In Tunisia and Morocco, which are Protectorates, the nationalist leaders have the letter of the law on their side; in Algeria, which is legally part of France, the reverse is true. But in neither case will the French setters accept the nationalist claims, because they fear it would leave them without any means of defending their rights in what they have come to regard as their homeland. It must be admitted that no one fears from the Tunisian nationalists anything like the discrimination applied in South Africa. But the strong moral guarantee afforded by so distinguished a personality as M. Bourguiba is valid only insofar as he, or his friends, control the government. Who can say to what extremes a National Assembly might go, in the joy and pride of new-found power? The French doctrine that whatever the National Assembly wills is law may then have fateful consequences.

Whether it be the lesser or the larger community which possesses the sovereign power in a pluricommunal state, the principle that the majority has unlimited authority to make the law is rife with dangers for any minority formally or effectively disenfranchised. There is no doubt moreover that communal antagonism becomes more rabid as one descends the social scale. It is the majority of the European settlers in South Africa which supports extreme policies of discrimination; again in North Africa, the most violent opposition to liberal policies comes from the lower strata of settlers, contrary to what is believed on a mythical basis by progressives at home. In short, the problem of the pluricommunal state seems to call for a government enjoying some independence from the drives of communal passion.

It is relevant that the organization of government in a multicommunal state has everywhere been found an intractable problem. In India, the distinction between Hindu and Moslem gave rise to partition. In the same manner, partition resulted in Palestine from the duality of Hebrew and Arab. North Africa now poses the same problem of duality. If French policy finds an adequate formula for self-government, theirs will be the first modern solution to the problems raised by the pluricommunal state, a solution in no way facilitated by the teaching which North African Moslem leaders have received in the French universities. They have learned there that "the law is the expression of the national will," a strong inducement to think that whatever the most numerous community may want will be the expression of justice. More empirical ideas on the nature of law and government might have been conducive to easier compromises.

III

Legality and Reality. But we have not as yet touched upon the most difficult part of the problem. While the main difficulty in the case of countries such as Tunisia and Morocco lies in the attitude of the settlers, all the moral and intellectual passions of Metropolitan France are involved in the case of territories such as Algeria and Africa south of the Sahara, which are legally part of France. The obstacles to self-government in those countries arise, strangely enough, not from French selfishness, but from French idealism.

When the Europeans first migrated overseas many were driven by the love of adventure, the lure of riches or the desire for fame; many others, however, thought of their ventures as missions to make known the true faith. Thus a strong strain of the apostolate entered into European expansion, and from the very beginning the Jesuits made a twofold effort: to bring the "savages" into the fold of Christianity, and to get these converts recognized by the European adventurers as co-equal with them.

From the outset, French colonization was deeply marked by the idea that the "savage heathen" were unlike us far more in the quality of heathen than in the quality of savage, and that they became "just like us" as soon as they were converted. This notion is clearly expressed in the charter which Richelieu granted in 1629 to the French West Indies Company, which prescribed that any Indian who became a convert acceded without any further formality to the full rights of a natural born Frenchman including the right of establishment in France on a basis of equality with all other subjects of the French King.

Here emerged two notions fundamental to French colonization: (1) it is a privilege to be a Frenchman, and (2) this privilege is obtained by the espousal of whatever is regarded as a morally determining factor, which at the time of Richelieu was faith. Nor did French sentiment rest on these propositions. By 1794, the National Convention of the French Revolution proclaimed that *all* inhabitants of territories under French rule, whatever their religious convictions, were free men and French citizens. And so it has remained to this day for the inhabitants of those territories which were French colonies at that time. Most of them, to be sure, were lost to English naval superiority in the Wars of the Revolution and of Napoleon. But an inhabitant of La Martinique or La Guadeloupe has been a French citizen for far longer than an inhabitant of Nice or of Chambery, since the latter until 1860 were subject to the King of Savoy. The Third Republic did not show the same enthusiasm for the granting of French citizenship. But in 1946 when the Constitution of the Fourth Republic integrated most of the former French Overseas Empire into the French Republic, it granted French citizenship to all the inhabitants.

As consequence, to the French mind, there is all the difference in the world between a Tunisian rebel who is agitating *for* the independence of his country and an Algerian rebel who is agitating *against* his country, i.e., France. In order to realize how the French feel about it, let the American reader imagine that the state of Mississippi proposed to secede from the American Union. An American citizen would regard this event in exactly the same light irrespective of whether it occurred while Mississippi had a "Caucasian" majority or had a colored majority; the latter are no less American than the former and no more entitled to break away from the American Union. Thus the inhabitants of all the territories integrated into the French Republic have, in French eyes, lost any right even to claim national independence. It would be a grievous misreading of the motives of the fathers of the French Constitution to believe that they had this objective in mind when they extended French citizenship to these people. They were conscious, not of taking something away, but of granting a great boon.

The real difference between the legal position and the actual position has tended to foster resentment rather than contentment. It is true that all Algerians and all Africans are Frenchmen, but it is not true that they have the same living standard, nor again is it true that they exercise the same political rights. If the overseas territories which are now component parts of the French Republic were represented in the Paris National Assembly on the basis of population–their population being about equivalent to that of Metropolitan France–one half of the French

Deputies would be elected in these overseas territories. In actual fact, the ratio is only about 12 percent, i.e., 68 Deputies out of 616.

It did not seem feasible to grant full voting rights to each and every inhabitant of the oversees territories, and transitory solutions were adopted of which the Algerian formula can be used as a significant example: all inhabitants of Algeria have a vote, but their votes do not count equally. There exists two bodies of electors unequal in numbers, which elect an equal number of deputies to the National Assembly in Paris as well as to an Algerian Assembly sitting in Algiers. The first body of electors is comprised of all French citizens of European origin, to which are added all the "Moslem Frenchmen" (the legal designation of Algerians not of European origin) with some minimum voting qualification such as possession of an elementary degree in education or service in the French army or the payment of a minimum tax. The remainder are collected in the second body. It is the aim of French policy to transfer an ever increasing number of "Moslem Frenchmen" into the First College. Thus the line of cleavage is not drawn on the basis of origin but on the basis of qualification. The "native" population (if that ambiguous term can be used when the great majority of Europeans in Algeria are themselves native to that country) is perhaps most aroused about the workings of this system on the municipal level. For it brings home to them the fact that municipal authorities are truly elected only where there is a European population, while they are nominated where the population is solely Moslem.

IV

On Being a Frenchman. This constitutional problem is magnified by a psychological one: in a Frenchman's eyes there exists no more desirable status than that of being a Frenchman; he understands that one should desire to become French, and indeed French nationality has been sought by large numbers of foreigners. He does not understand that one could wish to turn from French nationality to any other, and actually few have done so except in periods of persecution, such as the Revocation of the Edict of Nantes or the French Revolution, and, to a lesser degree, during the last war. All Frenchmen therefore believe that they have granted a great boon to residents of French overseas dependencies, and few stop to consider the actual reactions of the indigenous population. But whatever Frenchmen may believe, the acquisition of French nationality is satisfactory to foreigners only in proportion, first, to the absence of any formal alternative, and second, to the actual meaningfulness of the grant.

It was a more desirable thing to become French in 1794, when France ranked first among the nations, than in 1946. Moreover, there was no alternative at all for the emancipated slaves of the French American colonies. Take, on the other hand, the Moslem citizens of France. There is perhaps no more persistent cultural pattern than that of Islam, which shapes social life in all its aspects. A Moslem who has become a French citizen has not ceased to be a Moslem, and indeed this is recognized by French law which allows him to live under the Moslem law and the jurisdiction of Moslem courts. Thus he remains vividly conscious that his basic social culture (whatever his intellectual culture may be) is intrinsically different from that of other Frenchmen, a factor which does not intervene in the case of African Frenchmen who are not bound to a pre-existing highly evolved cultural pattern. Proceeding with the case of the French Moslem, we must also notice that he can look to independent Arab countries, and envision for himself an alternative destiny in an independent Arab state. More than that, the upper layer of the French Moslem citizens are aware of a superiority (which they owe to French culture) over the leading groups of a good many independent Arab states. They can therefore easily imagine themselves taking a major part in the leadership of the great Arab or Moslem world (two alternative concepts, each of which has its partisans).

Thus the mental image of "Frenchness" is made less appealing by virtue of an existing alternative. In short, the Moslem Frenchmen do not become French in the full sense of the word since they remain Moslems (this does not hold for Africans), and, on top of that, they can visualize another political destiny (this holds only to a lesser degree for Africans).

Another point needs to be considered here. While in Metropolitan France social distinctions are substantial, they are far smaller among Frenchmen of European origin living in a colony where only a very few are found in the very lowest economic or social brackets. Because in Africa Frenchmen are bureaucrats, entrepreneurs, managers, and, at the very lowest, foreman or skilled workers, the image of "Frenchness" is bound up in the native mind with the image of a certain minimum social status. Because the conveyance of French citizenship does not convey to the mass of those receiving it a social position similar to that enjoyed by French of European origin, it seems to the natives that they have been cheated of something which in their minds went with the quality of being French.

This sentiment is, of course, unreasonable; but it is not so unreasonable in the case of the most qualified natives, who feel that the acquired quality of being Frenchmen should give them more opportunities than in fact it does. Their complaint is commonly answered by the assertion that the Africans (or Moslems) to whom Europeans were preferred, were in fact *not* equally qualified. It is pointed out that even when the natives hold diplomas delivered by French universities, the natives are not equally qualified because diplomas are delivered to Africans and Moslems far more to reward attendance than to recognize achievements.

Be that as it may, the intellectual elite of French overseas dependencies feels cheated of the opportunity which citizenship of a great country should furnish. These people have a strong case. When regions differing very greatly in wealth are welded into the same State, it generally happens that the poorer regions send into the richer a stream of people who come to fill a great number of salaried positions, especially in the bureaucracy. France north of the Loire has a great number of bureaucrats who come from the less productive part of the country. The case of Corsica is even more characteristic: the large proportion of Corsicans in the French police and among the NCOs in the army is a well-known fact. The educated Africans or Moslems who are French citizens would be fully entitled to claim that openings should be made for them in Metropolitan France: this is implicit in the integration of the overseas territories with France. Quite evidently, it would bind these people to France were they to realize that, as Frenchmen, they enjoy opportunities which they would have to forego if they obtained national independence. To be sure, a number of instances of this kind can be cited: the president of the French Senate is a colored senator from Guyana; high positions in the French central administration are filled by Moslem Algerians. But these instances remain so few as to have only symbolic value. Their occurrence can be translated in the following language: "the example testifies that the French acknowledge the principle. But the example is so rare that it demonstrates French failure to apply the principle in fact." The distance between the ideal and reality is characteristic of French practice.

Since French citizenship does not in fact convey to Africans or Moslems many opportunities in Metropolitan France, they are all the more sensitive to the fact that the integration of their country with France excluded them from some local opportunities which independence would afford them. The relative scarcity of bureaucratic positions available to educated Moslems and Africans has been perhaps the major psychological factor in turning their minds toward political independence. This exclusion of the native is by no means a deliberate attitude of the French Government. It is much more the result of a closing of the ranks against outsiders on the part of bureaucrats coming from Metropolitan France. In the case of Tunisia, no single element has played so great a role in aggravating tensions as the closing of bureaucratic ranks against undoubtedly qualified Tunisians.[2]

V

From One Ideal to Another. The declaration that all inhabitants of Overseas France were equally Frenchmen was a great ideal, but it raised higher expectations than were or could be fulfilled, even if the pace had not been slowed by the social friction of a reluctant bureaucracy. As a consequence, hopes were in quick succession raised very high and then dashed, leaving a feeling of frustration and even of betrayal.

It was felt that the French had not really meant what they said–which was an error, for they did mean it albeit without taking steps to make their meaning operative. Quite a few Moslems and Africans came to think that the enjoyment of actual equality within the great French Republic straddling the Mediterranean was an illusion and that another and more attainable idea should be substituted, i.e., national independence. The progress through disappointment from one ideal to another can be illustrated in the career of the able Algerian leader Fehret Abbas, who began by agitating for the full exercise of French citizenship by Moslem Algerians and who, disappointed in this campaign, then rallied to the ideal of Algerian separatism.

Indeed, the full force of French education militated in favor of national independence rather than of a great blending of peoples within a vast commonwealth. For the history of France, which Africans and Moslems have been taught as a matter of course, underlines at every step the rejection of foreign rule. The kingdom of France arose in the tenth century as a token of the rejection by the French of the political unification of Western Christendom under an emperor who claimed to renew the Roman tradition. The kings of France were always meticulous to reject any semblance of subordination to the emperor: when the Emperor Charles the IV visited his nephew King Charles the Fifth of France, the latter mounted his uncle on a black horse while reserving a white one for himself as a symbol of sovereignty. The greatest hero of French history is Joan of Arc, whose feat is recounted as "ousting the foreigner," even though this foreigner was the French-speaking son-in-law of the former French king. France, throughout the nineteenth century, was the foremost exponent of the principle of nationalism, and the French could not be persuaded either by Proudhon or by Thiers that this principle would help to build up across the Rhine a dangerous threat to France. So wedded are the French to this principle that when their ally, the czar, was overthrown by revolution, and when their comrade in arms, the Russian people, stopped fighting by their side, Clemenceau gloried in this desertion saying that even though France has lost a great ally, she could rejoice because henceforth she could demand the national independence of Poland. Although the partition of Austria-Hungary at the end of the First World War was recognized by the foremost French diplomats as disastrous to the European equilibrium, it was favored by the full force of French public opinion, because several nations acquired thereby a political life of their own.

Such are the lessons which the Moslem or African people of France have learned from French education. Little wonder, then, that they should come to think in terms of national independence. But, on the other hand, French public opinion is traditionally attached to the ideal of complete national unity. If there is one point on which the Jacobins of the French Revolution had the full backing of public opinion, it was on their opposition to the Girondins, champions of local self-government, who were represented by their foes as standing for the dismemberment of France. French ideals thus war with one another. The American reader will find this exposition singularly lacking in economic terms. This is not for lack of awareness that the development of French overseas territories, while extremely costly to France, has been inadequate to raise rapidly the living standard of the population to the level of that of France proper. But the more one ponders the crisis unfolding in the various French overseas territories, the more one grows conscious that its main feature is a battle of ideals which takes place within the context of French thought and French political vocabulary. The main rebels against French rule in the French overseas territories are also the personalities least foreign to France: they can be recognized as conscious replicas of Lafayette, Mirabeau, or Robespierre. They are playing a role against France which is taken from a French script.

VI

The New "New World." There is a final problem too often obscured by the millennial hopes of new nations. Let us assume that all of Africa, with its vast spaces and its scant populations, is fragmented into sovereign states. Is it not clear that the emptiness of these states will attract the packed crowds of Asia? Have we any reason to suppose that Asian nations react differently to population pressures than those of the West? In short, it is conceivable that Africa may be the Asians' New World.

It surprises me to find how readily one assumes that economic progress is just a matter of know-how and capital, and how far one disregards the importance of natural resources. Why did the same people, in North America, forge ahead of their counterparts in Europe? Because emigration was a selection of the most enterprising, because they operated on a field less cluttered with regulations? These factors certainly contribute, but surely the main and decisive difference was the far greater abundance of natural resources. Nor am I thinking primarily of coal, oil and other raw materials, but chiefly of land. The formidable economic advantage which the U.S. has enjoyed over Europe can be reduced to the fact that Americans have been easily and amply fed by the effort of a far lesser part of their working population than has been possible within any other area of the world, so that a far greater percentage of the total work-time of the population has been available for other labors.

When we casually say that the other peoples of the world are to be raised to the American standard of living, I wish we were realistic enough to translate this statement into the physical terms it implies. The Paley Report gave the consumption of foods and raw materials per head in the U.S.: take this as the basis of the American standard of life, and multiply it b͜ the number of inhabitants of the earth. The first thing which will strike you is that there is simply not enough land available to sustain the cattle necessary to generalize American consumption of meat throughout the world. The extensive methods of cultivation which stand back of American industrialization and which industrialization has helped to develop, are not practical in Asia, where the problem is not to economize man-power in agriculture, but to economize the scarcer factor, land. The point has been effectively made that some of the areas we term "underdeveloped" are in fact over-cultivated, the intensive use of labor on land keeping more people alive on a given territory than we would deem feasible.[3] Obviously, in such cases, the population cannot afford animal foods which are more land-consuming than vegetal foods. In fact one may query whether the "European" peoples, with whom the consumption of animal foods is an index of the living standard, are not able to afford these animal foods because they occupy an inordinate fraction of the planet's surface; force them back into Europe and they would have to be vegetarians.

Moreover, it is obvious that where it takes much labor to produce little food, only a small fraction of the population is available for other economic functions. Industrialization is dependent upon agricultural improvement.[4] We can easily understand the formidable progress of industrialization in the world of "Europeans" if we think of the enormous areas of arable land which they have conquered. Taking the Europeans as a whole, the procuring of food has been enormously cheapened for them in terms of labor by the expansion of the territory they command.

In the abstract, one may conceive that the most densely populated areas of the world, such as Southeast Asia, should barter industrial wares for foods produced in the vast expanses of North America and Russia. In fact, the U.S. is certainly not prepared to be a massive importer of industrial goods produced with cheap labor.

Merely touching upon these problems suggests that a narrowing of the gap in the living standards of the Asian peoples and the American citizenry is in no sense probable. The inequality of physical assets is far too great. It further suggests that the ceaseless propounding of the American standard of living as a model for less favored nations implies a fallacy which must logically excite land-hunger in the closely packed populations of Asia. There are many subjective causes of imperialism, but there is also an objective cause: the insufficient carrying capacity of the territory one occupies and the availability of other territories over which one may spread and scatter. There is no such objective cause for Russian imperialism; but there is such an objective cause for Asian imperialism, and its most obvious goal is Africa.

It is one of our fondest delusions that all nations should be equally content if each obtains its political independence within the confines of the territory it happens to possess at this moment. This however implies a once-for-all attribution of natural resources, and an extremely unequal division of physical assets per head. This would not matter in a world where men might move freely; but that is excluded. In our world, where, under our Western teaching, people have been led to conceive the Good Life in terms of rising material standards, and governments have been made responsible for this increase, the struggle for land appears as a logical outcome.

Notes

1. "Arab" is of course an improper term to designate populations of very various origins. It is used here for the sake of brevity. The non-Europeans are officially designated as "Tunisians" and "Moroccans" in the two countries where they alone are "nationals"; in Algeria they are distinguished, when necessary, by the term "French Moslems."
2. The language of this paragraph should not be taken as implying that administrative careers are closed to Africans or Moslems, the reverse is true; but the quota of higher positions filled by Europeans is quite excessive.
3. Cf. N. Koestner, "Marginal Notes on the Problem of 'Underdeveloped Countries.'" Wierschaftdienst Kiel, May 1954.
4. Cf. Arthur Lewis, "Economic Development with Unlimited Supplies of Labor." *The Manchester School*, May 1954.

13

On the Character of the Soviet Economy

Man is free to choose his purpose: but once wedded to a purpose, he is bound to the conditions of its fulfillment. The avowed purpose of the Soviet government is to bring Russian industrial power, in the shortest possible time, to parity with that of the United States. There is nothing specifically "communist" in this purpose. Indeed it stands in stark contradiction to the Marx-Engels picture of a communist economy which would not be concerned with building-up of capacities but with their full employment for the consumer satisfaction of the workers. The purpose of the Soviet government might just as well be that of a modern Colbert whom we can imagine presiding over the eventually blended destinies of the six European nations which have begun to associate in the Coal-Steel Community.[1]

It is worth stressing that the Soviet program is the conscious and systematic imitation of something which exists, but which was not brought about either consciously or systematically. Take, for instance, steel: steel capacity did not, in the U.S., reach its successive levels because someone enjoying supreme power had decreed that steel capacity should reach such a level by such a date, but additions to capacity occurred in response to demands made upon it by steel-consuming industries, which, in turn, attuned their capacities to rising demand, ultimately consumer demand. There is no question in Russia of steel capacity growing under the prodding of demand: it must grow, period. Evidently if the growth of steel capacity is regarded as an end in itself, it can be best served by reserving all the steel presently produced for the building of more steel capacity.

Reprinted from the *The Bulletin of the Atomic Scientists*, Vol. 13 (November, 1957): 327–330. Reprinted by permission of *The Bulletin of the Atomic Scientists*, © 1957 by the Educational Foundation for Nuclear Science, 6042 South Kimbark Avenue, Chicago, Illinois 60637, USA.

This is, of course, driving things to the extreme; but it can serve at least to stress the orientation of Russian industry. Russian industry is, to a considerable degree, employed in producing industrial capacity. Of course every industrial nation has some part of its industrial plant engaged in producing plant and equipment. This is necessary in order that plant and equipment which wears down or becomes outdated can be replaced, and so that in every field the productive apparatus can be enlarged and improved.

But in Russia the production of plant and equipment has absolute priority, which is understandable enough, given the aim, which is to reach a stated level of productive capacity. According to the statistical publication which the Soviet government has recently brought out, industrial production in Russia consisted of consumer goods in the proportion of 66.7 percent in 1913, of 60.5 percent in 1928 (when total industrial production was no greater than in 1913, as far as one can tell on other authorities), and the proportion of consumer goods in total industrial production fell successively to 29.4 percent in 1955, the last figure given, producers' goods having risen to 70.6 percent of total industrial production. The Russian publication also gives indexes of growth of the two sectors of industry: all outside experts agree that these indexes are fantastically exaggerated, but the relation between the two indexes may presumably be trusted. From 1928 to 1955 it is claimed that the sector producing means of production multiplied its output almost thirty-nine times, while the sector producing consumer goods multiplied its own output only nine times.

The much faster expansion of the sector producing means of production has been obtained by a priority which is perhaps the decisive feature of the Russian economy. That sector, which bears the A label in Russian economic vocabulary (as against the B label for consumer goods industries) is bidden to produce means of production for itself instead of producing them for the consumer goods industries. The Soviet reasoning is that providing plant and equipment to consumer goods industries competes with providing the same to producer goods industries, and that the faster the A sector grows, the easier it will be for it then to fill out the voids existing in the plant and equipment of the consumer goods industries.

The logic of this reasoning cannot be attacked. It is quite true that the more steel that goes into not only motorcars but also the motorcar industries, the less there is available for building steel furnaces and hydraulic presses; and that the sooner you have a great deal of the latter, the easier you will find it to equip the motorcar industry.

Russian economic history from 1928 to date can be contrasted with American economic history up to 1914 as a thing different in kind: building as against growing. In the process of growth, the bones and the flesh develop together. In building, you first construct the skeleton, then you put on the flesh: that is the Russian formula–which is incidentally convenient for purposes of world power since it gives you means of war far in advance of your means of comfort.

Investment, Saving, and Political Structure

An economy is most easily understood if you analyze it in terms of concrete goods. The manpower of Russian industry has risen from less than 4 million in 1928 to approximately 18 million in 1956: this is about the same manpower as that of American industry. Russian industry however produces less of everything, and the difference in amounts produced is far more pronounced in consumer goods than it is in investment goods. There are indeed some investment goods which are produced in greater quantities in the USSR than in the U.S. In other terms, the percentage of resources going into investment activities is much higher in Russia than in America. If this fact is formulated in the language of national financial accounting, we have to say that the rate of investment within the industrial product is very much higher in Russia than in the U.S....

Marx's critique of the capitalist system was based upon his postulate that the whole of added value belonged by right to the workers: and therefore the distribution of profits was an expropriation of the workers. It was an injustice, but at the same time it was necessary. Only through profits, as he clearly saw, could there be reinvestment, building up of the productive apparatus. Therefore this injustice would have to endure until the productive apparatus had been sufficiently built up. When no further capital investment was necessary, then the capitalist would become unnecessary. But he would not readily perceive his redundance; therefore he would have to be forcibly done away with. His redundance would be revealed by the fact that he would be able to find no productive employment for the capital arising out of profits: opportunities to invest would have withered away, and therefore his levy upon added value would be useless and nefarious, depriving the working consumers of the buying power needed to absorb rising production.

The historical necessity of the capitalist's disappearance was based primarily upon the postulate, widely prevalent in Marx's day, of the dwindling opportunities for productive investment: this is to be found in Ricardo. It was based also on the assumption that capitalists would not allow workers to get directly or indirectly (through government redistribution) a rising share of added value. On the other hand, the capitalist was held necessary for the process of accumulation because Marx could not imagine (and here he was no doubt right) that the workers, if they received the whole of added value, would be willing to save a large part of it for investment.

The class struggle was regarded by Marx as a struggle over "value added," the workers wishing to obtain the whole of it and to apply it to consumption, the capitalists wanting to retain as much of it as possible, and to apply it to investment. The workers were bound to win this fight, but not as long as it was socially useful that accumulation should proceed. And therefore it was also a historical necessity that capitalists should retain their power to make profits as long as accumulation had to proceed.

Communism as Super-Capitalism

When things are looked at from this angle, it becomes quite clear that the Soviet government plays the part of the capitalist as seen by Marx. Just as Marx pictured the capitalist, the government gives the workers the smallest possible share of "added value" and retains the largest possible share in order to apply it to investment. No doubt a true democracy of workers would, within an individual company, assign a far greater part of the financial product to wages, and, within the nation, address a far larger share of activities to consumption-serving activities. This tendency must be overcome in the interests of accumulation, and therefore there must be a despotic authority to do it.

No such thing was conceived by Marx. While this point cannot be stressed here, it may be mentioned that the term, "dictatorship of the proletariat," was not understood by Marx to connote the strengthening of the state's power; the state, on the contrary, had to be destroyed root and branch, and by "dictatorship of the proletariat" Marx meant that workers' councils should be bound by no law until the liquidation of the privileged classes had been completed.

What interests us here however is simply the fact that in order to obtain rapid accumulation of productive assets, it is necessary to tilt the balance of power against the workers' eagerness to consume. This tilting was achieved in capitalist society, as Marx saw it, by the economic power of the capitalists, able to employ workers at a mere living wage. Why were they able to do so? As Marx saw it in England, there were three contributing factors: firstly, the rapid influx of candidates for industrial employment, due in small part to the rise in population and in major part to the flight from the fields. Secondly, because the capitalists owned the means of production and were free to give or deny employment: they held the whip-hand. Thirdly, they were able to do this because of the backing which the capitalists received from the state, which was a "class-state," the state of the capitalist class.

It is quite clear that in the capitalist countries of our day, there is no excess offer of manpower, thanks to policies of full employment. It is also clear that the government has ceased to be the wholehearted supporter of the employers as against the employees. Insofar as it departs from neutrality it does so in espousing the interests of the employees. Under such conditions, the ownership of the means of production does not give the capitalists the whip-hand over the workers, the power to dictate the share these will get.

On the other hand, we do find in Russia the precipitate influx of workers depressing the labor market which Marx observed in England in his day, and which led to the "hard times" described by Dickens. And we do find the solidarity between employers and government which Marx thought characteristic of capitalist society: this solidarity is based on the fact that the employers are the instruments of government, which is completely at one with them.

We are therefore tempted to conclude that Soviet communism as we see it today is a synthetic version of early industrial capitalism.

Are These Sacrifices Necessary?

A question, however, arises, which does not seem to have been asked in the leading circles of Soviet Russia: was it really necessary to reproduce, as it were systematically, all the most regrettable traits of capitalist growth, to condense and accentuate them? This is surely a relevant question, when Soviet economic development is imposed as a model upon the satellite European nations, accepted as a model by the leaders of Communist China, and suggested as a model for the underdeveloped countries of the world. There is no more urgent task for Western economists than to give an answer to this question, as upon this answer may turn the choices made by leaders of the uncommitted areas of the world.

Obviously, an adequate answer cannot be offered here. Some rough suggestions may, however, be put forward for further thought. To begin with, it is a puzzling fact that while the purpose of the Soviet leaders has been to repeat the American performance, their concept of procedure has not been taken from direct pondering of American growth but at second hand from Marx's analysis of British industrial growth...

Such a study would no doubt have brought to the fore, among other points, the enormous part played in American industrial growth by the high and rising productivity in agriculture, a feature to which American industrial workers owed their initially high living standards. The lack of any reference to the American experience seems all the more absurd on the part of the Russian leaders, since what they wished to emulate was the U.S., and since the natural resemblance of the USSR physical data was plainly to the U.S. and not to Britain. This neglect can be explained by mental enslavement to the Marxian model.

But let us take up the problem from another angle, and make the questionable assumption that the basic equipment of the USSR could not have been built up to its present pitch in the given period of time by any other procedure than that which was adopted.[2] Then the discussion might turn upon the question whether so steep a rise by so arduous a path was a desirable thing.

Let us further assume that Russia persists in its procedure of rapid growth, and therefore catches up with the U.S.[3] in basic capacities by a certain date T, and in production of consumer goods by a certain later date T'. Is anyone ready to argue that the total welfare of the Russian people between the years 1928 and T' will have been maximized by the procedure followed? Is it not far more plausible that the total welfare of the generations concerned would have been greater if a less arduous path had been followed?

It is natural to discount very distant satisfactions as against immediate satisfactions. Tinbergen has produced striking estimates of such discounting.[4] Acting as self-constituted "representatives" of the Russian people, the Soviet leaders seem to have turned things the other way round and to have set future satisfactions at a premium as against the present. But have they really reasoned in this manner? And have they not rather thought in terms of equalization of power?

For over a century, starting with Sismondi if not earlier,[5] there has been a ceaseless critique of capitalism, arguing that its unquestionable achievements in the building up of capacities were not worth the price paid in the uprooting and hustling of men, that in fact men would have been better off, and happier with a more leisurely pace of change than that forced upon them by capitalists and their sales pressure. It is interesting to find the communists enamored of the buildup achieved by the hated and despised capitalism, to the point of thinking that its speedy emulation justifies greater pressure upon men than was ever exerted under capitalism.

Notes

1. These nations, France, Western Germany, Italy, Belgium, the Netherlands, Luxembourg, muster together 160 million inhabitants. They are however far poorer in natural resources than either the U.S. or the USSR.
2. We can note this analogy in respect of steel production: in Russia it rose from 4.5 million tons in 1928 to 45 million tons in 1955. In the U.S. it rose from 4.5 million tons in 1894 to 45 million tons in 1917.
3. As far as one thinks of consumer goods, one should, of course, picture the catching up as involving equalization of consumer goods per capita; it one thinks of power, then the catching up is to be thought of as merely the equality of productive capacities between the two nations, regardless of differences in population.
4. See Tinbergen's remarkable article in the *Economic Journal*, December 1956.
5. One might say that this critique starts with Rousseau's *Discourse on the Sciences and the Arts*.

Part Three:

The Political Economy
of Natural Resources

*"In a highly organized society such as ours,
Nature disappears behind the mass of our fellow-
creatures; each individual believes that his living
depends on his relationship with his fellows, the
services he renders them, and the return he
receives for these; he has forgotten that he lives on
what the population of which he is a member can
draw from its natural environment. Everything he
makes use of seems to him to be the product of
human labor; this is true so far as concerns its
form; but its substance is obtained from Nature.
We recognize our borrowing from Nature in bread,
but we forget it in the airplane—in its body, whose
components are minerals, its rubber tires, and the
fuel it obtains from the bowels of the earth."*

—"From Political Economy to Political Ecology,"
1957

14

A Place to Live In

We are the first of mankind to see and sense the Earth as a small place. I can now hang upon my wall, just as easily as a picture of my own house, a photograph of our terrestrial ball taken from outer space. But the essential reason for our new assessment of our planet is our recent ability to move to almost any point of the sphere within a day or two. Distances have been contracted by a miraculous increase in our speed of displacement. It is a common saying that thought is quicker than action: this holds true in cases of imagination, not so in the case of more reflective use of the intellect. Our popular fiction now, boldly over-stepping our powers, sets its adventures in "The Galaxy"; in the meantime, however, our approach to our here-and-now problems is still weighted down by our age-old habits of slow movement. Our views lag far behind the change in our circumstances: this change deserves to be stressed.

The Revolution of Speed

For many centuries, the fastest means of land transport was by horse. Given roads or tracks, a horseman can cover seventy-five miles a day; across country, the cavalry of Alexander the Great is said to have covered the same distance in thirty-six hours: two thousand years later this was still accounted a remarkable performance. Cruising speeds maintained over a long journey were of course a good deal lower: an average of forty-five miles was very fair. Horse-drawn wagons, when loaded, could under the most favorable circumstances equal the achievement of a walker. Thus, during the long-lasting Age of the Horse, there was a

Reprinted from *Modern Age* 4 (Winter 1959/1960). Reprinted by permission of the Intercollegiate Studies Institute, 3901 Centerville Rd., P.O. Box 4431, Wilmington, Delaware 19807.

low "ceiling" on the speed of human displacement. This can be illustrated by an anecdote involving that exceptionally dynamic figure, Napoleon. In September 1805, he proposed to "fall upon the Austrians like a bolt," and for that purpose he transported himself in his specially equipped car from St. Cloud to Strasbourg in three days: this amounts to one hundred fifty miles a day, and involved the frequent change of the best horses available to the Emperor.

Not only was the horse slow according to our modern reckoning, but moreover the diffusion of its employment was slow. The horse was domesticated more than five thousand years ago in the great plains of Central Asia. But within classical Greece it was a scarce asset and its ownership a badge of class; the same situation obtained in the Roman Empire and in feudal Europe, which was all but overwhelmed on several occasions by an avalanche of Asiatic horsemen. Even though our children associate "Red Indians" with horses, we know that horses were introduced on the American continent only by Cortès, who owed his conquest of Mexico in no small part to the impression made upon the Aztecs by this hitherto unknown animal.

Turning our attention to sea transport we find that the transatlantic clippers, soon after the Napoleanic wars, held an average cruising speed of over one hundred fifty nautical miles per day on their westward journey, a performance which was halved on the eastward passage. Strangely enough, a Viking ship is said to have done as well a thousand years earlier, crossing from Norway to Iceland in four days at an average of one hundred fifty sea miles per day—or so a saga bids us believe. We have more solid authority, that of Thucydides and Xenophon, for the achievements of Athenian triremes twenty-five centuries ago: we are told of one such ship covering one-hundred sixty miles in twenty-four hours, and of another covering six hundred twenty miles in four and a half days—of course impelled by a combination of sail and oar. It seems then that the great gain in navigation which had been achieved over the years was not mainly one of speed: it was an enormous improvement in seaworthiness and manageability, the major step of which was made in the construction of the Portuguese caravels in the fifteenth century, thanks to which Columbus reached the New World.

It is indeed fascinating to think that an improvement in the design of the sailing ship, and mainly of its rudder, allowed the hub of the modern world to be transferred from the Mediterranean to the Atlantic: it would surely be wrong to say that this technical factor was the cause of the event, but it was its precondition. And if an alteration of means, relatively so small, has been followed by so major an alteration of circumstances, what can we not expect to follow now that man has made a prodigious break through the long-lasting ceiling on his speed?

The gain in speed achieved over the Age of the Horse ranges from ten to one in the case of the motorcar to as much as a hundred to one in the case of the jet airplane. The change seems even more sensational when we associate with the increase of speeds the increase of weights which can be moved. By far the most striking progress of human technique is that which affects the transportation of persons and goods. The economic benefits derived therefrom are too well known to need any stressing. Instead, I should like to draw attention to some of the political consequences.

Political Consequences of Speed

Let us compare the desks of Augustus, Jefferson, and Eisenhower. To all three desks come news "from all over the world." There is a great difference between the desk of Jefferson and that of Augustus: since a far smaller fraction of the world was known to the Roman emperor than to the American president, news came in from fewer points, and the geographic coverage of information was very much narrower. But there is a no less important difference between the desk of Jefferson and that of Eisenhower. News reaching Jefferson [was] affected with time lags which distance and difficulty of communication often made considerable. Therefore the picture of the world pieced together by Jefferson from all items of information was a picture made up of nonsimultaneous events and situations, even as is the case today with our picture of the heavens. Many "facts" he took into account had ceased to be "facts" by the time they had become "information" available to him. It is otherwise with Eisenhower: in his overall picture of the world there are no outdated elements; all the "facts" of which he is informed are "live facts," facts in being.

It is a novelty that information should be instantaneous. But it is an even more important novelty that action at a distance should be near-instantaneous. The Berlin airlift in 1948 was a striking demonstration in this respect, intervention in Korea another; the French airlift to Madagascar offers a recent illustration: a century and a half ago relief would have reached the island at best four months after the disaster, whereas in this case the delay was only three days.

Any increase in man's power involves greater possibilities not only for good but also for harm; while it is unhealthy to concentrate upon the latter, it is unwise to ignore them. In past ages mere distance afforded a protective cushion to local authorities and national security. Slow and costly communications opposed a physical obstacle to the centralization of decisions in a country's capital. As all incoming information had to be borne by messengers, and all outgoing orders to be conveyed in the same manner, no central government could bear the costs involved in keeping sufficiently informed about local conditions to make decisions concerning them. Further, in the case of any rapidly changing local situation, the time-lag between composing a report and receiving the corresponding instructions was apt to stultify the latter. Therefore it was in the very nature of things for local problems to be coped with by local authorities. And even if local dispositions ran counter to the will of the central government, it was such a complex and lengthy operation to bring agents of enforcement to bear that it was practical to let the local people settle their own affairs except in extreme cases. When such physical circumstances are kept in mind, it becomes clear that the opportunities for far-reaching dictation were insignificant compared to what they are today. Political despotism as we know it is a novel phenomenon. Not only were the kings of Western European states quite bereft of formal despotic authority; even the tsars and sultans and other Asiatic rulers, to whom despotic authority did belong, lacked the means to exercise this despotism throughout their vast empires.

It was an old Asiatic tag that if you wished to be safe from the will of the ruler you should stay away from his court; but now this is not enough; the ruler's eye and hand are everywhere. In the same manner it was an old European tag that if you wished to be safe from a surprise inroad of foreigners you had to stay away from the seashore. This latter idea dates back to the snatch raids of the Vikings. Seapower was always the power to surprise. But even in the heyday of England's mastery of the seas, the sharpest blows which England could deal at an enemy without warning were to pounce upon its merchant ships on the high seas and to bombard its naval forces in port. The more vital threat of invasion was one of which the intended victim inevitably obtained ample warning. It took a great deal of time to assemble infantry forces, which lumbered forward at a slow pace. It followed that the threatened nation was always at leisure to muster its own forces. Although it could be swamped by a great superiority of forces, it could not be struck down by surprise.

I clearly remember the discussions on the prevention of aggression which were initiated at the League of Nations thirty-five years ago; we then worked on timetables involving two assumptions. One was that quite some time would elapse during which the preparations of the aggressor would make his intentions manifest, and that this afforded a period for diplomatic intervention by the Council. The second assumption was that if the aggressor did indeed strike, the actual progress of his operations would be sluggish enough to allow the rescue of his victims by means of a long-drawn procedure comprising three stages: the formal decision by the Council to call upon member states, the mustering of forces by these states, and their combination on the field. It was stoutly maintained by British and Scandinavian representatives that the prior availability of some forces of intervention was unnecessary. All this implied a leisureliness which now seems quaint. Such procedures are clearly inadequate to the danger of a missile attack, where there is no preaggression period during which visible preparations invite diplomatic action, and no postaggression period during which the victim is still unharmed enough to be rescued by hastily joined international forces.

Thus we find that our gains in speed place the subject more in the hand of the ruler, and the nation more at the mercy of a foreign power than was the case until our time. This conclusion can be used to depress us or to fortify our spirit. It can fortify our spirit if we perceive these chances for evil as a challenge to mankind. By our own material achievement we are driven so to educate ourselves that we shall forbear from harmful uses of our powers.

Social Consequences of Speed

The population of the Earth has increased more since the beginning of our century than it had done in the preceding two hundred fifty years. Furthermore, the rate of growth is increasing: two hundred years ago it required a good one hundred fifty years for the doubling of the population; by a century ago, this duplication period had fallen to about one hundred ten years; on the basis of current trends, which may of course change, the duplicating period has shrunk to forty years. Demographers worry over this and foresee an overcrowded planet, but any difficulty due to mere numbers stands a long way in the future and can be coped with in ample time. Speed, however, is a much more effective and immediate cause of overcrowding. A simple comparison will show how this is so.

We all know that if we heat a gas, it seems to demand more space, and if we deny it that space it bursts the receptacle in which it was formerly held without difficulty. Chemists tell us that heating is nothing but speeding up the movements of the atoms composing the gas so that each travels faster and collides more frequently and violently with others: here we find overcrowding arising from speed, not numbers. We enjoy over atoms the fortunate superiority of being able to control our movements (and that of our vehicles) in order to avoid collisions; but to do this we must submit to traffic regulations, which extend downwards even to pedestrians. The importance of traffic problems, and the status of traffic authorities, is sure to rise beyond present recognition.

We have compared our gains in speed to what occurs as the result of heating; and indeed the comparison is justified, since heating is an input of energy, and we do increase, continuously and sharply, the input of energy into transportation, some of this energy going into the increase of the weights carried and a greater proportion into the increase of speeds. The comparison with heating can be used also to stress the point that speed, like heating, facilitates the mixing and combining of various substances. Difficulties of transport have in the past held back geographic movements of populations. In the nineteenth century the westward trek of the Americans and the northward trek of the Boers were regarded as epic, although in terms of "logistics" there was little difference between these migrations and the southward treks of the Germanic tribes which overran the Roman Empire, and historians have made it clear that these invaders were not at all numerous. Now, however, vast movements of population are physically feasible. As a consequence we must expect that the uneven distribution of world population over the surface of the planet will become an issue.

Reducing inequalities *within the nation* was the great theme of the last few generations in the various countries of the West, since people naturally compared their condition only with that of their neighbors. But we have invited the other nations of the world to take cognizance of our living standards. And while at present they are concerned to rival these standards on their own ground, should this hope prove fallacious (in part because of the unequal distribution of natural resources), the pressure to immigrate to countries which have achieved great success will be renewed, and it will pose moral and political problems.

One World

Two thousand years ago, enlightened Romans were wont to repeat a saying learnt from their Greek tutors: "Though mankind lies dispersed in many cities, yet it forms but one great City." This saying has become imbedded in Western education through Cicero, who repeatedly referred to the Society of Mankind. Thus when Wendell Willkie spoke of "One World," it seemed that the statement was at last acknowledging what philosophers had stressed for a long time. But the world today is "One" in a sense quite opposite to that which the Greek Stoics had in mind. The purpose of their saying was to contrast physical distance with moral proximity: moral nature made it as easy for men to get on together as physical nature made it difficult for them to come together. Now the situation with which we are faced is utterly different: it is one of physical proximity and moral distance.

Progress in transport has flung down the walls of distance which insulated the many human communities; but men have not rushed over these toppled walls to greet each other as long-lost brothers now enabled to merge in one great community. In North America and Australia the advent of Western man has led to the near-extinction of the natives rather than their combining with the newcomers in one society. The prolonged presence of Western man in Arab, African, and Asian countries has quickened a feeling of kinship, not with him but against him. Clearly nationalism is the great political force in our age of No-Distance. Nationalism made Hitler, and unmade him when he ran afoul of Russian nationalism, which alone saved Stalin's regime. Nor is the will to nationhood dependent upon actual oppression: men now define oppression as the denial of recognition as a separate and distinct sovereign community.

There seems to be no basis in fact for the idea that men are naturally prone to treat each other as brethren and have been artificially weaned by institutions from this original propensity. The only evidence which can be adduced in favor of this natural brotherhood is that all men seem to have a deep-seated reluctance to kill another man, a reluctance which is overcome only under the stress of fear or extreme excitement: hence the war dances required to put them in that unnatural mood. But "not killing" and "regarding as a brother" are very different attitudes, the second far richer in content. And the second is developed by institutions. It is quite impossible for us to estimate the number of distinct political communities which have arisen on our planet since the appearance of man. All but an infinitesimal fraction of these have disappeared; and, for want of any other means of picturing them, we pay a great deal of attention to the minute communities which have subsisted long enough to allow our anthropologists to examine them.

The feature common to all of these communities is an intense but narrowly restricted sense of fellowship. This makes us aware that the building of political societies which have mattered in history involved an enlargement, coupled with a weakening, of the sense of fellowship: our bond with a compatriot is nothing like the bond between members of a tribe; still it is a bond. And we may then think of the art of building large societies as the art of stretching bonds of fellowship as far as possible without snapping. The diffusion of a religion, of a language, of a legal system is here of far greater importance than the diffusion of tools and skills, though the importance of the latter is not negligible.

It would be mere wishful thinking, than which there is nothing more dangerous in the management of human affairs, to assert that mankind now forms One Great Society. This poses a problem because, and only because, mankind must increasingly be thought of as gathered in One Place. While it is certainly an obstacle to the achievement of human excellence that a society should be too small, it is far from clear that such excellence is fostered by increasing bigness. Greek society which has afforded us models in arts and philosophy was small: a constellation of towns of which the largest did not count a hundred thousand inhabitants. Even smaller was Jewish society, wherein was kindled the Light of this World. It is readily believable that the advocacy of the all embracing society by the late Greek philosophers was in no small measure a means of consoling themselves for their absorption in the vast Roman Empire, which never got near to the achievement of Athens alone.

But if it can be doubted that the hugeness of society is desirable, there is little doubt that the mixing together of distinct societies retaining their distinctive traits is a cause of trouble: it was long illustrated in the Ottoman Empire. Contrary to the dreams of those who see in world government a cure-all, experience proves that the unity of government by no means solves the problems raised by the distinctiveness of the communities over which it presides. Incidentally, in that event, the nature of things forbids that government should be of a representative character: if men attempted to make it such, it would be at worst representative of the dominant society and at best representative of the coalition of certain component societies against others. Representative government assumes that what is to be represented is a dominant opinion or feeling within one society.

Tensions between societies are not amenable to the remedy of a common government, unless it be a very authoritarian one. But on the other hand, when societies have distinct political existence, their conflicts are far more disastrous than those which occur between different States belonging to one and the same society. Burke explained the mildness of eighteen-century wars in Europe by the fact that the nations involved belonged to the same system of manners and could therefore contend only about some specific interest, which was not worth any great fury or havoc. It takes great folly to drive war to the extreme under such circumstances, and history offers but two such examples, the Peloponnesian War and the War of 1914. On the contrary, war between societies is by nature absolute since it is not a squabble occurring within the same frame of values, but rather one in which neither camp recognizes the values of the other: this is potentially a war of destruction. Such were the wars waged by the Mongols and the Turks against Europe—wars between societies.

At present the combination of strong diversity between societies and of effective physical proximity poses a political problem of major dimensions. It is just not good enough to think of it in terms borrowed from the experience of diplomacy between the states belonging to the same society.

Our Home

Underlying this paper is a feeling which it is perhaps time to express, an affection for the Earth similar in kind to that which our home and garden inspire, an awareness that our inheritance is precious and vulnerable. In most pre-Christian religions figured a cult of Mother-Earth, the Bountiful. She was the primeval giantess on which short-lived men scrabbled punily; from her flanks sprang all things necessary to the sustenance and enjoyment of life; her power was adored. The Earth is still our abode and provider, but the giantess now seems far smaller and the majestic processes of her life are not immune to interference. We know that we live upon a few feet of soil, with a few miles of atmosphere above us; we know that we can blight the soil and corrupt the air, that we can produce smog and dust bowls; we could poison the sea; we could melt the ice caps at the poles; we might kill off bacteria on which we depend, or propagate viruses mortal to us.

Therefore the juvenile pride which we have understandably taken in our fantastically increased ability to "exploit the Earth" should now give way to a more mature thoughtfulness in "husbanding the Earth." Man, impatient with the weakness of his hands, has transformed his weakness to strength: now his handling must become more discriminating and delicate. We are like children who, as they acquire vigor, must be made aware of their new capacity to injure. Many of us no doubt have had the experience of nursing with love in our maturity a small garden through which we had blundered brutally as small children, then deeming its riches unlimited: such is the experience which mankind is now repeating.

Now that we have reached the limits of the Earth, we understand: this is the land of promise, the land beyond Jordan, a land of milk and honey, to be enjoyed, and cherished, and tended.

The Capacity to Harm

I have traveled enough not to fall into the easy accusation that modern industry is responsible for defacing Earth. I know that shepherds, so favored by poets, can with their lambs and sheep cause the soil to become barren; I know that noble savages will burn down a forest to raise a crop, and move on to cause another desolation; I have seen the squalor of the Arab *medina* and of the Asiatic large town. Man is careless; and if our factories pour filth into our rivers, this is just in line with age-old behavior. Yet the combination of education and wealth always fosters in men the will to live in graceful surroundings, and if this is an attitude of individuals it may also be an attitude of communities. It was the attitude of Athenians, of Florentines. Surely, if they were wealthy enough to build themselves beautiful towns, so are we. The preoccupation with urban beauty seems to me to be rising in the United States; I find it to a lesser degree in Europe. Also it is an attitude of mature minds to be provident, to think of improving the home, the farm, or the plant. Certainly we can not blame our contemporaries for any lack of investment-consciousness, but this preoccupation has not yet, or at least not adequately, extended to the conservation of the very basis upon which our structures are reared: we do not realize that natural resources themselves are requiring upkeep. This basic capital of mankind is entered in our account books at zero, and so taken for granted that it receives no attention.

The time has come for a new spirit of "stewardship of the Earth." Every animal, however humble, provides for its offspring. As one ascends the chain of beings up to man, the period during which the young are protected by the parents stretches, allowing for more complete development. But man is unique in his determination to hand down to his adult successor some asset he has built up, to be enjoyed and improved by his son, and handed down to the grandson for further improvement. As this propensity is peculiar to man and has obviously served the progress of our species, I doubt whether the legislative fashion against it, however plausible on other grounds, is well founded. But we must at least transfer this fortunate propensity to the asset on which the children and grandchildren of all of us shall be dependent, our Earth itself.

In towns where we have no animal company other than that of an occasional cat or dog, and see no plant other than an occasional tree, we are apt to forget that Life, with a capital L, depends upon a complex combination of an immense variety of forms of life, between which the balance must be maintained. We may have air conditioning, but should be aware that the availability of breathable air depends upon a complex cycle of operations turning on green plants. All our devised processes in which we take justifiable pride are, as it were, derivations installed on natural circuits; and our increasing understanding of the latter not only conveys a greater power to exploit them but also implies a greater awareness of a duty to preserve them.

Cleverness and Thoughtfulness

Throughout the history of mankind, as we know it today, new procedures have been devised, new tools forged and new ways of life have been adopted. It is a truism that the pace of such change has undergone a formidable acceleration: but truisms are the best starting points for meditation. When a new procedure or new tool arose in the distant past, its use was only slowly generalized in the immediate environment and its geographic diffusion was even much slower. Inventions, far between in time and spreading sluggishly, slowly affected ways of life but did not revolutionize them: for instance, I deem it quite misleading to refer to the adoption of tilling as "the Agricultural Revolution"—a phrase which implies a turbulence of events which was lacking.

For many thousands of years men lived in a world where new practices were a rarity and old practices made up the bulk of their existence. While the impact of successive new practices successively altered the environment, this alteration was so leisurely that sons were, on the whole, adjusted to their world if only they acquired the skills of their fathers and were guided by the experience of their elders. But now discoveries so press upon one another, are so rapidly accepted and so widely put into operation, that a human generation lives in a world utterly different from that into which it was born; for instance, I was born in the year when the Wright brothers first succeeded in flying a few hundred yards, and flying has become my normal mode of transporting myself to and fro.

I marvel at the rapidity of human adjustment. Man, living in a sort of symbiosis with an ever-changing population of machines, reveals a flexibility of behavior which could hardly have been forecast. Moreover, while great individual inequalities are revealed in this capacity as in every other, they bear little apparent relation to hereditary background: given favorable early opportunities, the knack of handling complex machinery can be acquired quite rapidly by men born in the most primitive conditions. We are only beginning to discover man's cleverness.

It is again a truism to say that our thoughtfulness by no means keeps pace with this development. Prudence consists in picking out the good under the actual circumstances: faults against prudence are committed either if one fails to take full cognizance of the circumstances or if one despairs of picking out the good: such indeed are the two trends of contemporary thinking about our fast-changing world.

Certainly the stress upon our minds arising from the pace of change is unprecedented: no man in his right senses can help feeling that he is unequal to the challenge. Yet we must humbly dare to meet it.

15

From Political Economy to Political Ecology

This paper, presented here in a greatly abridged and somewhat re-
vised version, was inspired by serious concern about the difficulties
which Asian countries may encounter in their process of economic development. But, moreover, it reflects the author's belief that the dependence of human life upon other forms of life present at the surface of
the earth is insufficiently stressed.

It is all too readily assumed that Asian nations, because they are late
starters (with the exception of Japan) on the path of industrial development, have a relatively easy job, since they can draw freely upon the
know-how of advanced industrial nations, and since they have only to
repeat an already established pattern of development: the path to riches
has been plotted out for them. Many well-meaning people in the West
are fascinated by a classification of the nations of the earth according
to their national per capita income in dollars, and this calls to their
minds a ladder with India standing on the lowest rung and the U.S. on
the topmost.[1] They think of Indian development as a climb up the ladder by a repetition of the stages through which the U.S. has passed.

I regard such a picture as quite erroneous and dangerously misleading. It does not matter here that such comparisons of national incomes
are very faulty. My quarrel is with the assumption that all the Indians
have to do is to repeat a process carried out by Americans. (It will be
abundantly clear to the reader that the Russian pattern is by no means
more suitable. Indeed, Russian development is nothing but an attempt
to reproduce the American structure.) This assumption logically rests
upon an unformulated postulate: i.e., that the present situation of Indi-

From the *The Bulletin of the Atomic Scientists*, Vol. 13 (October, 1957): 287–291.
Reprinted by permission of *The Bulletin of the Atomic Scientists*, © 1957 by the
Educational Foundation for Nuclear Science, 6042 South Kimbark Avenue, Chicago,
Illinois 60637, USA.

ans is one in which Americans formerly found themselves and from which they moved forward to their present situation. If Americans could name some given moment of their past at which they were placed as Indians are today, then it would be plausible to say that the Indians have only to follow the path which Americans made. But it is not so. Early settlers in America had a far better life than the Indian masses of today and enjoyed infinitely more promising circumstances.

Let me stress a physical contrast. India today [1957] has 387 million people on a territory of 1,963 thousand square miles. This territory is hardly larger than that which in 1810 supported 7.2 million Americans (1,723 thousand square miles at that time). American economic development started under conditions of extreme abundance of natural resources relative to population. Indian economic development, on the other hand, starts under conditions of extreme abundance of population relative to natural resources.

Living standards in the U.S. were at all times high, because manpower was always scarce and therefore at a premium. Quite contrary conditions prevail in India. In all American productive processes, manpower was ever the scarce factor, which had to be economized: therefore America led the world in productivity of labor. But the scarce factor in Asia is not man, it is land, and that is the factor which has to be economized: husbandry is the Asian equivalent of American productivity.

The Underestimation of Natural Resources

The huge natural resources of the American continent have benefited Americans directly and Europeans indirectly. Their abundance has tended to make us forgetful of their importance. No doubt every lecturer in economics teaches his students that *output* is a result of three factors—labor, capital, and land (standing for all natural resources). But the emphasis is so very much on the first two that the third factor tends to be neglected.

This induces in the student a calm conviction that the flow of goods depends entirely on human labor. For though labor is only one of the two remaining factors, the student learns that the other—capital—represents the objects "given," at the moment under consideration, as the basis of production—objects which were themselves produced by labor at a previous period. Thus, the means of production are reduced to human labor, in its different forms—labor represented by its concrete results, and labor available.

While this method of presentation has its value, it has the great defect of suggesting that the flow of goods offered for the satisfaction of man's needs depends solely upon man's own effort, *completely independent of his natural surroundings*. People are not sufficiently clear that what we call "production" can never be anything but the processing of natural resources, and depends entirely on those resources, and it is imprudent to assume that any given form of economic development can be precisely duplicated in a very different natural environment.

Ecology

In a highly organized society such as ours, Nature disappears behind the mass of our fellow-creatures; each individual believes that his living depends on his relationship with his fellows, the services he renders them, and the return he receives for these; he has forgotten that he lives on what the population of which he is a member can draw from its natural environment. Everything he makes use of seems to him to be the product of human labor; this is true so far as concerns its form; but its substance is obtained from Nature. We recognize our borrowing from Nature in bread, but we forget it in the airplane—in its body, whose components are minerals, its rubber tires, and the fuel it obtains from the bowels of the earth.

Every living organism, without exception, attracts certain substances which it obtains from its environment, absorbs those substances, transforms them, and utilizes them. The growth of a whale, beginning with the egg, is a process of construction which, so far as concerns dependence on substances from outside itself, differs not a whit from the construction of a skyscraper; in both cases materials are taken, transformed, and adjusted according to a plan. The difference between the two operations is that the one is biological and the other rational, and that the one procedure is identical on every occasion, whereas the other is perfectible; whales were being constructed on the present pattern in the days when men were only building huts out of mud and the branches of trees.

Every form of life is inevitably a form of exploitation of its surroundings, and a civilization is merely a form of exploitation which has been developed by the exercise of intelligence. Such a form cannot be transported bodily from one set of circumstances to another very different set...

The Food-Producers

It is well known to every student that the march of the Industrial Revolution can be plotted in terms of a diminishing percentage of food producers within the working population. In the U.S. in 1956 employment in agriculture had fallen to 6.6 million people as against 58.4 [million] in other occupations. As American external trade in agricultural products was roughly balanced, this can again be expressed in the following manner: the population of the U.S. was fed by the labor of less than 4 percent of its number. Or, if we think, perhaps more properly, in terms of families, a farm population of little more than 20 million fed a total population of 170 million: one farm family fed six non-farm families besides itself.

This offers a striking contrast with what we may think of as typical medieval conditions: four peasant families feeding a total of five families. Clearly, the greater the proportion of non-farmers which can be fed by the farming population, the greater the quantity and variety of non-food goods which can be produced by the nation. Indeed Stalin was so obsessed by this thought that his Grand Design was essentially to transfer manpower from farming to non-farming occupations at breakneck speed. Indeed, the main factor in the fantastically rapid growth of industrial production in the U.S. is to be found in the multiplication of the industrial labor force (4.5 times). Obviously, in order that such a transfer of manpower should occur without a lowering of nutrition standards (which was not the case in Russia), it is necessary that productivity per head should grow apace in the farming population. In Russia mismanagement of the farm population hampered this process, the pace set being anyhow extremely hasty, but the inherent conditions of Russia are on the whole extremely favorable to the aforesaid transformation. Russia is so land-rich that in time it may approximate the American structure.

This, however, is certainly not the case in Asian countries. It is true that in the U.S. there are only less than 7 million land workers, but it is also true that there are 188 million hectares worked and 256 million hectares available for grazing. The abundance of the second factor contributes to make up total output with a scant labor force. In order to achieve a similar output with far less land, more men would be called for.

Change in Demographic Structure

We shall now make a rough and immediate application of the preceding concept. Without concerning ourselves with numerical precision, which is unnecessary for our purpose, let us say that the European Coal and Steel Community has the same population as the United States, and that it includes 21 million agricultural workers, against 7 million in the United States. We shall therefore assume that the best method of raising the standard of living of the Europeans is to bring the European demographic structure nearer to that of America. We shall reduce the number of farmers and increase their productivity; we shall increase the number of nonagricultural workers and raise their production. All this is correct, but within certain limits.

Let us now suppose that, by the wave of a magic wand, 14 million agricultural workers have been transferred from their fields to factories and offices. Waving her wand again, our helpful fairy provides the 7 million remaining agricultural workers with the same equipment possessed by their American equivalents; but she can do nothing about natural conditions: she cannot give our 7 million farm workers the same amount of land as their opposite numbers in America. The European Coal and Steel Community covers an area equal to about one-sixth of that of the United States. Owing to this fundamental difference, the output of our 7 million European farmers will be far below that of the Americans.

In the circumstances in which the magic wand has placed us, we Europeans shall doubtless produce more per man than in our present circumstances, at the cost of a greater expenditure of land per man. But as we shall be unable to parallel the expenditure of land per man which prevails in the United States, we shall certainly not attain the same production, and we shall fall below our own present production. Moreover, the transformation we have effected will call for a greater total expenditure of raw materials and energy, assuming that such expenditure increases *pari passu* with the number of non-agricultural workers.

It is important not to make productivity into a fetish. We live on products, not on productivity. In a closed economic system, the most effective agriculture is that which produces the desired quantity of foodstuffs, not that which shows the greatest productivity. Agricultural productivity might conceivably increase until there was only one agricultural worker left, but the rest of the population would not be there to admire this champion—it would have perished almost to a man.

A human community which is growing at the rate, let us say, of 1 percent per annum, requires, in order to maintain its subsistence level, an equal rate of increase in agricultural output, and in order to raise its subsistence level, a more rapid rate of increase in that output.

Consequently, the best agricultural procedures will be those which ensure the desired increase in agricultural foodstuffs with the least possible expenditure of labor. It immediately becomes evident that, all other factors being equal, the quantity of labor required to obtain a particular agricultural product will be in inverse ratio to the amount of agricultural land available. The less need there is to economize on the use of land, the greater the possibility of economizing on agricultural labor.

What is true of American agriculture is true of the American economic system as a whole; just as its expenditure of land per agricultural worker is very high, so is its expenditure of raw materials per industrial worker. To understand the peculiar characteristics of the American economy, we need only remember that the country is a veritable treasure-house of natural resources, so that the only problem facing the European settlers, who at first were few in number, was that of economizing their only rare resource—men—and their original concern was with what is now called "productivity."

Illusions Fostered by the Example of England

There is a tendency to overlook the unique character of the American situation, because England, the great object of the economists' admiration before the United States, was concerned with the same problems, despite its very different geographical characteristics.

Long before the United States, England transferred a gradually increasing fraction of its increasing population from agricultural to nonagricultural work; and its nonagricultural population used increasing quantities of raw materials in the process of production. Yet England's land resources were small, and though in coal output the limit seems only now to have been reached, the country's consumption of copper and lead, even before the end of the nineteenth century, was already far in excess of what could be obtained from its own soil.

Suppose a country with a much greater population, such as India, were to recapitulate the history of England. Let us imagine, for the sake of argument, that the population continues to increase at the rate of 1.25 percent per annum, so that in about forty-five years' time it will be as dense as that of the United Kingdom and its total figure will be 690 million; imagine that by that time India is a larger version of the present United Kingdom, and that its imports of raw materials bear the same proportion to its population; those imports will then be thirteen times higher than the present British imports. Where would those products be obtained, and how would they be paid for?

It may be objected that this supposition is completely fantastic. Agreed; but it is equally fantastic not to perceive that the English example, like the American example, cannot be imitated everywhere.

All plans and projects drawn up in any country of the world have the effect of increasing the demand for natural resources. The great inspiration common to them all is economy of labor, at a time when manpower is constantly increasing; and little thought is given to economizing natural resources, though these are limited.

The Hungry Machines

A short time ago, anxiety about natural resources was directed mainly to sources of energy—which was understandable, for coal and oil deposits are in the nature of "savings," which took thousands of years to accumulate and which are being expended very rapidly. There were many gloomy predictions about the exhaustion of oil supplies, in particular; but it was noticed that the discovery of fresh supplies kept pace with the annual extraction. Though it seems obvious that this cannot go on indefinitely, atomic energy has now appeared on the scene, overthrowing prophesies of a shortage of energy. It seems as though the fear of a shortage is less justified in regard to energy than anywhere else, for solar irradiation of the earth, measured in terms of coal, is in the neighborhood of 2,500 tons per hectare per annum. So the problem of the energy available for man's use is simply one of capturing that energy.

Neither is there any real justification for the fear that man will ultimately be faced with a shortage of the raw materials he obtains from ores. There are two reasons for this. In the first place, man's consumption of metals is not a complete waste of those metals; the metal used in the manufacture of a car may be thrown away when the car is worn out, but it is not lost, it can be recovered; the recovery and reprocessing of such materials will become an increasingly important activity and will do much to improve the appearance of suburban districts. The other reassuring reason is that the outer crust of the earth is one vast reserve of ores of various kinds. Obviously, the ores of the metals most familiar to us will gradually cease to be available in the form of rich deposits lying close to the surface, because such deposits, being easily handled, are the first to be exploited. But there is no reason to doubt that we shall succeed in taking advantage of deposits which are either far less rich or far less accessible; the progress of industrial power will in itself enable us to penetrate much farther below the earth's surface in our search for the raw material required by industry.

I do not think, therefore, that world industry, which calls for ever increasing quantities of raw materials and energy, is in danger of running short of these at any foreseeable time. But the gluttonous appetite of industry will lead to two consequences, one probable, the other certain. The probable consequence is that, to obtain the necessary raw materials will require an increasing industrial effort, and thus become more and more costly in terms of industrial products.

A Population of Machines

The other consequence is the following. The distribution of the raw materials needed for industry is, at a certain moment, a geographical fact. But that geographical fact can no longer be regarded as constant. In the first place, because the distribution over the earth's surface of a particular resource is affected by the exploitation of the different deposits at varying speeds; in the second place—and even more important—because industrial chemistry is conferring value upon resources which previously had none, and this is bound to lead to changes in the map of geographical reserves.

Incidentally, that map will acquire increasing importance. Industry arose in tiny patches of the globe; its products were rare and could be very profitably exchanged for raw materials which were of no value to those who supplied them, since they, having no industries themselves, could make no use of such materials. As industrialization spreads, the possessors of raw materials develop a clearer sense of their value, and international trade has to be carried on at rates more favorable to these raw materials and less favorable to the finished products.

If, as would appear, frenzied industrialization in the USSR manner is to become the ruling principle of every country, this will increase the tendency to surrender national raw materials only in exchange for foreign raw materials (processible and combustible materials) needed by the exporting country, and not in exchange for industrial products.

We may describe what is at present going on as the very rapid *populating of the world by machines*. The machine population made its first appearance in a small corner of the world, in Western Europe, and spread out at first in certain privileged directions and then in others. A population of machines which is less flourishing than another, owing to smaller resources, will ask that other to supply it with raw materials, but will have nothing to offer in exchange, since its own products will be inferior to those of the other: this is the position of Western Europe in relation to the United States.

Still considering machines as a population, we may say at present its distribution over the earth's surface is extremely unequal, but that this inequality will gradually diminish, while the machine-population density will increase in all areas. There seems to be little to impede this increase of density, as machines feed on dead matter of which there is an abundance in the earth's crust (as well as in the seas, which contain so great a quantity of mineral salts), and on energy which the sun supplies in abundance.

Destruction of the Conditions of Human Life

With the human population, matters are very different. Man feeds on living matter, which is incomparably rarer, on our planet, than dead matter. His feeding is essentially the transformation of another form of life, whether animal or vegetable, into human life. As everyone knows, any living matter, consumed by fire, is reduced to fairly simple chemical constituents, but in living matter those elements are present in combinations of tremendous complexity—a complexity such that very few protein molecules have ever been satisfactorily described; and we also know that these complex structures are built up, in the first place, in the vegetable kingdom alone. This leads the chemist to assert that all animals live as parasites on the vegetable kingdom, including man, whose parasitic activity is either direct, when he eats vegetable products, or indirect, when he eats herbivorous animals, or more indirect, when he eats carnivorous animals. It is in the sphere of his vital necessities that man has the least justification for calling himself "producer." The producer is the growing plant.

We may regard this from a different angle, if we remember that living matter does not travel by a one-way street, but follows a circuit, a cycle. We can then say that the human population forms part of an eco-system, in biotic fellowship with other forms of life. It is "vitally" interested—the word can be used here, for once, without exaggeration—in maintaining the ecosystem on which it depends for its food. In his everyday life, man is obliged to destroy other forms of life, but as a long-term policy he is obliged to preserve other forms of life. He does not always succeed in doing so, or in remembering the necessity.

Mr. Koestner suggests[2] that civilization has an inherent tendency to destroy the conditions required for human existence. It is an impressive fact that the finest archeological remains (of cities) have been found in semi-desert regions, and a map showing them would coincide, to a greater extent, with the present areas of depopulation and destitution. Mr. Koestner defines two present-day conditions which apply to the majority of very ancient centers of civilization: infertility and depopulation, or, in the valleys of great rivers, overpopulation of an agricultural character.

Let us see if we can illustrate these conditions by simple examples. During its earliest period, Rome was the fortress of a population of agricultural workers, who personally cultivated the surrounding fields.

During its second period, Rome grew rich on the tributes it exacted, and its buildings and ships increased rapidly in number. The inevitable result was the deforestation of the countryside and the disturbance of its natural water system. In a third phase, the increasing population of Rome and the increasingly high standard of living of the Romans called for considerable quantities of meat; and the Roman campagna, together with much of the country districts of Italy, became an area traversed by large herds of cattle. What ruined Italy was not so much the large estates but rather the repeated passage of flocks and herds across ground eroded by deforestation.

In the Far East and in Egypt, the course of development seems to have been different. As the population, and more especially the town population, increased, great irrigation works increased the fertility of the soil; but that soil was cultivated with ever increasing intensity, being thickly populated with agricultural workers who scratched a wretched subsistence from their labors.

Conclusion

My remarks have two purposes. One is to point out that, contrary to current beliefs, the Asian countries have a much harder task than ours was, because natural resources were far more readily available to us, whether we had them on our own territory, or whether the lack of competing demand allowed us to obtain them easily from abroad. Asian leaders will perforce have to keep this difference in circumstances in mind while planning their development, and we should be conscious of it while shaping our friendly policies toward them.

My second purpose is to alter our state of mind regarding natural resources. Western man has a narrowly anthropocentric view of the universe. Nothing seems to him precious and worth preserving, other than Man. He tends to count nothing as an expenditure, other than human effort: he does not seem to mind how much mineral matter he wastes and, far worse, how much living matter he destroys. He does not seem to realize at all that human life is a dependent part of a ecosystem of many different forms of life. As the world is ruled from towns where men are cut off from any form of life other than human, the feeling of belonging to an ecosystem is not revived. This results in a harsh and improvident treatment of things upon which we ultimately depend, such as water and trees.

Mankind has only quite recently, and in its lesser fraction, entered into the Industrial Age. Our power to tax Nature is increasing and is ever more widely used: it is also a power to destroy. This is a problem which begins to appear under certain aspects (pollution, erosion, local scarcity of water) even in resource-rich America: it must appear at an earlier stage in countries less fortunately endowed. My stand is not an anti-progressive one. I am aware that our techniques are not only capable of impairing but also of repairing natural resources, provided we put our minds to it. This will increasingly claim our attention, and it must claim attention in resource-poor countries, from the very inception of their development. More generally, we shall be led to regard Nature not as a store on which we can freely draw, but as a flow which we must be careful to replenish. It will greatly help us toward such an attitude to realize that human life is completely dependent upon a great company of other forms of existence. This is why I speak of Political Ecology.

Notes

1. Thus a recent publication of the Committee for Economic Development (Economic Development Assistance, April 1957) gives national income per head in India as $54 as against $2,000 in the U.S.
2. Mr. Koestner, an economist on the staff of the National Bank of Egypt, has some extremely interesting ideas on this subject, very few of which, unfortunately, have been published. Cf., however, *Marginal Notes on the Problem of "Underdeveloped" Countries*, published in English by Witschafsdienst, May 1954.

16

The Stewardship of the Earth

Human ambition in our day aims at settling the planets. Such a dream involves the problem of survival under environmental conditions far from those familiar to us. Landing upon the moon is but the first step: even for this, explorers must carry with them very much more than has been necessary for adventurers previously plunging into the deserts, torrid or glacial, of our Earthland. The very air, a free commodity all over our planet, becomes the most precious of products on these novel ventures, and the machinery for its regeneration is the indispensable key to exploration.

However inhospitable the moon, the planets promise to be worse. The moon is inhospitable by reason of deficiencies that can conceivably be remedied by "imports"; the planets, one hears, are far more actively inhospitable by reason of elemental forces that would buffet men out of existence.

The places to which we dispatch men carefully selected for their qualities bear no likeness to the Fortunate Islands of medieval imagination but resemble the place to which the wicked were then consigned. I do not question the capability of the human mind to meet progressively the challenge of such hostile environments. But surely many are the moments when the toughest of these future explorers will sigh for the kindness of the earth.

We see the opening of an era: it is an era of seeking beyond the confines of our atmosphere; may it be also an era of awakening to the bounties of our Earth.

As we learn what prodigies our engineers and chemists must accomplish to reproduce, in the astronauts' micro-capsule, the conditions which

Reprinted from *The Fitness of Man's Environment* (Washington, D.C.: Smithsonian Institution Press, 1968): 99–117, by permission of the publisher. Coyright © 1968 Smithsonian Institution.

are freely given to us in this vast capsule, our Earth with its atmosphere, is this not the occasion for a sense of wonder, and a feeling of tender respect for the abode of our kind?

The bounties of the Earth notwithstanding, it has proved possible, as we know all too well, for most of our kind in the past, and, alas, to this day, to live very miserably on this planet. Why? Because of blindness to the resources offered. We are cured of this blindness, at least in the advanced countries. Are we not still subject, however, to another blindness—lack of appreciation, lack of enjoyment? From such blindness follow lack of care of our inheritance, indifference to its deterioration, failure to improve it.

We esteem ourselves masters of the Earth. But should not an owner be the husbandman of his land? Must he not tend it as he uses it? Shall he not indeed delight in its beauty as well as enjoy its fruit?

"The Lord God planted man in a garden of delight, to dress it and to tend it" (Genesis 2:15). This I take to mean that the Earth has been given to us for our utility and enjoyment, but also entrusted to our care, that we should be its caretakers and gardeners.

A more naturalistic approach leads to the same recommendation. Through hundreds of millions of years, increasingly complex living systems—organisms—have arisen from an initial beginning as a shapeless jelly. In this great process of evolution, superiority has not meant independence. Those forms of life displaying the greater ability are dependent for their very existence upon those displaying lesser. The animal, which has locomotive ability, is a parasite on plants, and so are we, for all our achievements and pride. A mode of existence which confines us to cities where we encounter no form of life other than our own may be of bad counsel if we are to adopt a policy of ecological balance.

In a very few generations the Earth has become quite small. It was encompassed by human peregrination less than five centuries ago. In the days of Jefferson, human movement was still no faster, whether on land or sea, than it had been in classical Greece. The shrinking of the Earth began with steam and has been accelerated by the airplane, the age of which is just my own.

Now we can take pictures of our planet from outer space and have its image on our mantelpiece, even as that of our home. Shall we not therefore cherish it as our home? We have become ever more efficient slave-drivers of the forces of Nature. Should this lead us only to pridefulness, or also to a new regard for the vulnerability of the system upon which our existence depends?

Small children behave with thoughtless brutality in a garden which seems to them an expanse without limits; and because they are so small, their brutality does limited harm. But we who have grown up possess such powers that we cannot afford thoughtless brutality. The time has come for us to be husbandmen of the garden.

The more we think of ourselves as masters of the Earth, the more we must be concerned with its prudent stewardship.

As I understand this stewardship, it stretches all the way from the widest to the narrowest frameworks of our lives, from recognition that the atmosphere of the planet is far the most essential of our capital assets, to recognition that what we see from our window is an important element of our welfare and education.

Animals use their environment according to the prompting of their wants, heedless of the wreck they cause and of the litter they leave. There are some few exceptions, among which Man does not figure prominently. Man is fundamentally an untidy beast; so women have ever found; against this they have striven within the home. Let me suggest that the extension of this very same striving to the planet, as our home, is a great requirement of our time.

The language we use in relation to Nature is alarming; we speak of its conquest, of its exploitation; such terms have connotations of brutality, of misuse. Of such sins we are indeed guilty, and they may well be visited upon our descendants.

Perhaps the clearest progress that Man has made is in his entrepreneurial capacity, which means his disposition to look far ahead toward the provision of future services, for the procurement of which he neatly assembles, first in his mind, and subsequently in fact, a variety of ingredients.

I have just used the expression "neatly" which seems incompatible with the previous reproach of untidiness. But the two attributes are indeed compatible. The man who is concerned with a project is extremely thoughtful and careful in the marshaling of requirements, he pays great attention to the proper joining of parts, and, in short, displays the utmost tidiness in what is relevant to the project. But he does not care about what is irrelevant to the project, and therefore behaves carelessly with respect to that.

A striking illustration is offered by strip mining in the Kentucky hills, described by John O'Callaghan in the following terms: "The process consists in making a 40-foot incision around a hillside above the seam and scooping up the exposed coal.... The strippers, cutting with bulldozers along the seams high in the scented, tree-covered hillsides, are tossing down hundreds of tons of rocks, soil, and broken trees, which have engulfed homes and threaten to engulf more."[1]

Here we have a perfect instance of behavior which is both neat and messy. The earth cover is neatly cut out and messily dumped down. The whole operation is neat from the engineer's angle; the mess it creates in the valley is none of his concern. He has a well-defined purpose, which is to get the coal out by the most efficient means; that these should involve the brutalization of Nature and the spoiling of the environment is to him irrelevant.

It springs to our lips that this destruction instances the evils of capitalism. Alas, the root of the troubles lies even deeper! It lies in the inspiration of the operation which has the exclusive purpose of getting out the coal at the least cost. The least-cost principle is tied up in the case of the private corporation with the profit motive, but it is just as important to the public corporation, being then tied up with the service motive.

On the 21st of October, 1966, 144 people, including 116 children, were crushed to death in the village of Aberfan, Wales, by the sudden slipping down of a mountain of rubble taken from the mine over the years. This enormous accumulation, of the order of a million tons, stood 800 feet above the village until it suddenly crashed upon it. Was the improvident accumulation of this threatening mass the product of the grasping spirit of capitalist enterprise? Not so; in Britain the coal mines were nationalized twenty years ago; they are not run for profit. Absence of a profit-motive, however, does not alter the specific obligation of actual mine-managers, which is to get the coal out at least cost. Their very zeal in the performance of that office tends to cast out of their minds the side effects, actual or potential.[2]

What I wish to stress is that we damage our environment not only when we, as individuals, behave like uneducated brutes, but also when, as agents serving some useful social function, we conduct operations in a manner that is rational relative to that purpose but thoughtless and damaging with regard to the scene in general.

Let me again illustrate. Among the natural beauties which abound in England, none are more famous than those of the Lake District. These have been very seriously threatened, so much so that only government intervention has saved them. Threatened by whom? By a most high-minded, public-spirited body, the municipal officers of Manchester. The urban agglomeration thirsted for water. Very properly its officers were determined to provide it. For this laudable purpose they laid plans that might have drained the lakes. Can we blame them for attending to what was their problem?

This poses a very serious question. Adam Smith rightly pointed to the division of labor as the characteristic feature of the society then in the making. Division of labor has indeed developed, not only, as he described it, in terms of the hands that perform, but also in terms of the minds that conceive and design. Our fantastic progress in problem-solving is due to a mental attitude which cuts out of the vast and complex universe those elements which are operationally relevant to our specific concern.[3] This intellectual surgery, this "divide and conquer" method, has served us well in the advancement of knowledge and power. This may be the key to our having achieved the Industrial Revolution and the explanation of its not having been achieved many centuries earlier by China, which then stood so far ahead of us in every aspect of civilization. That this is indeed the case is strongly suggested by Joseph Needham's admirable comparison of ancient Chinese science and technology with that of the West.[4] The great advance which the Chinese had enjoyed was overcome and reversed, Needham argues, because they were wont to think in terms of general harmony rather than to single out what was germane to a specific problem.

Such a comparison leads us to recognize what I should venture to call an intellectual toughness. The Western intellectual is apt to condemn the toughness of other social groups, but his own very thinking is tough. This is noticeable when you seek to interest one of our technologists in some foreseeable side effects of the innovation he is working on. He is apt to shrug off the intervention: "That will be someone else's problem." It is highly probable that his attitude is a condition of his success. But the more we concede the legitimacy, even the inevitability, of this attitude, the more also we must recognize that our process of problem-solving is problem-generating. A simple instance is offered by the supersonic airliner, which solves the problem of faster transport but creates the problem—the extent of which is so far unknown—of the supersonic boom.

Our progress, then, is a complex of problem-solving and problem-creation. If we consider the progress achieved in a long period, we can observe that certain problems have been eagerly attended to and others left quite unattended. We can further observe that among the new problems generated by the problems solved, some have been dealt with and others not. Using these categories, what strikes us then is the *neglect of*

environmental problems. This I can illustrate by citing two wholly neglected formulators of environmental concerns.

The year is 1775, we are near Besançon, attending a ceremony; the
first stone of a new town is being laid. Now, explains the designer,
begins a new age—the age of industry—which calls for the gathering
of many workers around a factory. The whole of the mill town, he indi-
cates, should be planned to make life pleasant by providing for the
amenities and for making attractive the appearance of the proposed
buildings. The building of this mill town of Chaux—which stands to
this day a shining testimony to the vision of its architect, Claude-Nicolas
Ledoux—was indeed a great beginning; but it was a beginning without
a sequel.

In my distant youth I fostered the slogan *"Des Versailles pour le
Peuple"* to denote what seemed to me a natural concern for a democratic civilization; that is, to give to the many the aesthetic pleasures
and the educating influence of which only the few had previously understood the value. This has not occurred in the 150 years elapsed between Ledoux's effort and my outcry. What has occurred in the meantime
was the abominable drabness of tenements. Why?

From the painting of Renaissance Italy there surely springs to mind
the lesson that the scenery which forms the background of human existence flavors every moment of it. As soon as the artist had learned to
detach figures from the wall where they had been stuck poster-like in
Byzantine art, he opened up vistas behind these figures. The background
might be a perspective of architecture, as in the works of Carpaccio; of
nature, as in those of Georgione; or a blending of both, such as preferred by Raphael. More subtly it would be a glimpsing of nature through
an architectural framework, as in Perugino's art. Imagine rubbing out
the backgrounds of these painter's works: you will see that most of the
magic would be lost.

Did such paintings reflect a concern of the mighty for a seemly de-
cor of life, or did they foster it? Surely both. While medieval society
was concerned with bringing beauty to places of worship, the more
man-oriented society arising from the Renaissance was concerned with
the frame of its daily life. One would expect that, with the dawn of a
more philanthropic view of life, a concern with the human setting might
have been more generalized. Was it? Unfortunately, it was not so. The
rich of the 19th century apparently thought of "hands" as devoid of any
sensitivity, possessed of no eyes capable of enjoying beauty or suffering from ugliness. This may be due to the rise of a new class itself

insensitive to loveliness, preoccupied with power and pridefulness; that which Veblen has described.

Let us now move to another pioneer, Charles Fourier. Concern for the disfavored countries of the world is no novelty; it was displayed by Fourier 160 years ago, in 1808. It seemed to him that the great handicap under which these countries suffered was a matter of climate, and that climatic improvement should be sought—an improvement for which he rested his hopes upon the systematic control of vegetation.

Neither Fourier's suggestion nor Ledoux's actual start have been followed up.

I am quite incompetent to say whether modern science could contrive any improvement of the climate in the disadvantaged countries. I am quite sure, however, that the negative cannot be proved. I understand, indeed, that the prevention of hurricanes is not an unmanageable problem. Hurricane Betsy, hitting a rich country, caused havoc that was measurable financially. I gather that the insurers alone were called upon to meet obligations of well over 80 million dollars. If one thinks of such disasters striking countries which lack the same ability to duplicate assets, one feels that it would be a great boon to have a defense force to dispel these destroyers at their very inception. Just how much of the world's research-and-development is being directed to investigation of such possibilities? I gather also from experts that it is not too difficult to divert rainfall. Now if one thinks of the floods that inundated northern Italy—where two months' rainfall fell in two days—one is moved to ask whether some of this precipitation might not have been diverted to the sea if the state of the science were somewhat more advanced; i.e., if it had been somewhat more encouraged. It did not, in any case, require any scientific breakthrough to avoid the denuding of the hills which is said to have had so much to do with the floods that wrought havoc in Florence. To put it bluntly, these are not the sort of problems to which the bulk of our science and technology is addressed.

Ignorant as I am in this realm, I do not know just what the currents of heat spewed into the atmosphere by our centers of industry and population do to movements of the air. I regret this lack of information, but I regret even more that nobody else seems to be very much informed about it. Our atmosphere has only lately—and thanks to the mishaps of Los Angeles—become a subject of interest. From Los Angeles came Professor Neiburger's warning about the gradual piling up in our atmosphere of noxious products.[5] The atmosphere is, after all, not unlimited in extent, and if the refuse we send into it is not broken down, it may in time cause changes in surface conditions. This biological hazard may be uncertain and far removed. As against it, however, we have the clear, present, and growing unpleasantness of our environment. But here we come up against the difficulty that the defacing of nature, as it entails no financially measurable injury to persons, is an uncounted loss with no standing in our national accounts.

Those of us whose active life has spanned the years from 1929 to 1967 are conscious that the national store of plant and equipment we enjoy today is far superior to that existing in 1929, be it in the United States or in my country, France. If I may evoke personal memories, in the early years of the Great Depression we had to fight the quite fantastic belief that the great social disaster was due to what was then called "over-investment." We had to plead that the way out was *more* investment, and we did our best through our lifetime to introduce or invigorate the feeling that each generation owes it to its successors to hand down a much richer national store of plant equipment than it received.

We know that in the allocation of resources each year a large share must be allotted to the upkeep and improvement of plant, be it private (e.g., factories) or public (e.g., roads, schools, etc.). We should regard it as ridiculously shortsighted to care only for the accumulation of inventories and short-lived equipment and to disregard the plant. Yet we display this very shortsightedness when we neglect to care for the upkeep and improvement of our basic plant, nature. This natural plant is an inheritance which we hand down greatly deteriorated. Why have we been so careless?

Because the productive services of nature are free, the enjoyments nature provides are free, and therefore nature does not figure under capital assets in our view of things. Of this oversight I can offer a striking example. In our carefully designed input-output tables for the French economy, water does not figure as an input of the steel industry. This omission is quite justified in an economic table, water being but an infinitesimal item in the costs of the industry. But what this goes to show is that an economic view, in which things are seen in terms of financial costs, leads us to forget nature, and therefore to neglect what should be done, on the one hand, to preserve and improve it as a resource and, on the other, to preserve it as a source of enjoyment.

I have sometimes wondered whether, to redress the errors into which we are led by our way of thinking, we should not restore to rivers the status of persons, which pertained to them in pagan times. That this could well promote the efficient and farsighted use of resources has been demonstrated by my good friend Gilbert Tournier. President of the Compagnie Nationale du Rhône, he has been responsible for the most ample series of dams constructed in my country, which harness the forces of our most powerful rivers. This prince of engineers is also the author of entrancing films which chant the glory of the "deity Rhône." Let me hasten to add that he is a most devout Catholic; nobody in my country deems it at all strange that this Christian engineer, turning a part of God's creation to man's use, should express his respect for it in words, pictures, and treatment imbued with a reverence for nature.

I may be criticized for having intermingled in this paper concern for the potential dangers of a thoughtless handling of nature with an interest in the boon of an aesthetically pleasing environment.

I make no apologies for this intermingling. These two considerations are but different aspects of one subject. Surely what we are concerned about is the flowering of the "plant Man." Having ever used this expression of the poet Alfieri, I am especially pleased that an American commission, led by my friend Daniel Bell, should take as its theme the development of the human potential.

The flowering of the plant Man is greatly assisted by environmental conditions, which continuously flavor daily existence and educate our taste. For the fulfillment of these conditions, it is necessary that we regard it as a goal to place man in a garden of delight. And this will mean both a wise handling of the whole system of natural resources in general and a specific styling of the places where men live or work, or through which they travel daily.

It will also mean overcoming certain practical difficulties. The values relative to the general husbandry of resources do not at present figure in the operational calculus of agencies attending to specific wants. Nor can we expect a great deal from the ultimate power of the consumer because of the great difficulty of manifesting aesthetic preferences with respect to the environment by way of the marketplace. Market behavior cannot afford us any evaluation of the importance people attach to a seemly landscape, since most people have no possibility of gaining access to such a landscape.

No matter whether his qualifications be high or low, a man needs to be employed and must live within reach of his place of employment. Moreover, his wife must shop and often herself be employed and his children must be sent to school. Thus there are quite a number of constraints upon the family's location; these determine the area within which the family must settle and within which its choice of residence must be made. In most countries, obtaining living space of any kind is a problem and no choice is possible; in others, the choice is very restricted. The family takes what home it can get, regardless of setting. Generally it has no opportunity to manifest its preference for an aesthetic landscape.

We could have a market measure of the value placed upon the seemliness of the landscape only if people had a choice of equally convenient dwellings with different aesthetic qualities. While we lack any such measure, we can observe in Paris that the apartments which have been carved out of the Palais-Royal and look upon its enclosed garden are, notwithstanding their lack of elevators, priced far beyond others that are their equivalents in space but are devoid of aesthetic appeal.

Indeed, if you peruse a list of lodgings for rent or sale, you will find emphasis laid upon the view and upon its character (e.g., "view of Notre-Dame"). But it is not only in money that people are willing to pay for the aesthetic quality of the setting. They will also pay in fatigue. The cost may take the form of climbing up a staircase, in a long uncomfortable journey to work, in the inconvenience of shopping, etc.

It would be simple to contrast the migration of the American social elite to new suburbs and that of the French to the oldest parts of Paris or to ancient houses and farms around Paris. The motivation is, however, quite the same; it is the search of an aesthetically pleasing setting. It is our misfortune in France that we can turn only to what was done in the past in order to satisfy this urge; but no doubt this will change. The question of interest here, however, is not whether seemly surroundings shall be contrived for a few, as they are in some American suburbs, but whether they shall be contrived for the many and how this can be done.

It seems to me that the main object of a discussion bearing upon man's environment should be to find out the reasons for the miscarriage of the opportunities we are given, which are certainly no less than those of which the builders of an Italian city in the Renaissance availed themselves. Why does one shudder at the thought that as much housing as exists in France at present will be built there within the next thirty years? Why does one not think that the beauty of the country will enormously benefit therefrom, as it did from the construction boom which occurred after the Wars of Religion—that is, from the beginning of the seventeenth century onward?

Given this great building effort, what are the impediments to the provision of an enchanting framework for the many? Thinking in terms of my own country, I see chiefly three. First, an architect is much hindered when he is commissioned to provide only the dwellings in an urban agglomeration while responsibility for the schools, hospitals, etc. is given to others. A condition of harmony is that the design of the whole community be in the same hands. (I recognize that there are people more expert than I who urge that the effort to accommodate to what has been done by another affords inspiration, but I submit that the gap may be too large to bridge.)

The second point is cost. I hear all the architects concerned with housing projects complain about cost constraints. Cost constraints are the great excuse offered by our public jerry-builders. It does seem to me that a campaign of public education stressing the harm wrought by parsimony would do much to redress this difficulty. As an economist I see no case for keeping the cost of housing within the inhabitants' present capacity to pay. If you build so that rent (or staggered payments) corresponds to the present income of the occupant, you build in a manner not consonant with his future income or that of future occupants. Thus, the dwelling may soon have to be pulled down to make way for a better. Cheap building is associated with rapid obsolescence, itself a cause of high cost. If you build for a long term, social utility is better served. Of course, financial devices will have to be found to distribute the burden over time so that less of it falls to the first occupant, more to his successors. In short, the idea of a rapid write-off, much of which is bunched at the beginning, such as developed in the case of industrial equipment, should be inverted in the case of housing.

This principle recognizes that we build living quarters for a long time. This is a key consideration. The idea is very current that, as our society is characterized by change, housing projects should be regarded as camps to be pitched for us overnight and folded up on the morrow— except that overnight represents, say, fifteen years. In my opinion, this is a mistaken policy. A society characterized by rapid change is a society that changes its instruments rapidly, but living quarters are not in the category of instruments.

Our cities today reflect the momentous change in the nineteenth century when the age-old use of light tools by individual workers was superseded by the service of heavy machinery by clusters of workers. The machines were important and well housed; not so the men. There sprang up the deplorable agglomerations we all know so well, which can best be designated, in Orwellian style, as un-cities—human colonies lacking every one of those amenities and exercising none of those influences that in the past justified the identification of the words "city" and "civilization."

They were no more than the servants' quarters appended to the palaces of machines. Such subordination of housing to plant has no justification in our day. It is, moreover, nineteenth-century thinking to imagine that we must live increasingly huddled in and around the big cities. Every augmentation of the cities lends greater credibility to this conception and leads to the continuance of the phenomenon; yet the more the cities grow the closer they approach their death from congestion. We paradoxically cling to the expression of distance in terms of miles rather than minutes, and we still think in terms of transport rather than communication. Hence we crowd into the cities and their outskirts for the sake of a supposed convenience. And we pile city upon city. It seems strange to many Americans that the French equivalent of Cambridge (Mass.), Detroit, and Washington, should all be heaped together in Paris. No doubt New York, however, offers similar unnecessary conglomeration. It is a prescription for constriction. One of the great problems with which modern civilization must deal in the course of the coming generation is the urban bottleneck. The race between congestion and engineering devices to relieve that congestion is increasingly costly and will prove to be a losing game. The large city has outlived its civilizing purpose; it will go the way of the saber-toothed tiger.

It is fashionable to speculate upon the changes that may be brought about by a "New Age of Leisure." Let me stress that, even as things stand today, the job, including the trip to work, absorbs only some 10 percent of the time of all members of society. Whenever I say this, it causes surprise, but it can easily be verified. Allot 2,200 hours per year to work including the trip to work, note that this affects but about 42 percent of the population, set this total against the total of hours lived by all; it comes out at about 10 percent. Most of the remaining 90 percent is spent at home or in the neighborhood. Say that paid vacations away from home are going to cut into this ever more deeply, and that these involve the whole group; even so you can count on 80 percent of the time lived to be spent at home or in the neighborhood.

The importance of the amenities available in the neighborhood is thus evident. The houses in which we live should look upon a pleasing scene of playgrounds for the children, recreational facilities for teenagers and adults, promenades for the elderly, landscaping through which children can safely wend their way to school. The tunnels through which income-earners travel to work and return should be pleasantly screened. Presumably for some time we must still think of roads for that purpose, though underground railways would, of course, be more progressive.

When such railways are generally available, shelters should be provided in which cars could be stored out of sight; they are efficient instruments only when the purpose of movement is individualized. Reflecting the place education should have in the life of a family, homes should cluster around the schools and playgrounds, and it is to the potential capacity of the schools and playgrounds that the community must be adjusted in size if we are to have true cities. And it is around "places to live in" that work places must be sited.

The point I wish to make is that technological change determines what is feasible but not what is pleasant. Whether you live in 1768 or 1968, a pleasant room, a pleasant view, a pleasant walk, a handsome place of meeting are much the same. What is changed is not the desirable but—and this most fortunately—our ability to procure it for an ever widening percentage of the population. Our achievements in that direction would be much greater than they are if we were less muddled in our thinking. It is absurd to regard the increase in our technological capacities other than as a great boon; if people suffer from sorry or monstrous living conditions, it is because we have not made the right use of our opportunities. At the same time it is also absurd to regard technological progress as determining what is to be enjoyed. Technology is here to serve; it is, or should be, the handmaiden of amenity.

Architects are often criticized for not making sufficient use of the new means which technology makes available to them. I am incompetent to judge of the relevance of this criticism. But I would formulate and vigorously urge another. For my own taste, architects are far too preoccupied with keeping up with the Joneses of engineering. Engineers have achieved wondrous progress in providing us with means, but it is not for them to tell us that these means are the amenities with which we must make do. If we let them, they shall lead us in the direction opposite to what makes life pleasant.

Let me cite another example. I cross the Atlantic faster in an aircraft than in a steamship. This does not imply that I am more comfortable in the aircraft; it is the other way around. The astronauts go where man has never been before; this does not imply that they are more comfortable in their capsule than I am in my study; it is again very much the other way around. Now if the architect draws inspiration from a rocket capsule, he is apt to build something more impressive to the eye than pleasant for everyday life.

The engineer and the architect are in utterly different lines of business; one is concerned with enlarging our possibilities, the other with utilizing these possibilities to extend the framework of the good life. What the good life is does not change with technology. The engineer and the architect are meant here to symbolize two mental attitudes each of which is valid in its time and place. It seems reasonable to feel that where the bulk of the population lives very poorly, efficiency should be stressed, while as abundance develops, amenity should become the more important. Amazingly enough, the enhancement of the pleasantness of life seems by no means to keep pace with our growing productivity. In our age of efficiency, those properly concerned with the provision of amenities are so bankrupt of ideas that they turn to the imitation of the engineers.

Surely the architect lacks no indications of the qualities of the physical setting that contribute to the good life. First, he can find such indications in the testimony of the civilization of the past. He can observe what kind of physical settings the better-off have always contrived for themselves, noting their concern for the landscape, which was certainly far more pronounced, even, in Asian than in European societies. (See what Needham has to say on the subject in his great work, *Science and Civilization in China*.) Secondly, he can observe what tourists seek; on the one hand ancient cities that testify to the skill of earlier architects in designing a humane environment; on the other, natural environments— "unspoiled," as the advertisements put it.

To sum up what I have to say: men have not so changed that the pleasurable is changed. What *has* changed is the opportunity to procure the pleasurable for the many.

Recently I visited Warsaw for the first time since I was with the Polish army in the first days of the last war. I was immensely impressed by the rebuilding of the old town and the restoration of the seventeenth- and eighteenth-century buildings—not only the public buildings, but even the private houses—to their pristine condition and indeed beyond that. This fantastic achievement was undertaken at a time of utter misery, when Poland had suffered immense destruction. This was a heroic effort. Seeking explanations for the priority given the task, I received a variety of answers, all of which contained this common part; beauty is a public good and a formative influence for good.

In our far richer countries, can we not afford such a public good; do we not need a beneficent influence?

One of the most promising utterances of our times is the White House message of February 8, 1965. It contains in its exordium this remarkable statement: "The increasing tempo of urbanization and growth is already depriving many Americans of the right to live in decent surroundings."

The idea here put forward in the form of a "right to live in decent surroundings" is of the utmost importance. Obviously there can be no such right without the counterpart of a responsibility to contribute to the decency of the surroundings. The man who enjoys the use of a noisy toy like the outboard motor commits an indecency just as much as the industrialist who contaminates the water—indeed, he is more guilty because he affords no service as a counterpart.

The quality of our surroundings can be achieved, maintained, and enhanced only if people individually are made aware that the behavior that impairs them is indecent behavior. No such awareness is as yet widespread. Cain, after murdering his brother, said: "I am not my brother's keeper." Similarly, we protest, tacitly or otherwise, that we are not nature's keeper, and we are heedless of the injuries we inflict upon our surroundings

We can and we must spell out public policies for the control of all those forms of pollution with which we are debasing our environment and for the creation of harmonious cities, but we shall not achieve very impressive results unless education at the very earliest stage breathes into our conscience reverence for the earth's bounty, on which we depend, and regard for beauty as Man's only lasting achievement.

Surely the United States as the richest country of our world, should take the lead. When Italy held this position, in the late Middle Ages and during the Renaissance, it gave the world what is still our richest patrimony. Is it not time for her heirs to emulate her?

Notes

1. *Manchester Guardian Weekly*, July 10, 1965.
2. This view, which I first expressed in a February 1967 lecture, has since been confirmed by the Report of the British Tribunal of Inquiry, issued in July: "Tips are the discards of the coal-mining industry. Constituted of industrially-rejected materials, hitherto they have been largely banished from thought" (*Report of the Tribunal Appointed to Inquire into the Disaster at Aberfan*, H.L. 316, H.C. 553, H.M. Stationery Office).
3. This has been well brought out by Masanao Toda and Emir H. Shuford, Jr. in their paper "Utility, Induced Utilities, and Small Worlds," in *Behavioral Science*, vol. 10, no. 3.
4. Joseph Needham, *Science and Civilization in China*.. The volumes of this masterly work have been brought out in succession by the Cambridge University Press since 1954.
5. Morris Neiburger, "Diffusion and Air Pollution." In *Bulletin of the American Meteorological Society*, vol. 46, no. 3, March 1965.

17

An Economic View of Marine Problems

How has it come about that the sea, after being exploited by mankind for millennia, has suddenly become a *new* sort of theme? The primary cause of this important innovation is that a new perspective has been identified. The sea has always figured in the human mind as a fluid mass supporting sailing vessels and containing an astonishing variety of marine life. Navigators have long known that this aqueous mass was supported by a floor which geology later made an object of investigation. The ocean floor was not traditionally included in ordinary thought except perhaps as a subject for poetry or as a kind of cemetery for submerged ships and cities. Incipient awareness of the potential of submerged "soils" as exploitable land is "discovery" in the most literal sense; what was hitherto covered and hidden is now observed directly.

Deep-sea exploration by the Piccards and the Cousteaus had enchanted us with underwater seascapes and the ballets of their inhabitants, but modern research of a different sort reveals the deeps rich, for example, in petroleum and natural gas. With the discovery of such wealth, the problem of a new regime for the seas is posed.

The series of events that is supposed to culminate in an international agreement on a new regime for the sea was initiated by a declaration in 1945. This declaration was the first to deal a blow to the age-old regime and was animated solely by concern for the mineral wealth of the marine depths. Many other preoccupations might well have justified a new look at the old regime and intervention in the new, but those pre-

Reprinted from *The Tides of Change: Peace, Pollution, and Potential of the Oceans*, ed. by E. M. Borgese and D. Krieger (New York: Mason/Charter, 1975): 4-32. Translated from the French by James Albritton and John Wilkinson. Used by permission of the International Ocean Institute.

occupations are of secondary importance chronologically, and the attention given them has been minimal; we will thus begin historically.

The Truman Proclamation and the Continental Shelf

The point of departure was President Truman's proclamation of September 1945, stating that the United States government considered the
natural resources on and under the continental shelf, measured three
miles from the coastline, to be under U.S. control and jurisdiction. The
term *continental shelf* thus entered into diplomatic language. (There
was at that time undoubtedly a not inconsiderable agitation in the world's
chancelleries to find the term's meaning.)

Marine geologists had used *continental shelf* to mean the shallow,
submersed base, an extension of dry ground, out to the edge, at which
there is a slope (known as *continental*). At the base of this slope, a zone
of detritus stretches gradually to the ocean depths. To this was given
the designation *continental rise*. The ensemble of shelf, slope, and rise
came to be known as the "continental margin." All these terms have,
since 1945, become more or less well known to the laity.

For the scientist a change in profile marked off the continental shelf.
This appears at different depths, perhaps 20 to 550 meters, with an
average of 133 meters.[1]

The Truman administration preferred to define the shelf according
to its maximum depth ("isobath"), rather than by the borders suggested
by marine science. The proclamation used an isobath of 100 fathoms,
an arbitrary geologic line which, however, was *practically* significant,
that is, in terms of accessibility and, of course, *future* accessibility.
According to Senator Pell three years later, there was still no exploitation at a depth greater than 30 meters.[2] Since then, forecasts of accessibility have indicated far greater depths.

It should be noted that delimitation by isobath was generally accepted (but with the use of the metric system, so that a depth of 200
meters, for example, took the place of a 100-fathom measure, that is,
183 meters).

In a communiqué accompanying President Truman's proclamation,
it was explained that the decision taken by the American government
"would render possible an orderly development of an underwater area
of 750,000 square miles." This referred to the isobath of 100 fathoms;
the change to a depth of 200 meters meant an increase to 845,000 square
miles.[3] The margin of error in the estimations was probably substantially greater than the difference made by changing the reference isobath.

The 1945 figure was nearly two million square kilometers; the 1969 figure exceeded two million. This means that the underwater area over which the United States asserted jurisdiction is greater than the surface of the ten states of the European Common Market.

The Truman proclamation was a break with tradition. It occasioned widespread repercussions, the character—or rather, the characters—of which ought to be understood. These are two important subjects that are not dealt with in this article except for noting them summarily, in order to give more space to a discussion of the motives of the Truman administration in initiating an action that would lead to the overthrow of the *ancien regime* of the sea. Through discussion and analysis of these motives, we get into the *economics* of the ocean.

The Break with Tradition

I trust I will be pardoned for setting down a number of truisms: the sea does not lend itself to human habitation, but on the other hand, it does allow expeditious passage. Men can behave on the sea only as nomads. They cannot be sedentary beings.

On its surface the sea possesses little or nothing equivalent to those accidents of terrain that have served for centuries to mark off the domains of sovereignty or terrestrial dominion, and we cannot easily erect markers to delimit private preserves or properties. Because of this natural difference, the sea has not known the political divisions and private subdivisions that are characteristic of men's activities on land. It has not been subject to the complex and highly differentiated *institutional* evolution of the land.

In connection with the nomad-sedentary polarity, we know that terrestrial nomads have played a double role with regard to sedentary humans, the one beneficial to commerce, the other that of robbers, pillagers, and the like. Something analogous can be said of the role of sea nomads with respect to terrestrial sedentaries. But on the earth, the inimical role of nomads has usually predominated over the commercial, and social progress has been achieved by suppressing the nomads. Even when sea nomads were guilty of numerous attacks, accompanied by much cruelty and destruction, the *positive* side of their activity grew in importance and even became *decisively* important in the development of civilization. To judge matters in purely terrestrial terms, it can be said that the sea has remained in a prehistoric condition. Nonetheless, it is on, or in connection with, the sea that the forms of modern life have developed. For example, it was in the world's seaports that a blending of products and populations has often been achieved. (See, for example, the description of Antwerp by Luigi Guiccardini, 1572.) In these ports, there were many social innovations, and creative imagination was excited.[4] It was in connection with such places that the first industrial production—the construction of naval vessels—began.[5] Plato's works contain the well-known description of the shipyards of the Piraeus. In these ports *collective* commercial enterprise originated, as well as the concepts of insurance and double-entry bookkeeping.

At the beginning of his well-known codification of Maritime Laws[6] the jurist Pardessus said: "If civil laws be intimately connected with the nature of Government, its *mores* and national habits, the same cannot be said of the laws of maritime commerce. Produced in *every* locality by like needs, they derive from this fact a *universal* character corresponding to what Cicero well said of Natural Law: *'non opinione sed natura jure constitutum.'* Since they concern the *universe* in which navigators form a single family, so to speak, their spirit cannot change with national boundaries." I shall not stop to consider whether it is the similarity of needs or the absence of boundaries that brought about the uniformity Pardessus praised, but will be content to remark that the absence of boundaries endured for a long time because there was no particular point at which there was sufficient interest in changing this condition.

There was interest in the rights of access to those regions where terrestrial wealth could be extracted. It was this interest which caused conflict to break out between the Portuguese, who discovered the route to the East Indies, and the Dutch, who could not tolerate being excluded. (This particular dispute has remained a classical one because of the attention paid to it by Grotius.)

The interests of national commerce were finally reconciled with freedom of navigation by terrestrial customs arrangements. Moreover, it is conceivable that acceptance of the principle of nonintervention, with regard to naval vessels, encouraged *political* control of the territories that were sources of riches. In all historical periods, the principal economic interest in the sea has arisen from the *terrestrial riches* to which control of the sea lanes gave access. If the original concentrations of capital had to do with the sea, it was with the sea as a route to the riches of the earth. And though, in all ages, fishing in the sea has been practiced, it has remained until quite recently an activity more artisanal than industrial. In the legends of all countries the fisherman is represented as being poverty-stricken,[7] the commercial navigator *(viator)* and his sedentary associate *(stans)* as rich. When Grotius argues for the freedom of the seas, he is taking the position of large commercial enterprise.[8] In his *Mare Clausum*, Selden responded by defending the point of view of a national fisherman.

Countries relatively advanced in navigation were only minimally interested in protecting their local fisheries from foreigners. But they were always interested in opening navigation routes to foreign riches. So it was scarcely surprising that the concept of "open seas" came to prevail over that of "restricted" seas. Also, the doctrine established became one of open seas for *everyone*. The national state reserved for itself only a narrow strip of three miles from its coastline, a strip that was designated the "territorial sea."[9]

Did the United States break with this centuries-old order of things by its proclamation in 1945? Perhaps it did not wish specifically to do so, but intention is one thing and result another.

Repercussions of the Proclamation, or the Vindication of Selden

To go into the details of national reactions would be to digress from our subject, but let us keep in mind three aspects of these reactions:

First, there was no protest.

Second, there occurred a "generalization" of Washington's claims by every country possessing a marine littoral and a continental shelf adjacent to this littoral. This principle was the object of an international agreement signed at Geneva in 1958 under the auspices of the United Nations. This agreement, concerning the continental shelf, can hardly be said to have influenced world opinion, an opinion which was not conscious of the fact that the states having designs on the sea had divided up submerged "territories" among themselves in this manner. These territories, according to the conventional definition of the continental shelf, included a total area of 27 million kilometers, that is to say, an area greater than the surface of North America (21 1/2 million) or of the Soviet Union (22,400,000) and equal to that of Asia (the Soviet Union excluded). Moreover, the language of the agreement made the delimitation of the continental shelf nonlimitative, since the following was written into the first article of the agreement: "The term 'continental shelf' is used as referring (a) to the seabed and subsoil of the submarine areas adjacent to the coast, but outside the area of the territorial sea, to a depth of 200 meters or, beyond that limit, to where the depth of the superjacent waters admits of the exploitation of the natural resources of the said areas."[10]

It appears by now that the expression "continental shelf," originally borrowed from the geologists, was so far from its primary scientific meaning as to denote everything that technological progress allows.

Third, Washington's initiative called forth even more comprehensive claims. On October 11, 1946, the government at Buenos Aires seized the initiative by decreeing that the "sovereignty" (a term avoided in the Truman proclamation) of the Republic of Argentina extended not only over its continental shelf, but also over the waters covering it, described as the "epi-continental sea." The second article did indeed stipulate that the use of the epi-continental sea for navigation would not be affected. But *fishing* rights were clearly affected, and it is for this reason that I have used the expression "Selden's vindication."

Possibly the American decision in 1945 did not infringe on the international law that was operative up to that time, especially since it had to do with an entity which had never been the object of consideration, namely, the resources of the marine soil and subsoil. On the other hand, the Argentine decision undeniably impinged on the former regime of the oceans. There was flat opposition, which brought definite consequences. Would Buenos Aires ever have thought of the annexation of the epi-continental sea if there had been no Truman proclamation? The Argentineans, in a decree embracing something avoided by the Americans, were searching for a concrete technical equivalent.

In Buenos Aires and elsewhere, the question was probably seen as this: The United States is extending its political power to the marine resources, which their technical arm will enable them to attain; so, for we who do not possess an equal technological capacity, are there not other marine riches that we might lay hold of? Why should we not extend *our* political power to them?

Here I introduce the term *marine content,* which is alien to juridical and scientific language but which comes naturally to the mind of an economist, to contrast the use of the sea as an *infrastructure* of transportation with the *extraction of its contents*, living or non-living. If there is a historical reason for distinguishing between the new activity of submarine mining and the ancient activities of navigation and fishing, there is an analogous reason for lumping the activities dealing with marine content.

It was this analogy that caused the Latin Americans to lay claim on the riches contained *in* the epi-continental sea, as well as on those of its surface and bottom. The United States had "flown" the flag on the ocean bottoms; others had advanced theirs up to the surface.

It soon began to appear illogical to countries preoccupied with fishing rights to trace marine borders under their control with reference to the continental shelf or to some conventional definition of it. It was also inconvenient for those Latin American nations which bordered on the Pacific and which, consequently, had negligible expanses of continental shelf—judged from the geological, or conventional, point of view—to a depth of 200 meters. This situation produced the Declaration of Chile (June 25, 1947), announcing that the Chilean government was "extending protection and control" over a maritime zone extending 200 miles from its coastline. On August 18, 1952, the Declaration of Santiago followed, by which Chile, Ecuador, and Peru proclaimed exclusive sovereignty and jurisdiction over a maritime zone of a flat 200 miles, including the "subjacent" soil and subsoil.

The national claims that Washington had enunciated with respect to its continental shelf had not only been generalized, they had been transformed. A chain reaction at the international level had appeared, dislocating what had long been international space.

Matters might have taken a different turn. This was a time when the United Nations was beginning; it was one in which the United States enjoyed international prestige as no other country in modern times had; it was one that saw an American administration on the point of manifesting an unheard-of international conscience in its policies with respect not only to a devastated Europe but to the underdeveloped countries. Would its policies have been followed internationally if it had taken some initiative in modernizing the international regime? Could this administration have taken into account the new technical possibilities of exploitation of the deep seas, as well as working for the prudent management of the living resources of the seas? A great opportunity was missed—or more accurately, it was not perceived. Something very different was done, and we must find out why.

Motives in the Truman Proclamation

I do not know of any study by American political scientists of the decisions that led to the proclamation in September 1945 and am therefore reduced to conjecture. Here it seems appropriate to first eliminate the motives that are unlikely to have ever existed. Was it really urgent that American interests constitute a "game preserve"? Where were foreign interests armed with sufficient technologies and sufficient financial means even to appear to possess the ability to intrude into such a preserve? If the concept of a "game preserve" became a general one, might it not be disadvantageous to American interests, that is, to a technologically advanced country? Could any profitable reserving of two million square kilometers be worth more than the restriction of 25 million square kilometers? Have we before us an example of *protectionism* on the part of a country in an area in which it was technically superior? Did Great Britain offer an example of protectionism with regard to textile products at the beginning of the nineteenth century? A quick examination leads us to dismiss a protectionist motive.[11]

We *can* be fairly certain that the U.S. proclamation was instigated by the Department of the Interior, which argued, on one hand, that future supplies of hydrocarbons in the United States called for exploitation of the sea beyond the limits of the territorial waters (the traditional three miles), and, on the other, that large expenditures for research would not be taken on by American business if it did not obtain exclusive rights to explore and subsequently to exploit a given area of the sea. To obtain such concessions, however, it would be necessary to have an authority possessing powers to grant them. This step would be that the federal government would claim jurisdiction.

A second consideration was: Any petroleum produced beyond the borders of the U.S. could be brought into the American market only on the condition that it be accompanied by importation certificates, that is, be subject to quotas as well as entry duties. Exclusion of petroleum extracted beyond territorial waters from these inconveniences would be needed in order to extend federal jurisdiction.

It is fairly certain that both of these considerations were urged by the Interior Department in connection with the 1945 proclamation, since identical considerations were more recently advanced by the same agency, in order that federal jurisdiction not be limited to the 200-meter depth, but be extended to the continental slope and even to the continental rise, that is, to the entire continental margin.

Another consideration, different from the industrial preoccupations of the Interior Department, was added, probably in 1945. In the United States, the territorial waters within the standard limit of three miles were under the jurisdiction of the states bordering them and therefore of their respective state governments. Without federal intervention, the state governments might have secured the right of granting concessions beyond the limits of the jurisdiction, but the proclamation deprived them of this possibility by reserving this right to the federal government. What has been said about states' rights explains the expression, "outer continental shelf" that recurs again and again in federal documents. What is beyond territorial waters is under federal authority. In light of this consideration, the Truman proclamation assumes the aspect of a *precedent* for international authority. The proclamation restrains the states within their historical jurisdictions in order to subordinate to a common authority whatever might occur beyond them in the future.

The American Fear of Running Short

One might ask, why did the American government move so precipitously to encourage research on and exploitation of the high seas? It was obviously not for whatever financial gains exploitation would bring to the U.S. treasury. The royalties received in 1971 by the federal government for exploitation of petroleum and gas on the outer continental shelf amounted to a mere $346 million, of which $330 million came from the Gulf of Mexico and $16 million from California.[12] What appeared to have spurred the federal government was a psychological phenomenon that recurs time and again in the United States—anxiety about *future* supplies of petroleum.

The combination of the objective fact of prodigious wealth in natural resource, on one hand, and a highly subjective attitude related to the fear of shortages in these same resources, on the other, is a curious American trait in the eyes of Europeans. We witnessed an outbreak of this susceptibility at the time of the Korean War, in the panic buying of 1950. On the heels of this, President Truman ordered a study of the future availability of raw materials (up to 1975), a study that became famous as the Paley Report.[13]

This episode was only one extraordinary manifestation of an always latent, but easily aroused, anxiety. To advance a psychological hypothesis, I risk little in asserting that the very foundation of American culture is an amalgam of pietism and pragmatism. It is more than possible that the large-scale wastage of the Creator's gifts that characterizes American civilization inspires vague sentiments of guilt and anxiety about the rising level of expectations.

This same consciousness has recently erupted in a passionate concern for the environment. But whatever the moral foundation may be, American opinion has obviously been subjected frequently to periods of anxiety over natural resources, especially petroleum. This is easily understood, for just as the English model of growth involved coal and steam transportation, the American model was founded on petroleum and the means of transportation associated with it.

Ever since 1919, anxiety about future supplies of petroleum had been expressed over and over again. For example, a director of the Bureau of Mines averred that domestic fields could never suffice to meet national demands.[14] The director of the Geological Survey agreed: "Americans will either have to depend on foreign supplies, or consume less, or perhaps both."[15]

A member of the same bureau carried this alarmism further: "We should expect, unless consumption is slowed, to find ourselves dependent on foreign petroleum deposits to the tune of 150 to 200 million barrels a year—perhaps even by 1925.... Add to this the probability that in five years, perhaps even in three, production will have begun to lag because of exhaustion of reserves."[16]

Concerning the first statement, it might be said that the level of imports predicted was not reached until more than thirty years after the prediction. As for the second, American production (about 443 million barrels in 1920) had surpassed 1.7 billion in 1945. (Including off-shore production, it was 3.5 billion in 1971.)

These warnings coincided with a change of attitude on the part of American petroleum companies. Founded in a society that seemed to abound in deposits, why were they not, first of all, concerned with insuring their reserves? It is typical that Standard Oil (founded in 1870, eleven years after the discovery of petroleum in the United States) began as a corporation for refining and distribution, leaving research and extraction to private individuals, much in the manner of European milk companies today. On the other hand, west European corporations (especially in Holland and England) had to go prospecting to discover and exploit *outside* the nonproductive areas of Western Europe. As a result, they acquired concessions all over the globe, which later inspired American firms to do likewise. The dismemberment of the Ottoman Empire offered an opportunity of penetrating a highly attractive area. Expert opinion ought not only to have interested American firms, but to have encouraged the federal government to back up American claims vis-à-vis European firms that had been there first but which were scarcely hospitable to newcomers.

A comparison of 1920 (the year marking the take-off point of American enterprise in the petroleum basins of the Eastern hemisphere) and 1945 (the year of the take-off point in underwater exploitation) comes to mind. These two temporal points of departure appeared in their own time as necessary for the maintenance of the positions of American firms. The country that had made the principal contribution to making petroleum the vital fluid of industrial society could scarcely be expected to envisage any prospect of finding itself the first to be deprived of it. Yet this was conceivable in the future. The relation between *proved* reserves and current production is doubtless much too sensitive an indicator, for only a few years of slowdown in exploration are necessary for estimates to become worthless.[17](This actually happened during the Second World War.) After 1945 the stimulation of exploration reestablished the normal relation of 12 1/2 to 1. In studying this situation *after* recovery, it is possible to discern the sources of the Americans' anxiety.

By 1948 the United States was responsible for 58 percent of world production, whereas their own proved reserves amounted to not less than 36 percent of the proved reserves of the world. However, this proportion of the proved reserves greatly exaggerated the Americans' real share of world resources. The main point was that exploration in the United States was far more elaborate than anywhere else; proved reserves therefore represented a much larger proportion of actual unexploited resources than they did elsewhere.

One expert, Louis G. Weeks, whose reputation was to grow, has illuminated the situation. According to his geological estimates of world petroleum stocks, the original share of the United States came to only 18 percent of the total.[18] From this it followed that the U.S. share in presumed reserves must be very much smaller, perhaps as low as 10 percent.

Thus, light shed on the disproportion between geological stocks on American territory and the tempo of its exploitation obviously justified the attitude of American companies toward other regions where, according to Weeks, 400 billion barrels of presumably exploitable resources remained to be discovered[19] and also toward the continental shelves of the world, for which Weeks tentatively gave a similar figure.[20]

Orientation toward other regions of the world succeeded so well that by 1970, the five major American firms were extracting less than 26 percent of total production from North America (the United States and Canada); 60 percent of their total was derived from the Eastern hemisphere.[21]

It is impressive to contrast the progress of world production with that of the United States. Taking 1948 as a base, the index of American production in 1971 was 187 and world production 525; that is, the former had not even doubled, whereas the latter had increased more than fivefold.[22]

However, more interesting here is the orientation toward *offshore* production. In the available statistics, production is distributed according to country, with no distinction made between production on land and under the sea. The absence of this distinction in national statistics is based not only on law but on natural fact. Drilling under the sea has consisted primarily of following the course of known terrestrial deposits into the sea. Most exploiters were reluctant to advance into deep waters, given the technical difficulties that had to be surmounted. So when Humble Oil secured a lease for the exploitation of sectors lying between 300 and 1,800 feet deep in the Santa Barbara Channel (February 1968), the record depth of wells exploited was 140 feet[23] and therefore well within the limit of 100 fathoms (600 feet) assigned to the continental shelf by the 1945 proclamation. Technology advanced, however, with great speed. This rapid advance is illustrated by the fact that the first offshore drilling rig was set up in 1949; twenty years later, there were 199.[24] Technologically the effort was enormous. Even though it is clear that results remain to be seen, petroleum presently coming from underwater exploitation already comprises a substantial portion of world production. It may even be true that it constitutes one-fifth of total production.[25] If this estimate is valid, underwater production already equals the total world production of 1948.

Petroleum and the Sea

I do not believe I have been too much preoccupied with petroleum, for the whole process of overthrowing the older ocean regime began with the Truman proclamation, and the American decision was certainly made with petroleum problems uppermost in mind. The principal changes in the use of the seas during the last twenty-seven years have been tied in with the problems of petroleum. For example, navigation is today, as in all past times, by far the most important use of the sea for the global economy. During the period considered, we have witnessed the replacement of coal by petroleum as the principal energy source for navigation. We have observed the enormous development of the use of petroleum in maritime transportation. It represents not only the major portion of the mass transported (1.3 billion tons out of a total of 2.5 billion), but, calculated in terms of ton miles, it comprises 62 percent.[26] Calculated in this manner, transportation of petroleum has almost quadrupled, compared, say, to the total transportation of cereals, coal, and ferrous minerals. More than half the tonnage of petroleum transported by sea goes to western Europe. Crude oil constitutes more than two-thirds of all cargoes arriving in Europe by sea. The immense importance of petroleum in marine traffic clearly reflects the position it holds in our industrial civilization, which, beginning as a civilization of coal, quickly became a civilization of petroleum, or rather, of hydrocarbons, since the close chemical relative of petroleum, natural gas, is coming into ever wider use. Safe methods of volume reduction (by liquefaction) were the necessary condition for it to become, in turn, an object for important marine traffic.[27]

Hydrocarbons have become one of the foundations of economic life, not only as sources of energy,[28] but as a raw material from which the chemist is able to synthesize a great variety of materials. The ancient alchemists merely proposed to create *known* materials; today's chemists actually create new materials which possess the *desired properties*.

Even more rapid than the growth of hydrocarbons for the production of energy is the growth of their more complicated functions. In 1969 some 51 million tons of primary organic products were extracted from them, of which two-fifths were used to produce plastics. The volume of organic products derived from hydrocarbons is rising from 13 million tons in 1960 to an estimated 165 million tons in 1980. More to the point, for Europe, according to these estimates, it will rise in two decades (1960–80) from 2.3 million to 60 million tons.

As for plastics, the principal outlet for petrochemical products, production grew from one million tons in 1948 to 20 million today, and it is estimated that it will reach 90 million by 1980.

Taking volume of production as the base, the total production of plastics surpasses that of nonferrous metals; only wood, cement, and steel are produced in greater volume than plastics.[29]

The Maritime Problems of Petroleum

Since petroleum today is vital to the international economic system, it is understandable that the problems it poses are also international, problems such as those of its transportation in international spaces (seas interposed between national habitats). Such transportation is by tankers, the dimensions of which have grown enormously since the Second World War. The largest tanker thirty years ago had a capacity of 16,000 tons; in 1971 there were tankers in service with capacities of 230,000 tons, and tankers designed to hold 500,000 tons are under construction.

Basic concepts, which are limited by their terrestrial origin, must change. On sea, the transportational infrastructure is a "gift of nature" and does not naturally impose limits on vehicle size; on land, however, infrastructure must be planned. The legendary quarrel of Oedipus with his father, Laertes, broke out over the use of ruts and tracks for chariot traffic. We know the historical importance of the construction of the Roman roads and how crucial it was for European civilization when their maintenance was abandoned after the fall of the Western Roman Empire. We know that civilization then was confined to coastal zones and towns accessible by river. Land transportation only became important once again as a function of governmental investment in road construction. Then came the railroad era. It is significant that the first line was constructed in accordance with the proposal of Stephenson to bypass the ship canal dug by Lord Bridgewater.

Land vehicles have never been able to sustain traffic without planned and costly infrastructures. Since these infrastructures determined where one could take such vehicles, relatively small size and carrying capacity limited the dimensions of the vehicles and the loads they could carry. Little such limitation was necessary on the sea, where shippers can increase dimensions and cargo whenever it appears economical for them to do so. According to a study done three years ago, the cost per ton of transport is found to diminish by more than three-fourths in passing from tankers of 20,000 tons (dwt.) to tankers of the 230,000-ton class.[30] This economy of private costs of the shipper admittedly does not take into account the vast public expenditures to make seaports usable by oceangoing giants. In the absence of international agreement, port authorities are forced to assume these expenditures as best they can.[31]

The rapid growth of maritime traffic creates congestion in the straits, which sometimes leads to collisions. The Straits of Dover (in which traffic has grown to perhaps 700 vessels every twenty-four hours[32]) was the scene of forty collisions in four years, including a number of sinkings which made navigation even more dangerous, since the wreckage was not usually cleared from the sea floor. Due to their increasing size, tankers aggravate such congestion and increase the risk of collision. Moreover, because of their content, the rupture of hulls can cause serious pollution.

Giant tankers are subject to accident outside the straits. The *Torrey Canyon* episode made a profound impression on European opinion.

Arriving from the Persian Gulf, the *Torrey Canyon* was bound for Milford Haven and did not enter the channel at the widest point. It foolishly hugged the Scilly Islands at a speed of seventeen knots and ran aground on a reef fifteen miles from the westernmost point of England. The shock collapsed six of the eighteen reservoirs, which contained 117,000 tons of Kuwait crude oil. Since the hull was left to the action of the waves, all that was not pumped out of the reservoirs (which had in the beginning remained intact, or almost so) was spilled into the sea. For the effects on marine biology, see the study by J.E. Smith.[33]

One aspect, however, is worth mentioning. The *Torrey Canyon* was flying the Liberian flag and its commander had worked without interruption for 365 days. "Six months of uninterrupted tanker service are common; for, given the daily operational cost of £15,000, large tankers have to be in service from 350 to 355 days a year with less than 24-hour intervals for charging and discharging," wrote a commander of the British Navy in an article with the provocative title: "Can We Delay the Next Tanker Disaster?" [34] The article appeared after a series of major accidents had occurred, most of them involving vessels flying the Liberian flag. This provoked violent denunciations from the president of the British Union of Merchant Sailors, concerning vessels flying a flag of convenience, which allows ship owners to work officers and crew in a manner both harmful to them and dangerous to others.

Liberia has the largest fleet in the world today, yet the population of this country scarcely exceeds one million. The degree of Liberian economic development is revealed by the fact that, according to the most recent information, the country has fewer than 5,000 telephones. This farcical situation would defy the fantasies of the most imaginative authors; it is, indeed, almost a satire. It should be noted that the rapid development of the Liberian fleet has been accompanied by a decline of the American. This would represent a felicitous transfusion of money from the rich to the poor were the affair not a mere legal fiction.[35] All this would be very convenient for private interests, who wish to escape American taxation and regulation, were it not that its consequences are so grave (particularly considering the number of accidents that befall the Liberian fleet).

The gross insufficiency of *any* regime of freedom of the seas, in which ship owners are subject to such obligations as are prescribed by the country under whose flag the vessel navigates, is clear; the necessity for controlled international regulations becomes equally clear. It is necessary to emphasize (with Ranken) to what degree the organization of maritime transport lags behind that of aerial transport in nearly every respect. This lag is not surprising. The use of the medium of the air is a recent phenomenon which appeared rapidly in technically advanced countries. It called forth a vast amount of attention, and it was only natural that rational regulations would be enacted. On the other hand, use of the marine medium is ancient. Since established customs tend to correspond to long-existing conditions, it becomes difficult to replace antiquated regulations with rational rules that correspond to changed conditions. The difficulty is compounded by the fact that a far wider degree of consent is needed.

That petroleum plays a major role in maritime transportation and must therefore play a major role in maritime pollution was revealed to the world by the *Torrey Canyon* incident. Accidents are a massive and obvious source of pollution, but dumping into the sea was an unobserved source until very recently, when the nations involved, with some success, were able to reduce the practice of dumping at sea.

Accidents and dumping, taken together, have probably contributed less to pollution than hydrocarbon use on land, the end products of which reach the oceans by the winds and rivers, since synthetic compounds fabricated by the hydrocarbon industry are much more poisonous than the hydrocarbons themselves. For everything dumped into the sea by runoff from terrestrial sources (a veritable *cloaca maxima*), defense of the seas calls for the same kind of regulation that is observed on land. This is clearly a part of national sovereignty and comes under the competence of the Conference on the Environment. It is probably sufficient that such rules be adopted by those countries that are large per capita consumers of hydrocarbons. It would be premature to raise obstacles to the development of countries which remain small consumers, and their natural refusal to cooperate cannot be allowed to create valid excuses for others. But it would scarcely be unreasonable to require that drilling in the sea, an operation so likely to result in pollution, be made to obey universal safety regulations. I say "scarcely unreasonable," since they are in every case the operations of the same kind of technologists who are nearly always employees of international firms.

The Distribution of Submarine Basins

In terms of the wealth of the sea, hydrocarbons have already, in commercial value, outstripped the value of the production of the fishing industry, a lopsided tendency which seems certain to grow. Other raw materials extracted from the seas are, at least for the time being, of relatively little importance.[36]

It is generally admitted that further progress in world consumption of petroleum will cause increased demand on marine sources. The progress of technology permits the extraction of petroleum from ever-greater depths, hence each state, assuming that it has a coastline, will be interested in extending its jurisdiction as far out to sea as possible.[37]

We may ask why this apparent similarity of interests is illusory. Is it because different countries are unequally situated with regard to personnel and technology? Is it due to the difference of interests between the "advanced" and the "developing" countries? It is hard to understand why the state of technology in a given country would make such a difference. The most advanced techniques are (and will be) applied in the epi-continental seas of the least advanced countries of the world, as well as those of the most advanced countries, with arrangements made through concessions with firms on land. Also, given the large role played by petroleum royalties in the budgets of countries with weak economies, it would appear that they have an even greater interest in extending their control over underwater deposits than do the advanced countries.

The dividing line of *national interest* does not pass between the "advanced" and the "underdeveloped" countries; rather, it passes between those countries whose epi-continental sea seems promising and those for whom it does not.

It we take into consideration the volume of petroleum exploitation on the territories of the Third World, we see how little their location coincides with any concentration of population. In fact, petroleum royalties come mostly from desert areas. In 1970, for example, $5.5 billion royalties were paid out in the Eastern hemisphere among states whose total population was slightly less than 50 million—that is, a small fraction of that of the Third World. From this total (if we subtract Iran, with 29 million inhabitants, and Iraq, with 10 million), there remain less than 12 million inhabitants in states which together received $3.9 billion. (Saudi Arabia, with eight million inhabitants, $1.2 billion in royalties; Libya, with two million inhabitants, $1.3 billion in royalties; and, finally, Kuwait, Abu Zabi, Qatar, Bahrain, Oman and Dubay, taken together, with 1.2 million inhabitants, and $1.4 billion.[38]) Thus a disproportionately large share of royalties goes to a small fraction of the population of the Third World. This distribution of royalties is extremely unequal, quite simply as a result of natural endowments exceedingly unevenly distributed.

There is little reason to believe that the distribution of hydrocarbons in marine subsoils is less unevenly distributed.[39] There is even good reason to think that this unevenness will reinforce rather than correct the inequality already existing on land. The process of "diagenesis," the generative force in the creation of petroleum deposits, took place over millions of years, during which the earth-sea boundaries fluctuated widely. So it isn't surprising that the Mexican and Persian Gulfs, both of which possess great resources in petroleum in their emerged parts, are rich in their submerged parts.

Bearing in mind that prediction is made on the basis of present knowledge, it can be said that the countries already producing onshore petroleum can look forward to the exploitation of their epi-continental seas and therefore will be interested in seeing that the limits of national jurisdiction be pushed out as far as possible. This interest is heightened to the degree that national economies are weaker and, consequently, that their budgets are more dependent on royalties.

In the case of the other countries of the third world, for which neither past production nor the prospect of future exploration gives promise of underwater riches, do their interests lie in gambling by allying themselves with those claiming expansion of jurisdiction, or do they lie rather in sharing royalties collected by an international organization? Let us go further: if gain by expansion is chancy, it is nevertheless preferable to nothing, however slight the possibilities may be. On the other hand, sharing in internationally collected royalties will be zero if the sum of these royalties are zero. This sum is bound to be zero if resource exploitation is under the jurisdiction of the coastal state as far out as the resources can be exploited, as is provided by the Geneva Treaty of 1958. The result is the same if the elasticity of the boundary is replaced by an enlargement of the concept of shelf, so as to include the slope or the rise.[40]

Even if the limit of national jurisdiction is fixed at the 200-meter depth, and if all extraction beyond this point is regulated by, and royalties paid to, the international community rather than to the coastal state, the sum of these will remain too small for a long period to make any important contribution to international distribution.[41] On the other hand, they could be the means of *collective* enrichment. The question is: Is collective enrichment more urgent than progress in food production?

Primacies in Energy-Producing Matter

It is characteristic of modern society that marine space assumes new attractiveness as a source of energy-producing matter for the very good reason that modern society stands in marked contrast to all preceding societies, in being based on the consumption of energy-producing materials. In all anterior societies, action was produced by the expenditure of living energy, human or animal.[42] The great divide in the history of man is to be found at the point at which he began to use physical instead of physiological power. Our frame of reference was so closely tied to animal power that we still measure the work done by combustion engines in units of horsepower.

Industrial civilization was launched by "inputs" of coal; ever since, it has relied more and more on hydrocarbons. (Nuclear energy has so far played only a minor role.) The demand for energy-producing materials seems insatiable. This demand is destined not only to expand in the developed countries but also in the underdeveloped ones. Energy-producing matter furnished by non-living forms of life is, in this respect, the basis of our *material* civilization, and just here, lies the contrast with all preceding civilizations, as well as to primitive society. In the former, as in the latter, work was done by living species, human and animal, nourished by inputs of animate matter. In this sense, they were *biological* civilizations. What remains biological in our society is we ourselves, plus those inputs necessary for us to continue to live. We look for these inputs from living species, not from inorganic matter. We are fundamentally the supreme parasites on a vegetable base which *sometimes* feeds us directly, but more often through intermediate animals.

In order to merely exist, we require a quantitatively smaller input than that required for our civilization. According to a recent study, the material civilization of the United States requires a per capita input of energetic matter equivalent to 80 times the biological input necessary for the bare sustenance of an individual.

If there were merely small quantitative differences in our needs, the problem of an adequate food supply for an expanding population could be easily solved; for world consumption of energy materials is about twelve times the nutritional input needed to feed the population. Moreover, the progressing production of energy-producing materials is considerably greater than that of the population. However, there is a qualitative difference. We know how to feed ourselves only with living species. For long epochs, the human race was merely able to take them wherever they could be found and without having to be concerned about their reproduction. The result was that our ancestors were in a perpetual race with famine. Societies that existed by hunting and gathering were small, and extensive space was necessary for the survival of even small groups. After the Neolithic, man developed agriculture and stock-breeding, both of them qualitatively and endlessly improved on.

It seems strange that this improvement was not extended to the greater part of the surface of the globe, that is the seas, which cover 71 percent of it. In this respect, man has remained at the level of the hunting and gathering civilizations. It is, therefore, not surprising that most of the earth's surface furnishes, in tonnage, a mere 2 percent of man's food supply.[43]

This is a shocking state of affairs, given the lack of nourishment (especially that due to lack of protein) of a large part of the world's population and given, too, the concern frequently expressed about the *future*. We may well ask if it is not an inescapable conclusion that the contribution of the seas to human nutrition must become a major preoccupation of the international community.

Sea-Hunting

Since food production from marine spaces proceeds by way of hunting, this logically entails foreseeable results. Production is small even in those regions containing the greatest number of fish. The North Sea is exceptional, in that it yields five tons per square kilometer.[44] This amounts to a high yield compared with other zones, but even this figure means only 50 kilograms per hectare (2 1/2 acres).

In sea-hunting, the best-equipped hunters are advantageously situated. And the most mobile are in a favorable position to invade the least exploited zones to the detriment of those who have been using them, provided that reserved areas are not involved. "Technological progress often puts the most highly developed countries in a superior position, being able to dispatch their highly mechanized fleets far from their home bases. This, in turn, is liable to exhaust the resources near those very countries in which lack of protein is well attested."[45]

The Soviet Union's fleet is the main example of this invasion. It alone possesses 49 percent of the world's fishing vessels of more than 100 gross tons each. Soviet supremacy is easily explained by the fact that fishing activity was traditionally artisanal. When the transition was made from artisanal forms to "enterprise," this particular sphere of human activity did not greatly interest large established capital. Thus it is in countries where small private enterprise was abolished that the technologies of large-scale enterprise were first introduced.[46]

Most of us are familiar with the inevitable results—an increase in the volume of catch accompanied by a gradual depletion of the supply of fish. Fisheries volume doubles each decade but only by including a growing proportion (recently as much as 37 percent) of humanly non-consumable catches, which are turned into "fish meal." This "trash" catch is thus available for consumption, but one might ask: *whose* consumption? The answer is that since such meal is not readily acceptable to humans, it is consumed mainly by chickens and pigs.[47]

I cannot go into detail here about the high-level discussion presently going on among experts concerned with the "end limit" to fishery resources. I note only that it is not surprising that experts arrive at very different results because they envisage different total volumes of very different composition. In any case, the discussion relates to the "biological pyramid" of Schaefer, in accordance with which all forms of oceanic life rely on a base of phytoplankton, the "bed" of minute, stationary, or actually mobile, vegetable matter, which is capable of photosynthesis. (It is an excellent moral that all forms of life rely on the humblest.) These phytoplankton nourish a whole hierarchy of small animals—the zooplankton and certain herbivorous fish. The next higher level of fish are nourished by them, which, in turn, are nourished at a higher level, and so on. Gross "living volume" decreases from level to level by between 80 to 90 percent. Man, the supreme parasite, is nourished at, and by, the highest level. It goes without saying that the total volume to be obtained in this way depends on a more or less marked descent to productive lower levels.[48]

But, however they make their calculations, experts are unanimous in agreeing that species are ultimately exhaustible through over-exploitation, which prevents adequate reproduction. This concern was apparently never felt in past centuries. For example, Vattel remarked in 1758:

> It is manifest that the exploitation of the open sea, in navigation and fishing, is harmless and *inexhaustible*; he who navigates or fishes in the open seas disturbs no one, and the sea, in these two respects, can supply the needs of all men. But, even so, Nature does not give any man or men a right to expropriate for themselves resources whose use is innocent, inexhaustible and sufficient for all.[49]

I have emphasized Vattel's adjective "inexhaustible" because it can have two very different meanings. When the sea is an infrastructure for transportation, it is not, in this respect, exhaustible by the use made of it.[50] But we have to do with an entirely different matter when our concern is with exploitation of its *contents*, for any prey is exhaustible through bad management.

Let us continue a moment with Vattel. Drawing from the notion of *inexhaustible* the conclusion that "to undertake to make oneself the sole master and to exclude all others, constitutes the will without reason to deprive them of the benefits of Nature," he states by way of contrast: "Since the Earth is no longer able to supply of itself all necessary or useful things without cultivation to an extremely multiplied Human Species, it becomes convenient to introduce property rights, so that every person can apply himself with greater success to cultivating his fair share." This is the reasoning of Latin American countries when they undertook to assert jurisdiction over their epi-continental sea with regard to fishing. History had united the two ancient uses of the sea—navigation and fishing—and the "nature of things" reunited them, that is, pitted living content against material content. If sovereign states appropriate the material content of their continental shelves, there is no reason why they could not appropriate the living content of the epi-continental sea (and it is well known that the epi-continental seas are zones dense in marine fauna).

One might well think that the argument justifying the appropriation of epi-continental seas is stronger than the arguments for continental shelves. If living, as well as material, resources are vulnerable to exhaustion, living resources may be maintained and even improved through adequate care. This prospect of resource maintenance *and* improvement is indeed a proper justification of the right to exclude anyone who would disturb efficient and beneficent administration. On the other hand, we do not today have the confidence of eighteenth-century authors as to the automatic nature of the blessings of private enterprise. Granted that natural exhaustible riches should not be abandoned to pillage by irresponsible parties, we are not one whit assured that, once an "allottee" has been found, he will administer these resources in the long-term interest of mankind. Only a very short time has elapsed since we even began to recognize *at all* that wise administration of natural resources of our planet is a major problem.

"Poor" Countries and Fishing

It is understandable that poor countries would prefer to reserve to themselves the living riches in proximity to their coasts. Included in this "wealth," fishing is important to their economy for three reasons: (1) from a nutritional point of view, that is, as a means of nourishing their populations; (2) from an economic point of view, for exportation (Peru being the best example); and (3) from a social point of view, as affording the possibility of employment.

From the point of view of employment, it is necessary, I think, to set aside the traditional concepts of orthodox economists. According to them, it is better for the fish to be caught by foreigners *if* these foreigners bring to bear more efficient methods of production. But better for whom? Certainly not for the fishermen of some coastal country who will lose the occupation that gives them their livelihood or who, at the very least, will find such occupation much less profitable. Is it better for the proper use of the labor force of the coastal country in question? Almost certainly not, since such a country lacks the necessary capital for the creation of jobs and, moreover, cannot more productively employ unemployed fishermen. It can of course, *buy* the fish caught by others. But then, will such purchases be reasonably inexpensive? And, if so, inexpensive in what sense? Imports are inexpensive or expensive according to the "counterparts" one can furnish. It is precisely the problem of furnishing counterparts—acceptable exportations—that causes monumental difficulties for the underdeveloped countries.

It was reasonable for industrial England in the nineteenth century to allow most of its agricultural activity to disappear—first, because there was at that time a lively demand for British products abroad, and second, because there was a congestion of capital seeking to employ manual labor at home. Finally, this occurred because the manual labor transferred from agriculture to industry could supply a greater amount of foodstuffs through imports paid for by exports. But such conditions are the very opposite of what is found in the case of a poor country, which is bound to protect its fisheries and fishermen. This is the reason that impelled Ambassador Arvid Pardo to include Article 54 in his Ocean Space Draft Treaty: "The coastal state can reserve the exploitation of the living and non-living resources of its national ocean space to its nationals."[51] But if a country can have a negative interest in excluding others, one can also have a positive interest in developing the sources of its goods.

Here is a contrast between living and nonliving resources. Activity brought to bear on nonliving resources can only be by way of extraction—simple in principle but immensely difficult in execution, calling for the emplacement of sophisticated techniques and costly equipment. So a country that reserves its continental shelf to itself is obliged to manage its exploitation by way of granting concessions to enterprises possessing the necessary means. In the case of the poorer countries, this can only mean to foreign enterprise. The national state comes into the picture merely by being the granting agency for permits for exploration, concessions, *and* by taxation and reception of royalties.

The activity of extracting living resources can indeed be exercised by small local enterprise, but in that case, it must be kept in mind that extraction is not the only activity. Fortunately, marine populations can be developed through appropriate measures. (This was already the case 2,000 years ago for oysters, and, with the Japanese, for shrimp.) Moreover, such measures can be extended to numerous other species, depending on the support given to research and development in this field.[52] These maricultural activities are particularly promising for poor countries, since most operational expense essentially goes for manual labor. Therefore, the most useful contribution to be made in the area is adequate technology. (It should also be said that, as far as the techniques in question can be extended to nomadic species, they will probably prove to be beneficial to all coastal countries.)

Fascinating perspectives are offered by the "St. Croix experiment." Water drawn from a depth of 830 meters was sucked up to the surface and was found to be charged with nitrates and phosphates; that is, it carried fertilizers that enriched the phytoplankton, thereby making it capable of maintaining a denser fauna.[53] This means that the phenomenon of the Humboldt current (which produces the prodigious fecundity of the anchovies in Peruvian catches) was artificially reproduced. The authors of this experiment have publicized the value it represents for countries with steep continental shelves.

Lack of competence prohibits any further account by me of the prospects of mariculture. But it is unnecessary to possess much particular knowledge to sense that, of all the ocean research, the most vital is concerned with increasing its nutritional contribution. The only other research that rivals it in importance for the human species is concerned with the influence of the seas on climate. Unfortunately, neither the former nor the latter is at present very high on the scale of research-expenditure of the advanced countries.

Physical Residues—Moral Residues

And this leads us naturally to the problem of an international authority of the oceans, whatever its legal makeup is going to be. It would have a geographic domain, and it would have tasks to perform.

How will its geographic domain be defined? To put it quite crudely: as the residue of national claims. We have seen how the extent of these claims has been broadening. It is difficult to imagine an international agreement except on the basis of the most comprehensive and extensive national claims (ocean floor as well as superjacent waters; 200 miles, as in the Pardo proposal). Under these circumstances, the international authority will still retain a vast domain; but the revenues to be taken from this domain are an entirely different matter.

The revenues one naturally thinks of are those to be derived from the material resources of international ocean space. The first that come to mind are the hydrocarbons. But here we are faced not only with the problem of their accessibility in very deep waters (a problem which, in time, may be solved by technical progress) but with the question of their existence on the abyssal plains of the oceans. I say, "abyssal plains," given the present trend toward the extension of national jurisdiction, which potentially includes the possibility of engulfing the continental slopes and even the rises; the whole continental margin—way beyond the limits of the shelf itself.

Now, according to most geologists, it is highly unlikely that deposits of hydrocarbons exist outside the continental margins. The reason is clear. Essentially, hydrocarbon basins are cemeteries of living forms—liquid or gaseous collections of the debris of life. Logically, therefore, they should be found only in those areas where living forms existed for long periods in some density. It seems, however, that ever since the beginning of life, or at any rate, for a very long time, density has been a function of the vicinity near land. Even though the borders of continents have changed greatly in time, these changes have not affected the abyssal plains.

This opinion of the scholarly world, which I unfortunately must present here in a most summary way, is not conducive to encouraging enterprises to undertake expenditures for exploration which may have little chance of being profitable.

The revenues of the international authority from the exploitation of hydrocarbon resources depend, therefore, on the manner in which the limits of national jurisdiction are defined. Even supposing that these national jurisdictions leave a substantial portion of the continental margins to the authority, this authority would still have to persuade enterprises to look much further from shore for what they could find much closer, that is, to undertake more hazardous research and more difficult exploitation. In this, the authority could only succeed by offering much more favorable financial conditions; that is, concessions would have to be free and royalties small.

On the other hand, the abyssal plains abound in metals which can be scooped up from its surface. This is because the abyssal plain is part of the earth's crust, which is itself abundant in metals. But is it less costly to harvest ore-bearing nodules from the seabed surface at great sea depths than to mine metal which is buried, even at lesser depths, on the land? This is doubtful; if one wished larger royalties, he would discourage mining from the seabed.

But here is a consideration that is foreign to the calculations of business enterprise as it is constituted today: mining activities on the land are destructive of the environment and of people's habitats.

As early as 1920 Pigou deplored the fact that damage done to the landscape by mining was not accounted for in the usual calculations of national revenue.[54] In the summer of 1971, popular opinion in Great Britain rose against the government's encouragement of mining research in the national parks of the British Isles. The British government had voted a credit of 90 million pounds in support of the research of some 30 mining companies, of which the Rio Tinto is the most important. The Lake District, whose beauty is celebrated and much enjoyed by tourists, was to be prospected.

Two thoughts come to mind. First, it would be better to extract metals from the seabed, and second, the government must subsidize this type of research. Would it not be better, then, to subsidize it a little more in order to reorient it toward the seabed? It would be an excellent thing for the environment, but it would not be profitable to the international authority, since it would cost a great deal.

Here we come to the core of the contrast between two different concepts of an international authority for the oceans. According to one concept, its geographic domain would be a source of revenue which it could then redistribute in favor of the underdeveloped nations. This concept holds only if national jurisdiction is limited to the three-mile territorial sea. The international authority cannot play this role if its geographic domain is a residue whose material promise is small and far off.

Another concept of the authority is offered by *Pacem in Maribus*.* If national claims leave the authority with a physically insufficient resi-

---

*The reference is to the annual conferences of the International Ocean Institute, with headquarters in Malta. These conferences focused increasingly on the negotiations leading, in 1982, to the United Nations Convention on the Law of the Sea, and on the international agreements which followed [Eds.].

due, they still leave it with an immense, diversified, and capital residue on the moral level.

The authority would have to deal with all those issues which do not respond to private interests and to the short-term interests of enterprises or governments, in addition to long-term considerations on a planetary scale—more specifically, the various functions of ocean space and its uses by mankind. Some of these are as yet little understood by the public, such as the impact of the oceans on the earth's climate or their function as a recipient of waste disposal (*cloaca maxima*). Other uses are traditional (transportation and navigation). Still others have only recently begun to preoccupy public opinion (mining and recreation). On the basis of a full analysis of all of these functions, concrete proposals must be made for the improvement of services. If the resources are available, technical assistance must be given to the poorer countries, to enable them to profit from the services.

I am afraid it would be illusory to think an international institution could be vested with much real power. Its intellectual and moral power, instead, could be very great and therefore efficient. The very idea of an international authority responds to a vague but powerful feeling abroad today: *let us take care of this planet, for we will find no other one; let us use its resources with wisdom and equity.* Is not the best response to this sort of feeling the creation of an institution which would seek all the needed improvements in the uses of this the largest part of the globe?

Notes

1. According to the eminent marine geologist, K.O. Emery of Woods Hole. Many of my observations have been borrowed from Emery's numerous studies.
2. Hearings of the United States Senate Commission on Commerce, September-November 1969, p. 130.
3. These figures were given respectively by Russell Train and Senator Pell during the Senate hearings mentioned [above] at pp. 104 and 122.
4. It is certainly because ports were the locus of marvelous stories that Thomas More used this setting for the account of his Utopia, using the discourse of a fictitious Portuguese navigator (1518).
5. Galileo situated his dialogues (*Discorsi*) in the naval dockyard of Venice. In them, he wrote of the "Two New Sciences Relating to Mechanics and Motion" (Leyden, 1638).
6. Pardessus, *Collection des Lois Maritimes*, T.1, Paris, 1828.
7. The poor fisherman extracting treasure from the sea figures in all the legends of the world. It is characteristic that the fisher folk who played an important role in the War of Independence of the United Provinces called themselves "sea beggars."
8. We know that the attention Grotius gave to matters of the sea had its source in the mandate given him by the West Indies Company in order to justify the vio-

lent capture of a Portuguese galleon in the Straits of Malacca by one of its captains, Heemskirk. It was with this in mind that he wrote his *De Jure Praedae* in 1604. His famous *Mare liberum, seu de jure quod Batavis competit ad Indica Commercia* (1609) was taken from the 12th chapter of this great pleading (which was not published until 1868).

9. We have to go back to 1576 to find a more ambitious statement. Chapter 10 of the first book of Jean Bodin's *Six Livres de la Republique* briefly enunciates, after having stated that the coastal marshes and salt works can be private property: "But the rights of the sea belong only to a sovereign prince, who may impose charges out to 30 leagues from his territory, if there is no other sovereign prince to impede him from doing so..." (30 marine leagues are equal to 90 marine miles).

10. See the commentary of René-Jean Dupuy, in *La Souveraineté au XXe siecle*, R.J. Dupuy, ed. (Paris: Armand Colin, 1971).

11. Moreover, we can be sure that Washington foresaw and admitted the generalization of the claim it advanced. This can be found in the justification of the proclamation as first announced: first, there is a world need for new sources of petroleum and other materials; second, technological progress makes possible the exploitation of such resources in the subsoil of the continental slope, now or in the near future; and third, there exists a need for some recognized jurisdiction for the conservation and prudent exploitation of these resources. It is certain that Washington had communicated its intention, at least to the Mexican government, which was going to make an identical declaration the following month. The American government did not fear being imitated; it hoped to be. What displeased it was the transformation of this claim by the example of Argentina; and it was against this that diplomatic protestations were made.

12. *Petroleum Press Service* (March, 1972), p. iii (of the French edition).

13. *Resources for Freedom* (Washington, D.C.: Supt. of Doc., June 1952), 5 vol.

14. Van Manning, in *National Petroleum News*, October 20, 1919. In 1919 U.S. production comprised 64.3 percent of world production, but that only took care of national consumption.

15. George Otis Smith, *National Petroleum News*, May 5, 1920.

16. David White, "The Petroleum Resources of the World," in *The Annals* (May, 1920).

17. By which is implied both the discovery of new sources and raising (former) estimates of known sources through further exploration.

18. According to Weeks' estimation, the initial endowment of the earth was 610 billion barrels, of which 110 belonged to the U.S. The proportion is the interesting thing: quantitatively better estimates were made by Weeks, thanks to the progress of exploration. The figures for 1948 quoted here are found in the Paley Report, Vol. 2, p. 166.

19. The estimate of the resources remaining to be discovered is necessarily hazardous, since it is founded on a rough estimate of the initial geological stock. From this presumed initial value, one deducts the historical sum of what has already been extracted to the date of the statement, and the condition of the proved reserves at that date. The sum constitutes the presumed, and not the proved, resources. The known parts of the calculation are represented by the sum of the extractions which were made and the proved reserves, but the estimates of the initial stock progress with time and study. Thus in 1928, the estimate of the initial stock of the U.S. was on the order of 39 billion barrels; twenty years later, it was 110 billion.

20. Today, the estimates of 1948 appear much too small. At the World Congress on Petroleum, held in Moscow in 1971, Weeks presented a study entitled "Marine

Geology and Petroleum Resources," according to which the potential resources in hydrocarbons are:

Billions of Barrels in Petroleum Equivalent

Class of Source	Offshore	Ground	Total
Petroleum liquids	790	1,500	2,290
Petroleum gases	400	800	1,200
Secondary recovery of petroleum	360	1,000	1,360
Heavy petroleum sands	200	700	900
Total	1,750	4,000	5,750

Petroleum Press Service (September, 1971), French ed. p. 338.

21. As appears in the following table from data collected by the First National City Bank:

Firms	U.S.A. & Canada	The rest of the Western hemisphere	Eastern hemisphere	Total
		(production in thousands of barrels daily)		
Standard (N.J.)	1,116	1,455	2,094	4,665
Gulf	746	201	2,110	3,057
Texaco	905	258	1,824	2,987
Standard (Cal.)	537	68	1,799	2,404
Mobil	481	104	988	1,573
Total:	3,785	2,086	8,815	14,686

22. Even more striking was the reduction of the share of proved reserves of the U.S. in the total of the world proved reserves: the proportion fell to 6.6 percent at the end of 1969. One can surmise that the change of orientation toward exploration contributed to the drop.

23. *Ocean Industry* (January, 1971), p. 23.

24. *Ocean Industry* (September, 1970).

25. *Petroleum Press News* (September, 1971), reporting a statement by Weeks in Moscow.

26. According to an analysis by the Norwegian firm, Fernley and Egers (1971), in *Petroleum Press News* (March, 1972). For confirmation, OECD: *Maritime Transport* (Paris, 1971). The 62 percent figure mentioned breaks down as follows: raw petroleum, 55 percent and petroleum products, 7 percent.

27. This innovation is of French origin. It allowed the transportation of liquefied natural gas (GNL) by ad hoc vessels called méthaniers, from Algeria to the United Kingdom, beginning in 1964 and to the north of France, beginning in 1965.

28. In the U.S. in 1957, coal was still the principal source of energy: 44 percent of the total, 33 percent for petroleum and already 14 percent for natural gas. In 1970 petroleum comprised 44 percent, but the share of natural gas had grown even more, more than 33 percent.

29. The "world" production given here does not include the communist countries. *Petroleum Press New* (March, 1970), French ed., p. 89.

30. Cf. Requier-Desjardins, *L'evolution des transports maritimes et l'environment socioeconomique*. Memoire de Prospective Sociale de l'Université de Paris, I.

31. The instructive example of a large international firm might be cited. The firm erected its own terminal, which was adequate for handling vessels in the 230,000-

ton class; they took care to distribute their cargo in much smaller units at this terminal.

32. See the editorial in the *Guardian*, January 13, 1970, following a chain of accidents which resulted after the sinking of the cargo ship *Brandenburg*.

33. Smith, *Torrey Canyon Pollution and Marine Life: A Report by the Plymouth Laboratory of the Marine Biological Association of the United Kingdom* (Cambridge University Press, 1970).

34. M.B.F. Ranken, in *Ocean Industry* (June, 1971).

35. One of the effects of this transfer of flags is to render the American balance of payments more and more negative in the area of maritime transportation.

36. According to a recent estimate, the value of all such materials extracted represented only 1/12th of that of hydrocarbons. It must be noted, moreover, that of this 1/12th, chemical products from seawater (including water itself) comprise more than three quarters. The use of seawater does not pose any problems of delimitation. Data from the Dow Chemical Co. (1969), quoted by John Flipse, *Undersea Technology* (January, 1970), p. 45.

37. The most extreme thesis in this respect is that national jurisdiction would embrace not only the continental shelf, but also the continental slope and rise; in sum, all of the continental margin. This would be true to the extent that the neighboring country is far off; when it is close by, jurisdiction would extend to the median line.

38. *Petroleum Press Service* (September, 1971), French ed., p. 327.

39. According to L.G. Weeks, "In the underwater zone extending to a 300-metre depth, only 4% would be rich in petroleum."

40. If the continental shelf zone comprises 28 million square kilometers, and that of the continental rise, about 19 million square kilometers, the total margin covers about 15 percent of the total surface of the earth as a whole, 21 percent of ocean space, and is equal to 50 percent of dry land. According to the estimate of Menard and Smith, "Hyposometry of ocean basin provinces," *Journal of Geophysical Research*, vol. 1971 (1966), pp. 4305-25. Quoted by K.O. Emery in *Continental Margins of the World*, reprint (Woods Hole Oceanographic Institute, 1970).

41. Let us suppose the royalties to be $1 per barrel—a rate which is already being surpassed for the payment to the countries of OPEC—but, in order to encourage the enterprise to go beyond the 200-meter depth, one would have to be content with a lower rate. I leave to the reader the task of confronting the billions of barrels with the billions of inhabitants.

42. Energy from the wind, which is irregular, is, it seems to me, the only other source that can be mentioned as important before the use of combustible fossils.

43. In order of importance, in terms of tonnage, vegetables make up 4/5ths of our food, animals 1/5th, with marine animals making up 1/10th of this 1/5th. However, it should be noted at the same time that marine animals furnish 1/10th of the animal proteins needed and, in addition, are much easier to assimilate than vegetable proteins.

44. R. Letaconnoux, assistant director of the Institut Scientifique et des Techniques des Pêches Maritimes, in CNEXO, Colloque International sur l'Exploitation des Oceans, Bordeaux, March 1971, Theme II, vol. I.

45. P. Adam, Chief of the Division of Fisheries, OECD.

46. One might add another motivation: the country is poor in coastlines.

47. Lowering the cost of producing chickens by more than one-half in twenty years is due, to a great extent, to the use of fishmeal. Chapman, *Planning and Development in the Oceans*, p. 23.

48. For a clear statement of this, see J. A. Gulland, ed., *The Fish Resources of the Ocean*, FAO, 1970, pp. 307-19. One finds Schaefer's pyramid, which is quantified according to the following method: Schaefer assumes the annual fixation of carbon by the phytoplankton to be 19 billion tons; he accords the latter a tenfold living weight of 190 billion tons, from which, level by level, the living weight of each successive level is deduced through the application of a coefficient of ecological efficiency, on the basis of three hypotheses: an efficiency of 10, 15, or 20 percent, and the efficiency is probably not the same for the different changes in level.

49. M. de Vattel, *Le Droit des Gens ou Principes de la Loi Naturelle Appliqués a la conduite et aux affaires des Nations et des souverains*, London, 1758, p. 243, T.I.

50. It is subject to congestion in the straits, but that is another matter.

51. In this draft treaty, the national ocean space (I would prefer the term national marine space) is defined according to the formula advanced by the Latin American states—a belt of 200 marine miles.

52. See the work of the White Fish Authority in Great Britain on sand-dabs, turbots, sole, and the black coalfish: CNEXO, Theme II, vol. I.

53. O. A. Roels et al., "Nutrient-rich water: the most abundant resource of the deep sea," in *CNEXO, Colloque International sur l'Exploitation des Oceans*, Theme IV, vol. I.

54. A. C. Pigou, *The Economics of Welfare* (London, 1920).

18

Back to Basics: The Concrete Economy

A spell of anxiety has fallen over Europe, Japan, and the United States. After thirty years marked by the swiftest improvements ever seen in productivity, economic progress, and the quality of life, we suddenly face the question whether this drive toward ever stronger economies and ever greater affluence can be maintained, and if so, how? If not, what are the alternatives?

This worry logically calls for an understanding of the fuels that fire the engine of affluence. To what do we owe the facilities we presently enjoy? The answer lies in the realm of economics: factual, *concrete* economics. But it so happens that we are lacking in such a vulgar, down-to-earth economics, and in the future this discipline must be reborn. As an academic science, economics today operates at a very much higher level. It has been concerned with reasoning, neglectful of information. A Nobel prize winner, Wassily Leontief, outlined this problem in his presidential address delivered at the 83rd meeting of the American Economic Association on December 20, 1970. The title of his address sums up the problem clearly enough: "Theoretical Assumptions and Non-observed Facts."

The lecture begins with a true statement about the enormous prestige currently enjoyed by economics: "Economics today rides the crest of intellectual responsibility and popular acclaim." Leontif notes "the serious attention with which our pronouncements are received by the general public, hard-bitten politicians, and even skeptical businessmen" and goes on to castigate the irrelevance of the clever exercises in which economists delight.

Reprinted with permission from *The Futurist* 14 (June, 1980): 11–15, published by the World Future Society, 7910 Woodmont Avenue, Suite 450, Bethesda, Maryland 20814.

"The weak and all too slowly growing empirical foundation," says Leontief, "clearly cannot support the proliferating superstructure of pure—or should I say speculative—economic theory.... Unfortunately, anyone capable of learning elementary or, preferably, advanced calculus and algebra and acquiring acquaintance with the specialized terminology of economics can set himself up as a theorist. Unqualified enthusiasm for mathematical formulation tends often to conceal the ephemeral substantive content of the argument behind the formidable front of algebraic signs."

This castigation shall be regarded as well-deserved by anyone who takes the trouble—and enjoys the intellectual pleasure of—going through the preceding ten years of the *American Economic Review*, which published Leontief's address. I add "enjoys the pleasure" because it is a disposition of the human mind to enjoy logical reasoning, and indeed most of our sitting games imply such reasoning in different degrees. Chess, a very ancient game, is a notable instance. But then, in chess, all the practical data are known, fixed once and for all: the chessboard is ever the same, so are the pieces, so are the moves allowed to each. Thus successive generations of chess players can devise ever more ingenious tactics.

Economics offers the exactly opposite picture. The geopolitical chessboard is ever changing. The pieces on the board multiply continuously and undergo fantastic mutations allowing quite different moves. A lack of attention to these concrete changes banishes economic theorizing to the limbo of fancy.

The last few years have offered a most striking proof of this phenomenon. In the late 1960s, for example, the Organization for Economic Cooperation and Development (OECD), which is composed largely of Western European states but also includes the U.S., Australia, New Zealand, and Japan, called upon an international team of outstanding economists to foretell its economic growth in the 1970s. Their finding was that growth would be somewhat faster than in the previous decade: it had been 4.8 percent yearly, it would be 5.4 percent yearly—in other words, an increase of 70 percent during the 1970s as against 60 percent during the previous decade. As is well known, things turned out quite differently. We are now told to expect zero growth in 1980, and 20 million unemployed by the second half of the year.

What happened is common knowledge. It can be summarized as a political trend arising in a poor, sparsely populated and industrially backward geographic region whereby the march of the whole historical team of advanced countries has been shaken to the core. Yes, *to the core*, because since the days of James Watt, the inventor of the condensing steam engine and the man after whom the electrical "watt" is named, we in Europe, in the U.S. and later in Japan as well as Russia, have increasingly based our economic life upon machines fed by mineral fuels, and, over time, the role of petroleum has outpaced that of coal.

A century ago, feeding machines with coal was no problem in England, where coal was abundant. When later the United States started feeding its machines with oil, no problem was immediately apparent either, as the U.S. seemed abundantly provided with it.

When Europe turned to petroleum, however, little of which is to be found in its subsoil, it had to depend upon outside sources. This situation presented few difficulties as long as the lands from which oil could be obtained were themselves politically dependent on Europe. But by the early 1970s the days of colonial domination, when European entrepreneurs could routinely depend upon the backing of their governments, were past. With this loss of political control came a situation of pronounced dependence, and some keen Arab minds became aware of this dependence. Moreover, the power which now led the West, the U.S., was insistent upon the sovereignty of every state, and this is the very principle that Libyan Premier Quaddafi invoked in 1970 when he dealt forcefully with American exploitation of Libyan oil. In the meantime, American support of Israel antagonized the Arabs; hence the bold step of the OPEC cartel in October 1973. The decision to set prices at the will of the OPEC governments was a historic turning point.

Here, we find a political move with major economic consequences, a move made possible by the geographic localization of a mineral playing a major role in the economics of the world's wealthiest nations.

In the phrase just uttered, three terms that are hard to find in economic treatises figure prominently: *political*, *geographic*, and *mineral*.

The term "political" all but disappeared from many economic treatises a long time ago, even though governments around the world have been steadily assuming an increasingly important role in the economic realm. Such words as coal or oil simply do not figure in major economic treatises, such as Joseph A. Shumpeter's famous *History of Economic Analysis*. My favorite, Wesley C. Mitchell's *Types of Economic Theory* mentions coal just once: it is by reference to a British economist, Stanley Jevons, who published in 1865 a book entitled *The Coal Question*.

This contrasts with Adam Smith, who dealt with coal at length and repeatedly in his classic *Wealth of Nations*, even though it was as yet used only for heating. I shall not resist the pleasure of quoting one out of many tempting passages from that work, this one from Book V, chapter 2:

> In a country where the winters are so cold as in Great Britain, fuel is, during that season, in the strictest sense of the word, a necessary of life, not only for the purpose of dressing victuals, but for the comfortable subsistence of many different sorts of workmen, who work within doors: and coals are the cheapest of all fuel. The price of fuel has so important an influence upon that of labor, that all over Great Britain manufactures have confined themselves principally to the coal countries: other parts of the country, on account of the high price of this necessary article, not being able to work so cheap.

This immediately raises in the reader's mind a vivid picture of men tramping through the cold toward the workplace, stepping inside, and using the warmth of burning coal—coal carted in from neighboring mines—to coax the numbness from their stiff fingers. Such touches, evocative of realities, came naturally to Smith. Who indeed does not remember the life-like picture of the pin factory with which the *Wealth of Nations* opens.

Such illustrations are entirely foreign to modern economists, addicted to close reasoning in abstract terms. Economic growth has been their major theme since World War II. And, indeed, it is a most important theme. Is it not by the progress of production that people are afforded better technologies and more numerous conveniences? Is it not by way of more employment and increasing rewards that the working population is enabled to pay for increasing consumption? What was it that went so wrong in the 1930s as to cause the Great Depression, with its fall in production and consumption, its huge expansion of unemployment, and its nullification of investment? After such an experience— socially disastrous, politically dangerous (as it proved in Germany)— was it not the duty, indeed the mission, of economists to teach the way of avoiding any repetition of that catastrophe, to ensure the successful pursuit of beneficial growth?

This most laudable preoccupation, due to events, but also stimulated by the economic thought of John Maynard Keynes, inspired two generations of economists, at a time when their numbers multiplied, and their services were greatly welcomed. They attacked the problem of growth by reasoning upon the proper relation between investment, production, and consumption, to be financed by increasing employment and wages. To this macroeconomic vision, mathematical expressions were especially suitable, and they throve.

The post-World War II era was marked in the OECD countries by a great increase in governments' recourse to economists, and by a sustained pace of growth unprecedented in these countries' economic history. There is no good reason not to connect the two phenomena, not to give economists their due. But the more we do so, the more also we must reproach not a few of them for inadequate attention to accelerating inflation, and practically all of them for complete neglect of the role played by natural resources. It is upon the importance of the latter that I propose to insist.

Dependence Upon Nature Increases

Our species, as every other living species, has ever depended upon the gifts of nature. We have moved from our animal condition, very slowly for thousand of centuries, then at an increasing pace, toward getting more in quantity and kind from this source of life. Agriculture, undertaken no more than a few thousand years ago, was a momentous step forward, making it possible by regular harvest to support cities. Similarly, learning to fell trees and work their wood allowed navigation, and it is to trees that we owe the discovery of America.

Are we justified in deeming ourselves now less dependent upon nature? Assuredly not. Our demands upon it have very greatly increased; but our awareness of our continuing, even growing, dependence on nature has greatly declined. This is a psychological effect of our urban life-style. It is to money that we look for the satisfaction of our every need or desire, and because we are served by organizations, we are at most conscious of the workers who provide these services—our awareness does not reach back to the basic resources. Instead of opening our eyes to it, growth theorists ignore any mention of land or raw materials.

Yet, for those willing to see, the crucial importance of raw materials to sound industrial economies has long been evident. When the Korean War aroused the fear of an impending general war, for example, the resulting panic buying of raw materials generated a most important study, which should have made its mark upon the minds of economists and political leaders around the world. President Truman was inspired by circumstances to call in January 1951 for a study of how much more natural materials would be needed for the economic growth of the U.S. and also of the "free world," and how they would be procured.

The response to the president's request was prompt: an exhaustive, five-volume study, of the highest quality, conducted by Philip H. Coombs and completed in June 1952. Entitled *Resources for Freedom,* it is better known as the Paley Report (from the name of its chairman).

This I regard as by far my most important lesson in economics (of which I have been an assiduous reader for fifty-nine years).

Indeed a single page, at the opening of the first volume, by itself produced an intellectual shock. Under the title "in 1950, the U.S. consumed 2.7 billion tons of materials," stood the bare outline of a human form attended by the statement "averaging 36,000 pounds per citizen." What a striking figure! How impressive a quantity! In a semicircle beneath the silhouette, these 36,000 pounds were divided into various kinds of materials. Fuels formed the largest parcel at 14,400 pounds; next the construction materials (10,000 pounds, attended by 800 pounds of miscellaneous nonmetallics); then 5,700 pounds of agricultural materials; and finally 5,100 pounds of metallic ore.

Surely, the most interesting comparison was that of fuels with agricultural materials, especially since the report indicated that of these agricultural products no more than 1,600 pounds went to food. Thus food for people turned out to be, in volume, only one-ninth as great as food for machines.

This exposition of facts made it clear that the most advanced nation was also the most demanding upon nature. Of course the American nation had huge spaces with a great variety of soils and subsoils. It could live very amply upon this natural wealth at small cost, indeed at a cost in labor that grew progressively smaller the more that labor was augmented by powerful machinery. Why powerful? Because it was sustained increasingly by fuels extracted from the subsoil.

Indeed the whole economy had its basis in machinery, and machinery had its sustenance first in coal (which started with Watt) and later in petroleum—the later fuel being both cheaper and more convenient.

Thus I realized that economic growth was not so much the fruit of increasing capital (a monetary source) as of power (a source obtained from nature). This shook to the core the prevailing, and then unquestioned, belief that a future of ever more consumption was guaranteed by the march of ever more investment. What, in fact, such a future depended upon was getting more out of nature.

Just as we needed food for our sustenance, we needed fodder for the machines on which we depended to an ever greater degree. And just as food comes from the soil, this fodder came from the subsoil. But the two are different in an important respect: we know that we must take care of the soil, while in the case of coal or oil we simply delve into natural, irreplaceable reserves, with no possibility of replenishing them and very little thought for their natural limits.

The Rise and Fall of the Cheap-Energy Era

Over the past two or three centuries, domineering Western civilization has been able to easily satisfy its increasing needs by obtaining natural goods abroad, where they were in greatest abundance and cheapest.

Two examples from recent history illustrate this point, and reveal, in the second case, how what would seem to be a wise monetary choice can lead to harsh consequences in concrete terms.

In the mid-nineteenth century, Great Britain, whose population and industrial might were at the time both growing rapidly, made up its mind to seek food for its population abroad. The speed with which Great Britain came to depend upon this imported food is strikingly illustrated by Michael George Mulhall in his *Dictionary of Statistics,* published in 1892. According to Mulhall, native wheat was adequate to feed 19 million of Great Britain's inhabitants in 1860, but less than 12 million in 1889; thus imported wheat fed 26 million Britons in 1889, as against 9.5 million in 1860. In different terms, and perhaps even more strikingly, Mulhall stated that the British were dependent upon imported wheat on 122 days of the year 1860, and on 251 days of the year 1889. Similarly, but to a lesser degree, the British depended upon imported meat on twenty-six days of the year 1860, but by 1889 this dependence had risen to as much as 142 days.

What was the initial reason for Great Britain's recourse to foods from abroad? A very simple one: they were cheaper.

In 1948, just a century after Sir Robert Peel succeeded in having passed the bill that opened the British market to the free entry of wheat from abroad, the beginning of noteworthy oil imports from the Middle East reached the United States. Oil imports jumped from 600,000 barrels in April of 1948 to 4 million barrels in December.

For the U.S., rich in oil as well as coal and natural gas, imported oil merely supplemented the national supply; it served as a means of sparing national reserves. Not so in Western Europe, where oil and gas were not then regionally available. Only coal and hydraulic power were widely used, and the coal was notably more expensive than coal in the U.S. Indeed, after World War II coal miners in Western Europe were told that they had a great mission, that economic recovery depended upon their striving to restore prewar output. This goal was achieved in

1957, with 492 million tons of coal being produced in Western Europe. But, by that time, interest in coal as a power source had flagged; in that same year, oil imports from the Middle East reached 80 million tons. This imported oil was incredibly cheap, easy to manage, and could be used not only for motoring (its primary use in years past) but as an all but complete substitute for coal. Furthermore, a ton of oil contains almost one-third more energy than a ton of coal.

Specifically, a ton of oil is said to contain 10 million kilocalories. Thus a barrel, of which there are roughly 7.3 per ton, contains something like 1,364,000 kilocalories. If one wishes to understand fully the incredible amount of energy contained in a barrel of oil, one need only to compare it with the energy used in human labor: the great physical effort of a coal minor burns roughly eight calories per minute while the average effort of the manual worker in our day is two to four calories per minute.

Oil, this incomparable source of energy, was indeed a boon. It is no wonder that Western Europe adopted it with enthusiasm; in fact, the consumption of oil in Western Europe during the post World War II period increased more rapidly than anyone would have guessed. For example, the Paley Report of 1952 made predictions about the consumption of oil in Western Europe and the U.S. in 1975. Their prediction for the U.S. was reached a bit ahead of schedule, in 1970. But consumption of oil in Western Europe in 1970 was already three times as great as the Paley report's predictions for 1975! And European consumption was not far from equaling that of the U.S.

By 1970, imported oil made up nearly 60 percent of Europe's energy consumption and 70 percent of Japan's, while in the U.S. imported oil accounted for little more than 10 percent of total energy consumption at that time. This steady flow of imported oil surely played an important role in the economic surge of Europe and Japan, oil being obtained for all of the twenty years from 1950 to 1970 at an incredibly low price— hovering around $2 per barrel and tending downwards.

During the same twenty years between 1950 and 1970, the cost of living rose continuously in advanced nations, despite the fact that their economies were fueled by a source of energy—oil—the price of which actually declined. The next ten years would see, on the contrary, a multiplication of the price of oil. For the moment [1980] it is fifteen times as costly as it was a decade ago; soon it may be more. Considering oil's value, the countless ways in which it can be used, and its crucial importance to industrial economies, I cannot consider $30 or more per barrel as too costly. What is deplorable is the brutal precipitousness of the price change, which caused economic disarray not only in wealthy countries but developing countries as well. And although harm was indeed done by the suddenness of the price rise, harm was also done by the previous cheapness, inducing prodigious wastefulness of a most precious material—an exhaustible treasure. Not only was such a wastefulness harmful in itself, but it also closed people's minds to the possibility of more durable forms of energy. During the 1950s pleas for the study of solar energy encountered only laughter.

If one stops to consider these two recent stages of oil history, they both seem shocking: first, a thoughtless depletion, a treasure accumulated over millions of years cheaply flung to the winds; second, with the realization of this treasure's true value, the sudden rise to power of nations that had done little toward its discovery and availability, but who now find themselves in a position of political lordship. Both stages reflect a woeful disregard of what we owe to nature.

Is it still plausible, given such events as we can witness, to speak of economics as if it were independent of politics, or even of nature? To emphasize speculative and theoretical economics at the expense of concrete economics? And are there not specific resources that have commanding roles in national economies around the world, and thus in the international economy as well? The task ahead for the discipline of economics is to probe the concrete changes taking place around the world and identify exactly which resources and products are most important, where they may be obtained, and, not incidentally, from whom. In sum, we should descend from the ethereal heights of theory and speculation and admit the crucial role that politics, nature, and other earthly influences play in economics. We should return to a realistic understanding of the workings of the concrete economy.

Index

Abbas, Fehret, 207
Abramovitz, Moses, 42
accounting, 44
Adam, P., 292, n. 45
advertising, 113
agriculture, 45, 107, 209–10, 213, 218–19, 238–45, 282, 285, 299
Alexander the Great, 223
Alfieri, Conte Vittorio, 79, 120, 255
Ambelin, Robert, 74, n. 8
amenity, 37–52, 115–117
Antipho, 54, 55
architects, 256–61
Aristotle, viii, 2
Athens, 79, 100
Augustus, 225

Balzac, Honoré de 123
Beckman, Gaston, 74, n. 4
Bell, Daniel, 255
Benes, Eduard, vii
Berdyaev, N. A., 145
biological pyramid, 283
Boas, Sarah Claire, vii
Bodin, Jean, 290, n. 9
Boltz, C. L., 136, n. 21
Bonald, Louis, 80, 94, n. 7
Bourguiba, Habib, 201
Boyd, William, 94, n. 5
Brutus, 101
building, 256–57
Burke, Edmund, 25, 231

Cairncross, A. K., 196
capitalism, 97, 137–53, 216, 217, 218, 250
Carpaccio, Vittore, 252
Cicero, 101, 229, 266
City of Science, 170, 176
Clark, Colin, 55, 56
Clemenceau, Georges, 208
climate control, 253–54

coal, 61, 131, 138, 209, 249, 250, 271–75, 281, 297–302
Colbert, Jean-Baptiste, 213
Colette, vii
collectivism, 97
colonialism, 197–210
Columbus, 224
commerce, 56, 101, 197–98, 265–66
Commission for Planning (France), 1
Commission of National Accounts (France), 1
communism, 37, 97, 216–18
Conan, A. R., 195
Constant, Benjamin, 25
Constantine, 101
consumption, 33
convertibility (currency), 182–95
Coombs, Philip H., 299
Corneille, Pierre, 90
Cortès, 224
Cousteau, Jacques-Yves, 263

D'Aguesseau, Chancellor, 118, n. 9, 146
D'Holbach, 146
Day, A. C. L., 196, 196, n. 3
de Grazia, Sebastian, 86
de Jouvenel, Bertrand, vii, 1, 4, 5, 6, 7, 9, 14, n. 8
de Jouvenel, Raoul, vii
de Malebranche, Nicolas, 167
de Mirabeau, Marquis, 9, 50
de Vattel, Emerich, 283, 284
Descartes, René 147, 148
Devons, Ely, 133
Dickens, Charles, 217
Dorfman, Robert, 136, n. 20
Dreyfus, Alfred, vii
Dupuy, René-Jean, 290, n. 10

economic planning, 97
economic progress, 39–40, 107, 110, 111, 123, 209, 295